Juvenile Reform
in the Progressive Era

WILLIAM R. GEORGE AND THE
JUNIOR REPUBLIC MOVEMENT

William R. "Daddy" George, 1914

Juvenile Reform
in the Progressive Era

WILLIAM R. GEORGE AND THE
JUNIOR REPUBLIC MOVEMENT

————*by* JACK M. HOLL

Cornell University Press ✧ ITHACA AND LONDON

First published 1971 by Cornell University Press.

Published in the United Kingdom by Cornell University Press Ltd., 2-4 Brook Street, London W1Y 1AA

International Standard Book Number 0-8014-0623-4
Library of Congress Catalog Card Number 72-148020

PRINTED IN THE UNITED STATES OF AMERICA
BY VAIL-BALLOU PRESS, INC.

To Jackie

PREFACE

——————— Our schools are more than educational institutions. They stand as cultural monuments to the aspirations and faith of the American people. Throughout American history, our school buildings, student bodies, curriculums, and prevailing educational philosophies have reflected both the breadth and the limitations of our political, economic, and social vision. As one of our most important institutions of social control and social mobility, the schools have had to define explicitly or implicitly the nature of man and his relationship to society. Years ago, R. Freeman Butts noted, in his book *A Cultural History of Education*, that what goes on in the classrooms is affected by "the whole matrix of political, economic, social and religious institutions as well as [by] the beliefs, ideas and ideals that guide a people in their private and public endeavors." [1] The school in turn has been an important innovating force within our culture. Social and cultural historians have long understood this, as the vast bibliography in the history of education indicates.

Our prisons are also cultural monuments, a fact we have recognized not quite so readily. Yet how a society treats its

[1] R. Freeman Butts, *A Cultural History of Education* (New York, 1947), v.

vii

deviants and criminals provides a significant insight into basic social values. Americans are quick to detect dark national characteristics embodied in the prison schemes of Russians, Germans, and Chinese. But we have tended not to look at our own jails, reformatories, and prisons for clues to the American national character. Like the schools, however, our penal institutions, their inmates, the prison regime, and the prevailing theories of prison discipline also reflect American political, economic, and social assumptions. American correctional institutions are governed by the same conclusions regarding man and his relationship to society that shape our educational establishments. Sing Sing Prison, for example, was as much an archetypal institution of ante-bellum America as was Horace Mann's common school. Not that the prisons simply caricature only the negative side of national character. Both school and prison are institutions of social control that rest upon similar cultural presuppositions; both reflect our society's fears and hopes as well as its anxieties and ambitions.

Nowhere is the interrelationship between the school and the prison more evident than in the Progressive Era, 1890–1916, when educational and penal reform complemented each other. And in few institutions can this connection be seen more clearly than in the George Junior Republic. Founded near Ithaca, at Freeville, New York, in 1895, the self-governing Junior Republic was a rural haven for delinquent, dependent, and immigrant youth. At the same time, it became an important laboratory for educational and penal experiments. Much of the New Penology was first tested at Freeville, under the leadership of William R. George and Thomas Mott Osborne, and the Junior Republic exported progressive education to Cuba, the Philippines, and England. Confusion among observers over whether the Junior Republic was a reform school or a preparatory school was not at all accidental.

If school and prison reform was one program undertaken by the Progressive generation, another, in the words of Samuel P. Hays, was to "organize or perish." Hays, Robert Wiebe, and Roy Lubove have characterized the Progressive Era as the age of organization and professionalization.[2] Yet the organizational impulse did not go unchallenged, especially among school and correctional reformers. Historians have seen too sharp a break between ante-bellum and Progressive reform and thus have underestimated the persistence of older concepts of poverty, crime, and will. Not all of the "old ideas" were strictly conservative, however. George's and Osborne's constant fight against social welfare bureaucracy made them leading spokesmen for both new and old anti-institutional reforms.

Borrowing terminology from John L. Thomas, I have described the George Junior Republic as an "anti-institutional institution."[3] Although seemingly contradictory, the term should not cause the reader difficulty. The purpose of the Junior Republic was to defend and promote America's principal political, economic, and religious institutions. Nevertheless, the Junior Republic movement attracted many friends and supporters who were intrigued by the utopian implications of the Republic's program. In most instances, the rhetoric of self-government and self-support obscured the differences between the right and left wings of the Junior Republic movement, although when he became aware of the differences, George usually opposed his more radical friends.

[2] Samuel P. Hays, *The Response to Industrialism, 1885–1914* (Chicago, 1957), 48–70; Robert Wiebe, *The Search for Order, 1877–1920* (New York, 1967); Roy Lubove, *The Professional Altruist: The Emergence of Social Work as a Career, 1880–1930* (Cambridge, Mass., 1965).
[3] John L. Thomas, "Romantic Reform in America, 1815–1865," *American Quarterly*, XVII (Winter 1965), 656–681.

Thus the anti-institutional potentiality of the Junior Republic idea, which George never fully understood, was only finally realized in independent schools such as England's Little Commonwealth and A. S. Neil's Summerhill.

On another level, George and Osborne were more clearly anti-institutional. They took part in the Progressive challenge to American penal and educational institutions. If certain critics were more profound in their analysis of the institutions of social control, few were more outraged by the Old Penology and the classical school than the two New York reformers. Yet although they would have welcomed the chance to dismantle the Elmira Reformatory because it subverted democratic ideals, George and Osborne are best described as conservative reformers whose criticism of educational and penal institutions can be read as a radical critique designed to gain conservative ends.

It was on yet a third level that George was most unquestionably anti-institutional. Throughout his career he distrusted and opposed the professionalization and bureaucratization of reform. He preferred to have little to do with superintendents and inhibiting regulatory agencies. His standard complaint was that professionals and absentee officials usually failed to understand the dynamic principle of the juvenile community. Most institutional managers placed efficiency and security highest on their scale of institutional values. The management of the institution became an end in itself, with professional recognition frequently given to success in administration rather than in reform of persons. Institutions tended to become worlds of their own, heavily encumbered with regulations designed to protect themselves from outside investigation. In the process, George believed, the individuality of the children was lost and basic human values were sacrificed. As we shall see, George and his followers hoped to establish institutions in which the integrity of each person was reinforced by giving him a meaningful role in his own education or rehabilitation. This was accomplished in the Republic by providing its citizens with real choices and responsibilities within an institutional setting that reproduced the conditions of the "real world" as closely as possible. George liked to call the Junior Republic "a village just like any other village," a reminder that the George Junior Republic neither looked like nor was administered like any other institution. The only alternative to the bureaucratic institution, most Progressives believed, was an institution whose organization and control rested in the hands of a single, inspirational leader such as "Daddy" George. But George hoped to find a middle ground between institutional regularity and his individual leadership. It was his ambition to prove that "Republic principles"—and not his personality—would guarantee the long-range success of the Republic movement.

This book, then, is neither the history of an institution nor a biography of a reformer. Rather, it is a history of an antiinstitutional movement conceived, developed, and promoted by William R. George, Thomas Mott Osborne, and the many friends and supporters of the George Junior Republic.

The narrative begins at the Junior Republic in Freeville, New York, during the height of the Progressive Era and thereafter follows the story backward and forward in time and across the Atlantic and Pacific oceans. On occasion the founder and Freeville are left far behind. Some readers may be disappointed because important administrative and financial details relating to the Junior Republic have been slighted, or because friends, co-workers, and leaders have been omitted from the study. I would refer those who want to read a detailed history of the George Junior Republic to William R. George's *The Junior Republic* (New York, 1910), which remains an excellent account of the first decade and a half of the Junior Republic. In addition, Frances Keefe has written a fine study of William R. George and the Junior Republic: "The Development of William Reuben (Daddy) George's Educational Ideas and Practices from 1866 to 1914" (Ed.D. dissertation, Cornell University, 1967). Keefe's study is especially rich in detail and answers most questions concerning personalities and events at the George Junior Republic.

It would be incorrect to conclude that the George Junior Republic is extinct, or even moribund. In the three decades since the death of its founder, the Junior Republic has continued to grow under the leadership of Donald T. Urquhart, son-in-law of William R. George. Urquhart, who has served the Republic cause for more than forty years, became executive director during the depression decade. From those discouraging years when the Republic occupied 400 acres and had but fifteen citizens, he has guided it through its diamond anniversary, celebrated on June 5–7, 1970. Seventy-five years after its founding the George Junior Republic continues to provide education and training to approximately 100 boys and 50 girls on its 1,000-acre campus. Recently, the *Junior Republic Citizen* (Summer 1970) announced the beginning of construction on two buildings in the Junior Republic's seven-million-dollar expansion program. Other Junior Republics still operate at Litchfield, Connecticut, and Grove City, Pennsylvania. The California George Junior Republic at Chino still functions, although under another name. According to the *GJR Bulletin* (June-July 1970), Donald Urquhart has also been helpful in planning a new institution at Lafayette, Colorado, which will be known as the Colorado Junior Republic.

I regret that I have had to neglect one of the Republic's most important personalities, Mrs. William R. George. Esther

George was more than the proverbial "power behind the throne" and an inspiration to her peripatetic huband. But in her role as a jealous guardian of George's prerogatives and a fierce critic of his detractors, she has appeared defensive rather than creative. For years, Esther George served as the Republic's unofficial archivist; the material she so carefully saved, collected, copied, and clipped now makes up the George Junior Republic Papers deposited with Cornell University's Collection of Regional History and University Archives. Without her work this study would not have been possible. Jacob Smith summed it up best: "Never had a man a wife more loyal, more solicitous, or more willing to sacrifice than 'Mrs. Daddy.' In remembering him we must not forget her because she surrendered much that he might be free to fulfill his mission." [4]

The manuscript sources cited in the notes, except when otherwise noted, and the originals of the illustrations are preserved in the Cornell Collection. I am grateful to Cornell University for permission to quote from the letters of William R. George and Mrs. George and to reproduce the photographs.

I am also grateful for the assistance of William R. George's daughter and son-in-law, Edith and Malcolm Freeborn. The Freeborns shared with me their reminiscences, private papers, books, and George's diaries, which have now been deposited in the George collection at Cornell. Equally important, they have been generous with their encouragement and understanding.

The literary heirs of persons quoted here have been generous in granting permission to print previously unpublished materials. I wish to thank the following persons for their

[4] Jacob G. Smith, " 'Daddy' George," introduction to William R. George, *The Adult Minor* (New York, 1937), xix.

cooperation: Lithgow Osborne, Charles B. Dawson, W. Stewart Hotchkiss, Helen Mellinkoff, Epes D. Miller, J. Riis Owre, Malcolm E. Peabody, Frank A. Ross, Dorothy Miller Schwab, Robinson B. Stowe, Josephine Strain, and the Visiting Nurse Service of New York.

For assistance and courtesy given during my research, I want to thank the staff of the Collection of Regional History and University Archives at Cornell University, especially Edith Fox, Herbert Finch, and Barbara Shepherd; Gould Colman, director of Cornell's Oral History Program; the staff of the manuscript collection at Syracuse University; and the library staff at Williams College, especially Nancy MacFadyen. Further, I would like to acknowledge the generous assistance given me by Williams College through the Class of 1900 Fund and the Summer Humanities Grant. I wish to thank the New York State Historical Association for permission to use material originally published in my article "The George Junior Republic and the Varieties of Progressive Reform," *New York History*, L (January 1969), 43–60.

Several friends and colleagues have significantly helped me with the manuscript. Arthur Zilversmit of Lake Forest College, W. David Lewis of the University of Buffalo, and Philip Cantelon of Williams College, having read the entire manuscript, offered valuable criticism and advice. I am indebted to Terry Perlin of Williams College and Robert Kleck of Dartmouth for their assistance in special problems, and to Robert Claridge for his excellent research into the origins of the reformatory movement. William Brazill of Michigan State University offered witty commentary and valuable suggestions.

I am indebted to Jean Donati, Mary Maughlin, and James D. Sanford for their proofreading chores, and to my wife, Jacqueline, for the many hours she devoted to typing the manuscript.

My greatest intellectual debt is to David B. Davis, who first suggested the topic to me. As a teacher, critic, and friend, he patiently guided my research in its early stages and, in his own work, set an exciting example of accomplishment. It was Professor Davis who taught me that scholarship, which has its own rewards, need not always be a lonely pursuit.

JACK M. HOLL

Washington, D.C.

CONTENTS

ILLUSTRATIONS

Juvenile Reform
in the Progressive Era

WILLIAM R. GEORGE AND THE
JUNIOR REPUBLIC MOVEMENT

I

THE JUNIOR REPUBLIC
IN THE PROGRESSIVE ERA

——————— A dark **V** etched itself against the autumn sky. A small flock of Canada Geese, not yet five minutes off Cayuga Lake and still low, winged southward over the tiny station in Freeville. The expectant crowd at the station was hardly aware of the passing season. The date was November 3, 1911, and Theodore Roosevelt, at the urging of his daughter, was on his way to visit the George Junior Republic and fulfill a promise he had made years earlier to William R. George. In 1911 the Progressive Era was approaching its zenith, and the visit of the former president and associate editor of *The Outlook*, a year before the election of 1912, once again enabled Roosevelt to reaffirm his active support for Progressive social reform.

i

During his term as police commissioner of New York City, Roosevelt had taken great interest in a wide variety of social workers and their projects. His closeness to Jacob Riis is well known.[1] Lillian Wald, Robert de Forest, Samuel McCune

[1] Roy Lubove, *The Progressives and the Slums: Tenement House Reform in New York City, 1890–1917* (Pittsburgh, 1962), 124–125.

Lindsay, Jane Addams, and Paul U. Kellogg were among other social workers with whom Roosevelt was intimate.[2] Willam R. George, tall, heavy-set, and youthfully good-natured, must be added to this list. Introduced to Roosevelt by Jacob Riis, George quickly interested the police commissioner in his plan to open a year-round camp for destitute and delinquent children. Roosevelt and Riis, George proudly confessed, were responsible for the successful transformation of Freeville's Fresh Air Camp into the George Junior Republic in 1895. Roosevelt's interest in the Junior Republic came at a time when most of George's friends scoffed at the scheme. Without Roosevelt's support and encouragement, George later reflected, the experimental Junior Republic would not have survived its pioneer years.[3] Nor did Roosevelt merely regard the Junior Republic as a passing curiosity. A week before his election as Vice President of the United States in 1900, Governor Roosevelt ordered his train to make an unscheduled stop in Freeville so that he might address the citizens of the George Junior Republic.[4] He had carefully followed the progress of the Junior Republic, Roosevelt told the assembled crowd. Expressing his desire to return someday for a close inspection of the Republic, he continued, "In this splendid Republic of yours you are doing the very things that I am trying to uphold—the dignity of labor, the principles of right

[2] Allen F. Davis, " 'Theodore Roosevelt—Social Worker,' A Note," *Mid-America*, XLVIII (Jan. 1966), 58–62.

[3] William R. George, "The Roosevelt Story," undated MS. George Junior Republic Papers, Collection Regional History and University Archives, Cornell University, Ithaca, New York. Unless otherwise noted, all MS citations are from this collection.

[4] Roosevelt, en route to address a political rally in Ithaca, personally ordered the stop in Freeville, although he had refused all other invitations to speak along the way.

and wrong—and the splendid energetic way in which you set about it has won my respect and esteem." [5]

During the ensuing years Roosevelt's admiration for the Junior Republic venture did not wane. Yet on his return to Freeville eleven years later, he was surprised at the scope and depth of the work. "I had expected to be pleased and interested," Roosevelt later remarked, "but my interest and pleasure far outran even my expectations." [6] Roosevelt's reaction was not at all unusual. Even though at first they might be skeptical, few visitors to the George Junior Republic could resist its charm and fascination. Edwin Markham was so enthralled by the work that he spent five days studying the Republic, and upon the conclusion of his visit left behind a signed poem as a memento. [7] At the end of his two-day inspection of the Junior Republic, General Robert Baden-Powell, the founder of the Boy Scouts, remarked that the Junior Republic was the most interesting sight he had seen in America. [8] Scores of other prominent visitors—John R. Commons, Washington Gladden, Ben B. Lindsey, Charles W. Eliot, Charles Evans Hughes, and Andrew Dickson White, to name but a few—left behind similar testimonials.

As his train approached the Republic grounds, Roosevelt immediately noticed the absence of institutional features. The Republic had no walls or fences, or even any plainly discernible boundaries. The buildings—a few old farm houses, a couple of barns, some small cottages scattered here and there, a school, a church, a town hall, and a water tower (none of

---

[5] Ithaca *Daily Journal*, Nov. 1, 1900.

[6] Theodore Roosevelt, "The Junior Republic," *The Outlook*, C (Jan. 20, 1912), 117.

[7] Edwin Markham to William R. George, Sept. 8, 1899.

[8] Mrs. William R. George to Ben B. Lindsey, Feb. 21, 1912.

them painted a uniform color)—could have been the center of almost any village in the Finger Lakes region of upstate New York. Travelers on the Lehigh Valley Railroad, it was reported, passed through the Junior Republic without realizing there was anything special about the village they could see so clearly from their car windows. Even on his guided tour, Roosevelt saw little that was unique about the Junior Republic. A few boys loitering in front of the post office, children playing in the school yard, and the casual bargaining at the country store were the most noteworthy activities he could discern. It did not take long, however, for Roosevelt to recognize that the very "normality" of these routine activities reflected the vital principle of the Junior Republic. Except for a small gang of prisoners breaking rocks by the side of the road, there was no evidence of institutional coercion, restraint, or discipline. The citizen policeman walked his beat as in any village, but social control depended primarily on the normal relationships that would be found in any community—employer to employee, entrepreneur to client, and friend to neighbor. In fact, so important was the appearance of normality to the Republic, that the pace of life was just the opposite of that of the country at large: the more distinguished the guest, the more "normal" was the Republic routine. Roosevelt did not miss this point and subtly remarked how pleased he was that everything went on as usual during his presence.[9] "The Junior Republic is just exactly what . . . Thomas Mott Osborne has called it," Roosevelt marveled. "It is a laboratory experiment in democracy." [10]

He noted that the Junior Republic motto, "Nothing without Labor," was rigidly followed. The boys Roosevelt had seen loitering in front of the general store, George explained,

[9] Mrs. William R. George to Ben B. Lindsey, Nov. 4, 1911.
[10] Roosevelt, "The Junior Republic," 117.

were mostly new arrivals. Upon his enrollment, each had been given three days' wages, but would receive nothing more unless he earned it. The boys were free to spend their money as they wished, and could work, play ball, or lie on the grass; that was their privilege. But at dinner time, each must have the price of his meal, or he wouldn't eat; and at night, each must have the price of his room, or he wouldn't sleep. For the shiftless and idle within the Republic there was soon hunger and want. The Republic citizen must either work or starve, George told Roosevelt.

Work, however, was not difficult to find, nor was it unduly arduous. In return for employment in the carpentry shop, printing shop, farm, bakery, public works projects, hotels, and restaurants, citizens were paid in Republic money. With their earnings they purchased food, lodging, clothing, and whatever luxuries they could afford. Thrifty and industrious citizens obviously lived better than the less provident. Most prosperous citizens ate at the best Republic restaurants and slept in the finest cottages. The poorest citizens ate at the "Beanery" and slept on the top floor of the hotel in a dormitory called "the Garroot." A citizen who became completely indigent was given free lodging at the jail for three days. Thereafter he was arrested as a vagrant and worked without pay. It did not take long for even the dullest to perceive the advantages of holding a regular job. Since almost the entire citizenry of the Junior Republic was gainfully employed, George explained, there naturally arose a demand for the strictest enforcement of law and order and the protection of the rights of private property.

The Junior Republic's self-government feature most interested Roosevelt. Like many others who had heard of the Junior Republic, he had suspected that the self-government scheme might be counterfeit. "I had been told before I went there," he wrote, "that the boys and girls literally govern themselves, that there was practically no government whatever from outside; but I had not been able to realize that the statement was to be taken as exactly true." [11] The citizens of the Junior Republic, all boys and girls between the ages of sixteen and twenty-one (Roosevelt noted that "woman suffrage was accepted as a matter of course in the real democracy of the Junior Republic"), had almost total independence in managing their own affairs. Roosevelt discovered that the citizens had written their own constitution and laws, elected their own executive and legislative officers, conducted their own courts under judges of their own choosing, and punished lawbreakers through a penal system administered by themselves. The effect was astounding. The whole Republic was busy, and everyone seemed happy. As he passed from the post office, the country store and the farm, to the Republic capitol and courthouse, Roosevelt found no evidence of discontent. The Republic, as far as he could tell, was a model of industry, prosperity, and order.

On the courthouse steps, George observed that few citizens at first supported law and order as a matter of principle, but all of them obeyed Junior Republic laws as a matter of self-interest. Only after the child learned the lesson of "doing good for policy's sake," George continued, was it possible to teach him "to do good for its own sake." Roosevelt's visit to the Republic court, therefore, was the most instructive episode of his tour, for it was there that he observed most closely the interaction among the three basic moral classes of the juvenile society: the criminal, the law-abiding hedonist, and the civic idealist. In every case brought before the Republic court the two law-abiding classes found common cause against the

11 *Ibid.*

criminal element. "An offense committed by one of their number," Roosevelt observed, "is thought to be an offense, not against some outsider or outside body with whom or with which they have no special connection, but against themselves." [12]

The punishments meted out by the court were real and severe. Most convicted offenders were sentenced to labor "on the gang," as the boys called it. Reduced to the status of convict (in the early days of the Republic the prisoners even wore stripes and marched in lock step), the prisoner exchanged his name for a number, was charged to a keeper, and then led away to his cell in the Republic jail. Until his release, the convict worked at hard labor without wages, receiving abundant but plain food. Sentimentality was not wasted on the criminal. Roosevelt noted that no outsider, not even George, operated the prison system. Prison discipline was maintained by "the citizens themselves, the boys and girls, on their own initiative." [13]

It was obvious to Roosevelt why the Junior Republic was better governed and more prosperous than the Great Republic, though both were supposedly founded on identical principles of self-government and self-support. The small size of the junior community (there were about 200 citizens living on 250 acres of farmland) reduced the possibility that the citizen could escape the economic or social consequences of his behavior. Furthermore, the simplicity of Republic life enabled each child to comprehend the dynamics of his society. The fundamental lessons taught by the Republic regime could hardly be misunderstood. Lastly, George, though never directly interfering with the government, was a powerful and charismatic personality who helped shape and guide the de-

[12] *Ibid.*, 118.   [13] *Ibid.*, 119.

velopment of the community even more than he allowed himself to believe.[14] George always argued that the Junior Republic superintendent directed best by not directing at all, but this did not mean that he exercised no control over the affairs of the Republic. His function was to make sure that adult helpers, who served as the Republic's employers, conducted their activities as if they were employers in the Great Republic. In his role as superintendent, George not only guaranteed that the Junior Republic was conducted as an "exact miniature of a well-ordered town," but he served benevolently as "Daddy" George as well. Roosevelt admired the machinery of the Junior Republic, but he stressed that he trusted more the individual—"the power, the will, the good sense and the initiative"—that was behind the machinery. In Roosevelt's judgment "Daddy" George, with his love, compassion, and moral guidance, was as essential to the success of the Republic as the economic and governmental principles on which it was founded.[15]

Before he arrived in Freeville, Roosevelt may have regarded the Junior Republic as simply an interesting and picturesque experiment in social philanthropy, but he soon discovered

[14] Shortly after the founding of the Junior Republic in 1895, George served as its president. He resigned within a year, however, and never afterward took direct part in the government. Thomas Mott Osborne, as Chief Justice of the Republic's Supreme Court, created in response to a demand from the citizens, served chiefly to mitigate the harsh penalties meted out by overzealous citizen judges.

[15] Roosevelt, "The Junior Republic," 119. George never admitted that his personality was essential to the success of the Junior Republic. Most observers, however, thinking they were complimenting George, testified that his role was absolutely vital. The best statement of the principles of the Junior Republic as George conceived them can be found in William R. George, *The Junior Republic* (New York, 1910), *passim*. A later publication, which, though brief, reflects some of his ultimate conclusions, is George's *Junior Republic Principles and Bulletins* (Freeville, N.Y., 1941), *passim*.

that it was no experiment at all. Unperturbed that he had not discovered something new, Roosevelt praised the Junior Republic precisely because it embodied a new application of a very old principle—the application of democracy to the correction of delinquency and dependency. The Junior Republic was, in the real and deepest sense of the word, a reformatory. This did not mean that the Junior Republic was simply a progressive correctional institution. Among its citizens, the former President noted, were immigrant children from urban slums, poor children taking advantage of the Republic's educational opportunities, children from wealthy homes, and wards of the state. Only about a third of the citizens came to the Republic through suspended sentence or probation by the courts. The Junior Republic was not a reform school but a refuge for the destitute and neglected. Juvenile delinquents were admitted in full equality with the child who had never committed a crime. Most amazing of all, Roosevelt wrote, "is that he [the delinquent] is about as apt to turn out to be a first-class citizen, not merely of the Junior Republic, but of the larger republic, the republic of the American Nation, when he graduates into it." Roosevelt abandoned whatever reservation he might have had regarding the Junior Republic and in the idiom of the day concluded: "The place is a manufactory of citizens, men and women, and I do not know of any place better worth visiting, nor any place better calculated to produce in the mind of the visitor a healthy modesty about drawing conclusions too rapidly from any one set of observations." [16]

ii

Roosevelt's enthusiasm for the George Junior Republic must be taken seriously. Had the former President been the

[16] Roosevelt, "The Junior Republic," 117.

only prominent Progressive to endorse George and his work, the Junior Republic might still be dismissed as a quaint and rather insignificant manifestation of American romanticism. Among the Progressives themselves, however, the Junior Republic was almost universally praised. As if not to be outdone by his great rival, Woodrow Wilson published an open letter to the citizens of the National Junior Republic (established at Annapolis Junction, Maryland) reminding his young readers that government in its original and ancient definition implied self-control and self-government as much as it meant control and government of others. The Junior Republic was to be praised, Wilson believed, because it taught the boys that self-government did not emanate from the city hall, nor the state capitol, nor the national congress, but began in his own heart.[17]

Lyman Abbott, Roosevelt's associate and editor-in-chief of *The Outlook*, reflected that the principles which George discovered and applied in the creation of the George Junior Republic were worthy of study by "all students of political philosophy, and of all legislators—municipal, State, [and] National." [18] Nor was Abbott's recommendation a product of momentary enthusiasm. In the twenty-year period roughly encompassing the Progressive Era (1896–1916), *The Outlook* published over fifteen articles and editorials about the Junior Republic.

One of the first was written by the Reverend Washington Gladden, who visited the Junior Republic in the summer of 1896, a year after its founding. In the midst of the com-

[17] Woodrow Wilson, "What Is Government and How Can a Boy Early Learn Its Value?" *Republic News*, printed by the National Junior Republic Press, March 1912.

[18] Lyman Abbott, "A Republic in a Republic," *The Outlook*, LXXXVIII (Feb. 15, 1908), 351–354.

parative chaos and confusion of a new social experiment, Gladden could write: "It is clear that this Junior Republic has caught the idea—quite a number of ideas—that a large share of our senior republicans—makers of laws, platform orators, administrators of charity—have failed to catch." If even a few hundred Republic graduates could be distributed among the urban populations, Gladden declared somewhat optimistically, they might prove to be the catalyst that would spark urban reform.[19]

Several popular magazines, some of them having little or no Progressive persuasion, praised the Junior Republic. *Harper's Weekly* proclaimed the Junior Republic "one of the most fascinating studies in sociology and human nature that is to be found." Frank Munsey's *Argosy* lauded the Junior Republic plan by concluding that "[it] is one of the most novel, original, and successful solutions to the perplexing slum question." *Strand, McClure's, World's Work, Century, Gunton's Magazine,* the *Nineteenth Century,* and the *Review of Reviews* were among other periodicals conspicuous in their support of the Republic. *Charities* (and later its successor, *Survey*), origrnally a house organ for the New York Charity Organization Society, kept its readers informed on the progress of the movement from the Republic's eighth anniversary in 1903 until George's death in 1936.[20]

[19] Washington Gladden, "The Junior Republic at Freeville," *The Outlook,* LIV (Oct. 31, 1896), 781.

[20] E. S. Martin, "This Busy World," *Harper's Weekly,* XLV (Jan. 12, 1901), 41; "The End of the Century: An Epitome of Things of Current Interest—The George Junior Republic," *The Argosy,* XXI (Jan. 1896), 301–305; James Wilson, "Citizens in Little," *Strand Magazine,* XIV (Sept. 1897), 209–215; Mary G. Humphreys, "The Smallest Republic in the World," *McClure's Magazine,* IX (July 1897), 731–746; Lyman Beecher Stowe, "What To Do with a Boy," *World's Work,* XXVI (June 1913), 190–195; A. K. Fallows, "Fair Play for Wayward Children," *Century,* LXXIII (Dec. 1906), 259–263;

A number of professional journals also ran articles on the the work in Freeville. A. E. Winship, editor of Boston's *Journal of Education*, became an early and devoted disciple of the Junior Republic and not only thoroughly described George's work in the pages of his journal, but lectured about it as well. Other articles appeared in the *Journal of Educational Psychology*, which publicized the pioneering work the Republic had done in psychological testing, and in the *Journal of Criminal Law*, which testified to the international appeal of the movement.[21]

What had attracted such a varied group of observers, participants, and supporters to the George Junior Republic? First of all, scores of newspapers recognized the Republic's human-interest value and ran countless stories giving the Republic valuable publicity and editorial support. William Randolph Hearst's New York *Journal*, attempting to emulate the *Tribune's* Fresh Air Fund, conducted an unsuccessful campaign to raise $20,000 for the Republic. Contributing $5,000 itself, the *Journal* blatantly appealed to the most conservative and self-interested instincts of its readers. Not only was the Junior Republic properly altruistic, the *Journal* pointed out, but it was also extremely utilitarian. A contribution to the Junior

Charles Burr Todd, "Civics and Education," *Gunton's Magazine*, Nov. 1898, 349–360; Rose C. Barran, "The George Junior Republic," *Nineteenth Century*, LXVI (Sept. 1909), 503–508; Albert Shaw, "Vacation Camps and Boys' Republics," *Review of Reviews*, XIII (May 1896), 572–576; John A. Parker, "The Eighth Anniversary of the George Junior Republic," *Charities*, XI (July 18, 1903), 65. Articles in *Survey* appeared on the following dates: Aug. 2, 1913; March 14, 1914; May 19, 1917; Sept. 16, 1921; Oct. 15, 1922; and May 8, 1936.

[21] A. E. Winship, "The George Junior Republic," *Journal of Education*, LXXI (March 10, 1910), 260–261; H. M. Jennings and A. L. Hallock, "Benet-Simon Tests at the George Junior Republic," *Journal of Educational Psychology*, Oct. 1913, 471–475; "Junior Republics in England," *Journal of Criminal Law*, III (Sept. 1912), 470–472.

"Daddy" George (center) with some citizens of the Junior Republic, about
[18]96. On his right, in the back row, is Jacob G. Smith, the first citizen and
[fir]st citizen president of the Republic.

The George Junior Republic, about 1902. Pioneer Cottage, the original Re-
[p]ublic farm house, is in the center.

The Court, about 1905, with a citizen judge presiding.

The Republic Store, about 1910, where citizens exchanged Republic currenc
for groceries.

Republic was not charity, the editors insisted, but a prudent and wise investment. "These children of the streets are the Anarchists, the enemies of order and of capital of the future," the newspaper warned. The cost of the Junior Republic was trifling, the *Journal* concluded, compared to the threat of uncontrolled street gangs to the capitalist class.[22] The *Journal's* campaign collapsed when the trustees of the Republic, fearing that Hearst was only using the Republic as a circulation-building gimmick, refused to cooperate.[23] The trustees had been much more pleased with an editorial in the New York *Evening News* which accepted the essence of the *Journal* argument but couched it in more acceptably "liberal" language. Pointing to the brutalizing environment of the urban slums, the *Evening News* compared the Junior Republic to the recently founded College Settlement House as an aid to the juvenile problem.[24]

Another group which contributed significantly to the Junior Republic was composed of local businessmen, women's clubs, missionary guilds, Christian Endeavor Societies, Sunday schools, and other church-related organizations. The Junior Republic appealed to both the charitable and booster impulses of Finger Lakes businessmen. The George Junior Republic and the Chautauqua lectures on the banks of Fall Creek pro-

[22] "A Few Words to the Rich Citizens of New York about the Junior Republic," editorial, New York *Journal*, July 15, 1896.

[23] Thomas Mott Osborne to George Foster Peabody, July 2, 1897, Letterbook, Thomas Mott Osborne Papers, Syracuse University. Letterbook contains several related letters.

[24] New York *Evening Telegram*, Oct. 1, 1895. Other major newspapers reporting on the Junior Republic were: Boston *Evening Telegram*, Brooklyn *Daily Eagle*, Chicago *Tribune*, *Christian Science Monitor*, Los Angeles *Examiner*, Los Angeles *Times*, Newark *Evening News*, New York *Evening Post*, New York *Herald*, New York *Times*, New York *Tribune*, New York *World*, Philadelphia *Record*, Pittsburgh *Post*, Portland *Oregonian*, and Syracuse *Post-Standard*.

vided two of the principal summer attractions for the area.[25] Ithaca businessmen embraced George in the same manner in which they patronized prominent local clergymen and Cornell professors. Their affection for George was genuine and honest, because George himself was one of the biggest boosters of all.[26] Fearing the growing power of labor and the new immigrants, local businessmen found a common cause in George's vision of a classless society based upon the sound principles of democratic capitalism. Thus as George gained respectability and status through his membership in Rotary, reform-minded businessmen earned a measure of good will and status through their promotion of the ideals of the Junior Republic.[27]

Women's clubs and organizations were responsible for founding at least five of the seven Junior Republics that became affiliated as the National Association of Junior Republics,[28] and no Republic grew and prospered without their

[25] Ithaca *Daily News,* June 26, 1897.

[26] George was elected to Rotary in 1921 and faithfully attended weekly meetings, even during his extensive travels and lecture tours (George Junior Republic Papers record George's Rotary attendance). The businessmen's esteem was documented at a banquet on Feb. 8, 1908, at which George was presented with a gold watch. "Testimonial Banquet Given by the Citizens of Ithaca to Mr. William R. George: With Addresses by Ambassador Andrew D. White, Mayor Jared T. Newman, Mr. W. R. George and Others," George Junior Republic Papers.

[27] No one has documented the role of businessmen in Progressive reform so well as Robert Wiebe, *Businessmen and Reform: A Study of the Progressive Movement* (Cambridge, Mass., 1962).

[28] There were the California Junior Republic at Chino; the National Junior Republic at Annapolis Junction, Md.; the George Junior Republic of New Jersey at Flemington Junction, N.J.; the Connecticut George Junior Republic at Litchfield, Conn.; the Strawbridge-Brophy Junior Republic at Morristown, N.J.; the Carter Junior Republic at Redington, Pa.

devoted assistance. Federated Women's Clubs, Ladies Aid Societies, benefit bazaars, and individual philanthropy were an indispensable source of Republic income. Women held from one-quarter to one-half of the seats on the Board of Trustees of all but two of the Republics and fully outnumbered men endorsing the movement. Although numerous women wrote articles publicizing the work of the Republic, few carefully analyzed their motives for supporting it. One of those who did was Mrs. Charles W. Fairbanks, the wife of the Vice President. Most obviously, she noted in 1902, the Junior Republics provided an outlet for the increased leisure and restlessness of America's emancipated womanhood.[29] As they were freed from drudgery and chores at home, women were able to devote more time to reform activities. But, Mrs. Fairbanks suggested, the emancipation was not achieved without misgiving. As the women's role in the family declined, as the functions of the home were assumed by the factory and state, American leisure-class women were threatened by "useless idleness." [30] The Junior Republic was "essentially a feminine conception," Mrs. Fairbanks believed. "Every mother, indeed every woman, knows that while the man is a boy his instincts should be developed, and the citizen who graduates from the Junior Republic enters upon his manly life equipped as a very knight of progress." [31] Thus perhaps what is not so

[29] Mrs. Charles W. Fairbanks, "The Value of Women's Societies," New York *Press*, June 29, 1902.

[30] Christopher Lasch, *The New Radicalism in America* (New York, 1965), 46–47.

[31] Mrs. Fairbanks, "The Value of Women's Societies." No adequate interpretation or analysis of the role of women in the Progressive movement has been written. B. O. Flower's *Progressive Men, Women, and Movements of the Past Twenty-Five Years* (Boston, 1914) presented a commendably broad view of Progressivism which was subsequently eclipsed by political history. Lasch's provocative chapter

obvious is close to the truth; scores of well-born women such as Mrs. Fairbanks discovered that the urban poor were not alone in their use of the Junior Republic as a surrogate family.

Bishops Frederick D. Huntington and Henry C. Potter, the Reverend Washington Gladden, and Rabbi Stephen S. Wise lent the Junior Republic movement the prestige of Social Gospel and Reform Judaism.[32] Recently, several historians have demonstrated that some Progressives sought a secular expression for old New England piety and moralism. Jane Addams, Robert Woods, Graham Taylor, and William R.

"Women as Alien" (*The New Radicalism in America*) is narrowly interpretive. Anne F. Scott, "After Suffrage: Southern Women in the Twenties," *Journal of Southern History*, XXX (Aug. 1964), 298–318, confines her analysis to one decade and region. Several recent publications, though not explicitly feminist history, have abundantly documented the vital contribution of women to the Progressive movement. Robert H. Bremner, *From the Depths: The Discovery of Poverty in the United States* (New York, 1956); Frank Bruno, Jr., and Louis Towley, *Trends in Social Work, 1874–1956* (New York, 1957); Jeremy Felt, *Hostages of Fortune: Child Labor Reform in New York State* (Syracuse, N.Y., 1965); Roy Lubove, *The Professional Altruist: The Emergence of Social Work as a Career, 1880–1930* (Cambridge, Mass., 1965).

[32] Stephen S. Wise to George, Jan. 2, 1911, and Jan. 31, 1912; Washington Gladden, "The Junior Republic at Freeville." Wise sent several children to the Junior Republic and Gladden sponsored unsuccessful efforts to establish a Junior Republic in Ohio (George, "Report to the National Association of Junior Republics," Jan. 3, 1914). Henry C. Potter attended several meetings of the Republic Board of Trustees in the years 1903–1906. He prepared one of the first ecumenical manuals of devotion for the Junior Republic chapel, which was endorsed by Edward G. Andrews, Bishop of the Methodist Episcopal Church; Charles Cuthbert Hall, president of Union Theological Seminary; and William H. P. Fauce, president of Brown University (George, untitled MS, April 12, 1933). For a discussion of the work of Huntington and Potter, see Henry F. May, *Protestant Churches and Industrial America* (New York, 1949), 178–181.

George were only a few of the Progressives who found in social reform a surrogate for religion.[33] But most of the church-related groups that supported George found the Junior Republic an ideal channel for their more traditional missionary zeal. Often lacking ready cash to support either foreign mission work or the home missions of their churches in distant cities, local churches welcomed the opportunity to aid the boys and girls at Freeville. The Junior Republic conveniently allowed them to contribute what they had and immediately witness the results of their charity. Books, food, clothing, and blankets were typical contributions from this type of source. Religious services at the Republic were often conducted by volunteers who practiced the arts of evangelism on the Republic citizens. During a typical week, according to one account, a missionary from one of Charles Cuthbert Hall's East Side Missions gave "a plain religious talk, accompanied with numerous hymns from one of Mr. Sankey's books." That same evening a student from the Auburn Presbyterian Seminary gave a talk on Asiatic heathenism, again accompanied with hymns. Later in the week, a Wednesday evening prayer service was conducted by a Christian Endeavor Society.[34] George was so successful in keeping religious differences in balance that Bishop Thomas F. Hickey, vicar-general of the diocese of Rochester, gave permission for Catholic children to enroll at the Republic and attend Catholic services held in the Re-

[33] Among the historians noting the religious content of Progressive reform are: Lasch, *The New Radicalism in America*, 6–11; George Mowry, *The Era of Theodore Roosevelt, 1900–1912* (New York, 1958), 87; Carl N. Degler, *Out of Our Past* (New York, 1959), 370; Louise C. Wade, *Graham Taylor, 1851–1938* (Chicago, 1964), 83–116. Mrs. Wade's chapter on "Religion and Social Action" is especially excellent. See also May, *Protestant Churches and Industrial America*, *passim*.
[34] David F. Lincoln, "The George Junior Republic," *The Coming Age*, Jan. 1900, 42–44.

public chapel.[35] Though few of the contributions were large, individual and church-related philanthropy, coupled with the fund-raising of the Ladies Aid Society, constituted the major source of Republic income in its early years.[36]

The most prestigious and influential supporters of the George Junior Republic were the group who made up the Board of Trustees and the Advisory Council. For the most part they were well-to-do, well-bred young professional and businessmen of native New England stock. Although in some

[35] George to Bishop Hickey, Feb. 23, 1911.

[36] George and Lyman Beecher Stowe, *Citizens Made and Remade* (New York, 1912), 30–31; "Minutes—George Junior Republic Association, 1903–1906." The George Junior Republic Account Books cover only the years 1913–1920. There are several lists of contributors in the George Junior Republic Papers. One of the most interesting, titled simply "List of Subscriptions and Donations," was probably compiled in 1896. Not all of those on this list were local supporters by any means. John D. Rockefeller's $100 contribution was one of the largest, exceeded only by the $300 given by Bishop Huntington's church. The Five Points Mission contributed $45 and the Christian Endeavor Society of New York City gave $95.75. The list contains 93 contributors whose gifts totaled $1821.54. If the four contributors who gave $100 or more are excluded, the donations of the remaining 89 averaged $12.

Another list, dated 1897, records that the Fourth Presbyterian Church of New York City sent a crate of 25 Bibles, 10 Testaments, 2 Books of Proverbs, and 30 miscellaneous books. Other contributions were a printing press, blackboards, baseball and football equipment, prison uniforms, a harrow, mower, rake, cultivator, 8 turkeys (killed but not dressed), a bathtub, wallpaper, wire, nails, pails, and magazines given by assorted friends, clubs, churches, aid societies, and anonymous donors. A third list reveals that V. Everit Macy and Gerrit Smith Miller gave the Republic a herd of registered Holstein cattle; Macy also donated a cottage and the Millers contributed a library of 500 books, 60 acres of land, an 11-acre athletic field, the Republic barn and dairy building, the Print Shop, and a cottage and remodeled the Republic Hotel and government and store buildings. The list of contributors is long, and I shall conclude by noting that John D. Rockefeller gave a cottage and the government buildings.

instances the George Junior Republic was their primary interest, it was rarely their sole involvement in reform.[37] Superficially, this collection of reformers resembled the group of "typical" Progressives described by Richard Hofstadter and George Mowry.[38] It is probably axiomatic that reformers in a dynamic society are influenced in one way or another by a "status revolution." Their writings and correspondence reveal that they were fearful, but not because they felt themselves overshadowed or threatened by the growing power of industrial wealth. On the contrary, their greatest concern was directed toward the opposite end of the social-economic spectrum, and their support of the George Junior Republic indicated a greater anxiety over the growing lawlessness in the urban slums than over the burgeoning power of the robber barons.[39] The trustees of the Junior Republic never

[37] Many of their names are quite familiar to the student of Progressivism: Bishop F. D. Huntington, Lyman Abbott, William F. Blackman, John R. Commons, John S. Huyler, William H. Maxwell, Thomas Mott Osborne, Charles H. Parkhurst, Jacob A. Riis, Albert Shaw, Josiah Strong, George Hamilton Dean, V. Everit Macy, Gerrit Smith Miller, E. E. Olcott, Frederick Almy, Henry C. Potter, Phillip Cabot, Jeremiah Jenks, Lyman Beecher Stowe, Alexander Forbes, and W. Cameron Forbes. Those on the first half of the list, including Josiah Strong, served on the Junior Republic Advisory Council in 1896. Those on the second half of the list, beginning with Dean, served a term on the Board of Trustees. The above list comprises slightly less than half the number of those who served on the two boards. The rest were primarily local businessmen, bankers, and lawyers from the Finger Lakes region and New York City.

[38] Hofstader, *The Age of Reform* (New York, 1955), 131-148; Mowry, *The California Progressives* (Berkeley, 1951), 86-104; Mowry, *The Era of Theodore Roosevelt*, 85-105.

[39] Lyman Abbott, "A Republic in A Republic"; William F. Blackman, "The George Junior Republic," *Yale Review*, V (Aug. 1896), 212-213; John R. Commons, "The Junior Republic," *American Journal of Sociology*, III (Nov. 1897, Jan. 1898), 281-296, 433-448; Alexander Forbes, "The George Junior Republic: A Community Vital to

hesitated to accept gratefully the contributions of John D. Rockefeller and Andrew Carnegie,[40] and unself-consciously solicited subscriptions from the nation's wealthy.[41] Two of their number, financier V. Everit Macy and E. E. Olcott, President of the Hudson River Day Line, were among Wall Street's most prominent businessmen and W. Cameron Forbes, who became governor-general of the Philippines under Taft, was a partner of J. M. Forbes and Company, Boston. There is no evidence that the rest of the men on the Advisory Council or Board of Trustees felt intimidated by their intimate association with American capitalists. Certainly none of them

the United States," pamphlet (Freeville, N.Y., 1925); Mrs. Gerrit Smith Miller, "Girl Citizens," MS, c. 1898; Thomas Mott Osborne, "The Way to Train a Boy," Buffalo *Express*, Feb. 10, 1902; Albert Shaw, "The Smallest Republic in the World," *Review of Reviews*, XVI (July 1897), 70–71; Jacob Riis, "Introduction," MS; and Lyman Beecher Stowe, "What To Do with a Boy," *World's Work*, XXVI (June 1913), 190–195.

[40] "List of Subscriptions and Donations," c. 1898; Pittsburgh *Post*, Dec. 4, 1909. Carnegie, for his part, mentioned the George Junior Republic in a speech, "What Our Republic Is about These Days," before the National Liberal Club of London, May 1910 (James Bentham to George, April 10, 1910).

[41] Frederick Almy arranged for Charles Waterhouse Goodyear of Buffalo to head the Republic Aid Society in that city (Almy to George, July 12, 1909). Waldo Forbes, successfully soliciting a testimonial from Andrew Dickson White, stated, "We hope to raise $20,000 in Boston and it ought to be possible to get as much in New York" (Forbes to White, Nov. 1912, White Papers, Cornell University). T. M. Osborne to John D. Rockefeller, Jr., Feb. 20, 1901; Osborne to Andrew Carnegie, Feb. 20, 1901; Osborne to Frederick Almy, Feb. 28, 1901 (Osborne got $1,000 and a promise of a building from Rockefeller); Osborne to Herbert Lehman, March 27, 1901, Letterbook, Osborne Papers, Syracuse University. The New York *Observer*, Dec. 31, 1903, reported a benefit at the Waldorf-Astoria attended principally by railroad and financial leaders.

had suffered loss of status or respect in their commitment to the George Junior Republic.

What is most striking about this last group of Progressives is that they were in revolt against neither the present nor the past. Their problem was not how to restore their status or escape their history, but how to live up to their heritage. Consider the backgrounds of four of the most important functionaries of the Republic: Gerrit Smith Miller, one of the largest contributors; Lyman Beecher Stowe, general secretary of the National Association of Junior Republics; Alexander Forbes, president of the Board of Trustees, 1927–1965; and Thomas Mott Osborne, president of the Board of Trustees, 1897–1913. Each man was a Harvard graduate, and each bore the stamp of Charles W. Eliot, who blessed their efforts.[42] Like the crowd of Mugwumps and young Progressives who poured out of Harvard at the end of the nineteenth century, they were convinced they had been endowed with intellectual and moral superiority. Though each successfully pursued his own material interest, none was able to put behind him the conviction that his privilege carried with it solemn duties. Their sense of moral stewardship was not entirely a product of Harvard, however.

They were all third-generation descendants of illustrious ante-bellum reformers. Thomas Mott Osborne was the great-nephew of Lucretia Mott, Alexander Forbes was the grandson of Ralph Waldo Emerson, Gerrit Smith Miller was the grandson of Gerrit Smith, and Lyman Beecher Stowe was the grandson of Harriet Beecher Stowe. Each was haunted by his

[42] In the New York *Tribune*, Nov. 2, 1900, Eliot wrote, "The George Junior Republic is a very interesting attempt to work a real reform in boys whose characters have been marred, or lost in the unfavorable environments of our large cities."

ancestor's epic struggle for social justice; each basked in an ante-bellum glory he could not share. As young boys, they were reminded of the sacrifices their own fathers had made in the Civil War. As young men they plunged headlong into Progressive reform because they were desperately seeking a suitable battleground for democracy, and not because they were being pursued by howling *nouveaux-riches*. Their fathers had emancipated the Negro, and they now sought to save the urban poor. The blight of urban poverty and the corruption of urban politics was to them what the plantation system and the old "slavocracy" had been to their forebears. Their response to the "status revolution" may have played a role in their decision to become reformers, but it was a reaction rooted in ante-bellum reform and passed along for three generations.[43]

Osborne, perhaps the most famous of the four, shared with George the distinction of being one of the most important Progressives of upstate New York. Osborne traced his ancestry to Richard Osborne who sailed from England in 1634 and settled in Hingham, Massachusetts Bay Colony. Though an old, industrious, and conservative family, few Osbornes achieved notable distinction before Thomas Mott Osborne.

[43] For a similar argument with respect to Massachusetts Mugwumps, see Geoffrey Blodgett, *The Gentle Reformers: Massachusetts Democrats in the Cleveland Era* (Cambridge, Mass., 1966), 19–47. No single document can be quoted to substantiate the above generalizations. An intensive study of this fascinating quartet would be interesting. Unfortunately Stowe's and Forbes' papers have not been found. Because a tragic fire destroyed the Miller home at Peterboro, New York, the Gerrit Smith Miller collection in Syracuse University is disappointing. The Thomas Mott Osborne Papers at Syracuse have not been completely catalogued and significant years are not available. My judgments are mainly based on the reading of innumerable letters in the George Junior Republic collection at Cornell University.

His father, David Munson Osborne, a pioneer American industrialist, was the founder of D. M. Osborne and Company, an agricultural implements factory in Auburn, New York. Osborne fortunes were multiplied by the Civil War, but though hard-working and colorless, the family was by no means *nouveau* to Auburn's society. They were members of the "South Street aristocracy," and their home was but a short distance from the Seward Mansion, the residence of Lincoln's Secretary of State. From his father, Osborne not only obtained the advantages of a Harvard education, leisure, and travel, but he inherited the wealth to finance his philanthropic experiments.[44]

From his mother's side of the family Osborne inherited his reforming zeal. Eliza Wright Osborne was the daughter of David and Martha Coffin Wright. Both the Wrights and the Coffins had been prominent Quaker families in the colonial era. The Coffins, originally a Nantucket family, were especially active reformers. Martha Coffin, and her more famous sister, Lucretia Coffin Mott, were among the leaders of the ante-bellum woman suffrage movement. Martha, Thomas Mott Osborne's grandmother, was an organizer of the famous Woman's Rights Convention called by Lucretia Mott and Elizabeth Cady Stanton in Seneca Falls, New York, in July 1848. Later, Osborne's mother took up the battle for equal rights for women. Consequently, Osborne's earliest recollec-

[44] Rudolph W. Chamberlain, *There Is No Truce: A Life of Thomas Mott Osborne* (New York, 1935), 27–31. Chamberlain, who had access to all the family papers, is the major source on the following section. Frank Tannenbaum, *Osborne of Sing Sing* (Chapel Hill, N.C., 1933), 59–71, and Charles F. Rattigan's pamphlet "Honorable Thomas Mott Osborne" (published by the Democratic General Committee of Cayuga County, 1910), provided additional information. The Osborne papers at Syracuse University yielded little information on Osborne's private life.

tions were of meetings held in the family home on South Street attended by Elizabeth Cady Stanton, Susan B. Anthony, the Motts, the Garrisons, and others. His aunt, Ellen Wright, married William Lloyd Garrison, Jr. (Osborne himself later married Agnes Devens, the niece-in-law of James Russell Lowell.) As a young boy, he accompanied his mother to conventions and meetings. Later at Harvard he witnessed the lingering afterglow of the great abolitionist crusade.

Osborne seems to have acquired much of his mother's romanticism. He viewed life as a morality play with virtue and vice struggling for the soul of mankind. Human nature was inherently good, he believed, evil and corruption being the products of environment and association. The reformer's obligation was to resurrect the latent dignity and goodness of man by purging the society of temptations and raising in their stead sound and inspirational institutions. In the battle for social decency Osborne admitted no middle ground. Possessing the romantics' intolerance for accommodation, he could more easily bear ignorance in his adversaries than disagreement with his friends. Those who rejected his theories he judged either incredibly stupid or morally corrupt. In any event, even well-meaning criticism by a friend often led to an acrimonious dispute ending in permanent alienation. Osborne's friendships with both William R. George and Theodore Roosevelt were terminated in this manner. His most perceptive biographer, Rudolph Chamberlain, has concluded:

The intensity of Osborne's likes and dislikes was heightened by an absolute confidence in his own perceptions. It is inaccurate to say that Osborne possessed ideas. Ideas possessed him. The assumption of infallibility which his assertions often carried was not, however, the dogmatism of an opinionated man. He rarely took credit for inventing an idea. He presumed only to uncover or restate a truth which had always existed. It was something outside of himself, having an independent existence of its own, like one of the eternal verities. Once freed from the dust of centuries, anyone could see it and understand it.[45]

Chamberlain has suggested that Osborne's inheritance created within him a complex and double personality. Intensely proud of his family's militant liberalism, he was also the son of American industrial capitalism. In his youth, Osborne's romanticism was always tempered by the demands of the business world. True to his father, he was intellectually a realist and a pragmatist. His father, a stolid and practical man, had sacrificed everything—labor, time, and health—to build D. M. Osborne and Company. The son never for a moment doubted where his duty lay. At the age of twenty-six, just three weeks after his father's death, he sat grimly behind the president's desk. Caught between his father's dynamic present and his mother's heroic past, young Osborne, sensitive, gregarious, and ambitious, was gripped by an internal tension he could not resolve. It was rumored that once the new president had put his mind to it, he accomplished in one or two days as much as the older men did in a week. But just as often, the young executive was discovered at his desk diligently planning the next production of the Auburn Amateur Dramatic Club, a group of local players he organized shortly after his return from college.

His marriage to Agnes Devens and his expanding community activities dampened his restlessness.[46] It is possible that Osborne's energies would have been consumed indefinitely by the demands of his business, family, and community. But the

[45] Chamberlain, *There Is No Truce*, 17–18.

[46] Osborne became a member of the school board, a trustee of the Auburn Savings Bank, a member of the Board of Trade and the City Club. Wells College elected him a trustee, and he lectured on business administration at Cornell University.

sudden death of his wife in 1896 upset the delicate equilibrium of his life. Osborne had long chafed at the tedium of a business career. When theatrical productions failed to provide him adequate release, he turned to masquerade. Dressing himself as an old peddler, or a down-and-out bum, Osborne found release from the humdrum routine of the business office. For a short period of time, the young romantic could be someone else, transcending the cares and responsibilities of his position while partaking of life from an alien perspective. Agnes, who had provided an important release for Osborne's inner tensions, had held his fantasies somewhat in check. But with her death, he could no longer find adequate sanctuary from the burdens of his father's business.

Trips abroad and increased community work (he became mayor of Auburn in 1902, served as public service commissioner under Charles Evans Hughes, and was boomed for governor in 1910) only seemed to heighten the void in his life. More and more frequently he relied upon his masquerades to fill the quiet, lonely hours. An embarrassment to his family, Osborne became so skillful that he could fool his own relatives, and among strangers he was never unmasked. His wigs, make-up, and old clothes became a passport to high, and sometimes dangerous, adventure. Although originally his disguises served only his romantic inclination, Osborne gradually discovered that his charades fulfilled a dual function. In a manner similar to Jacob Riis and the muckrakers, Osborne found masquerading an excellent outlet for his rational, empirical nature. As a job applicant at his own factory, he could investigate the hiring practices of his foremen. As a worker in his own plant, he searched for employee discontent and maltreatment. Mayor Osborne, dressed as a derelict, roamed Auburn's streets unobtrusively listening for complaints against the town administration. Saloons illegally serving liquor on Sundays or after hours were raided after the police were mysteriously tipped off concerning their operation. Vice dens and gambling joints were closed by the Mayor without previous hint that he had knowledge of their existence. The master disguise provided an ideal cover for Osborne's zeal for observing the realities of life. His mask provided him with the anonymity necessary for gathering unprejudiced facts and dates. A benevolent muckraker, Osborne not only knew how the other half lived, he took pride in sharing their life.

Osborne's family and associates did not enthusiastically endorse his adventures, however. His friend F. W. Richardson of Auburn invited him on an excursion to investigate the newly founded George Junior Republic. The discovery of the juvenile community provided Osborne with a solution to his problems. The model community furnished him an ideal stage upon which to play his romantic role and provided a worthy cause for his idealistic and reformist impulses. As Chief Justice of the Republic Supreme Court, as "Uncle Tom" to scores of young boys, as an itinerant organ grinder who was unrecognized by his closest Republic "pals," Osborne safely played the roles he loved so well. The Junior Republic provided a second important outlet for Osborne. As chairman of the Junior Republic Board of Trustees, he became the chief financial and business advisor to William R. George. David Munson Osborne's son thus vindicated his practical, rationalistic talents while gradually transforming his hobby into his vocation. The George Junior Republic allowed a perfect compromise between the heritage of the Coffins and the Motts and the endowment of D. M. Osborne and Company. As he invested his father's capital in the cause of Progressive reform, Osborne was confident that he had become the steward of an ideal in which he could place absolute faith.[47]

It is not my desire to minimize the seriousness of the un-

[47] Chamberlain, *There Is No Truce, passim.*

healthy social conditions Osborne sought to correct through his work with the Junior Republic, nor to imply that his reforms were less worthy because he had personal motives for pursuing them. Whatever else he may have been, Osborne was no Don Quixote. He no doubt believed in the Golden Age of his grandparents, but he set his face resolutely toward the future. His own words speak eloquently of his conversion to the Junior Republic movement:

At first I thought the Junior Republic was a very picturesque and interesting philanthropic experiment, that proceeded along the normal grooves of a child's nature, instead of trying to go across them.

Then I found that it was no experiment at all; that it was the residuum of a series of experiments—that the existing elements in the system were there for the very reason that experience had proved them successful.

Then I discovered that the Junior Republic was in its essential features a perfectly natural evolution from a benevolent tyranny, which, seeking to do its highest duty to the human beings under its charge, had unexpectedly blossomed into a self-governing community.

Then it came to me that what Mr. George had really discovered was a new application of a very old principle—nothing less than *Democracy* itself applied to a very puzzling problem— with results that were wonderfully, startlingly successful.

Then I found that for many of the problems of our great Republic I could gain light by studying the little Republic; and I called "a laboratory experiment in Democracy." [48]

The factors which carried Osborne into Progressive reform may not have been typical, but his rhetorical response to the

[48] Osborne, "Introduction," in George, *The Junior Republic*, ix–x. Some of Osborne's language was almost identical to Roosevelt's *Outlook* article. In all probability the former president borrowed liberally from his hosts.

plight of the urban poor certainly was. Osborne and his friends strove mightily to save democracy for America, and they all believed that democracy was its own best cure. "What the Republic has shown," he wrote to a Boston friend, "is that with healthy physical and social conditions and with society reduced to its simplest terms, the child of bad inheritance and . . . bad environment tends to right himself and throw off both the physical and moral disease." [49] Osborne was one of the first to detect that the Junior Republic principle could be expanded beyond limits of the Junior Republic, and that its basic components could be introduced into schools, prisons, and other institutions. Declining a position with Spencer Trask Company, Osborne explained that he could not bear to sacrifice his work with the Junior Republic. "I regard that as of more importance to the future than anything else I am interested in," he wrote Trask, "and if I had to give up everything else I should feel that it was my duty to serve the little Republic. I dare say you will think this exaggerated, but I assure you that the importance of Mr. George's work cannot be overestimated. Jail reform, prison reform, school reform and the literal perfection of Democracy lies in it." [50]

A few miles to the east, in Syracuse, New York, John R. Commons also looked benevolently upon the little experiment. Then a teacher of economics at Syracuse University, Commons organized field trips for his students to the Elmira Reformatory, the Auburn Prison, and the George Junior Republic. Intrigued by the juvenile community, a study of the Republic was undertaken as the class project for the spring of 1897, and the results were later published in a two-part

[49] Osborne to Mrs. L. F. Deland, April 11, 1900, Osborne Papers, Syracuse University.
[50] Osborne to Trask, May 29, 1905, Osborne Papers.

article for the *American Journal of Sociology*.[51] Though a professed socialist, Commons applauded the self-help and individualistic principles of the institution. Granting that at one time or another most of the devices used by the Junior Republic had been tried in reformatories, schools, and child-saving institutions, Commons reminded his readers that it remained for George "to begin at the foundation and to build up a complete system, untrammeled by traditions, institutions, or trustees." Because of its fame, charm, and apparent simplicity, Commons warned, there was a tendency to view the Junior Republic as fanciful and harmless philanthropy, yet to do so would obscure the fact that the Junior Republic had met "the most fundamental practical problem of sociology— the education of personal character for both individual and social responsibilities." [52]

In February 1899, just before he was fired from Syracuse University for his radical views,[53] Commons recommended one of his students for employment at the George Junior Republic.[54] George welcomed student help at the Junior Republic and had been ably assisted by the students of Liberty Hyde Bailey and Isaac P. Roberts of the Cornell University College of Agriculture.[55] College graduates, many of whom had spent some time working in settlement houses, frequently wrote George asking for positions. George hired them whenever possible, but a limited budget often restricted the number of young social workers he could employ. He accepted an unlimited number of volunteers, however, and during the sum-

[51] John R. Commons, *Myself* (New York, 1934), 55.

[52] Commons, "The Junior Republic, I," *American Journal of Sociology*, III (Nov. 1897), 281.

[53] Lafayette G. Harter, Jr., *John R. Commons: His Assault on Laissez Faire* (Corvallis, Ore., 1962), 21.

[54] Commons to George, Feb. 3, 1899.

[55] Ithaca *Daily News*, June 26, 1897.

mer months when the citizen population increased, much of the additional burden on the regular staff was relieved by students, many of whom, being under twenty-one, became regular citizens of the Republic.

The Freeville volunteers found their work challenging and exhilarating. Their studies with Commons or with Frank Fetter and Jeremiah Jenks of Cornell taught them the value of direct contact with the poor. Coming from well-to-do middle-class families, most students had confronted poverty only vicariously in *How the Other Half Lives, The Dangerous Classes of New York,* and *The Jukes.* Encouraged by their professors, they trooped to the Junior Republic, which became a practical graduate school for testing their newly acquired theories on unfamiliar problems and peoples. Weary of the pointless good will of their college days, hungry for excitement and challenge, the students pursued experience and reality. Had these same students lived in the cities, they would have joined a settlement house. In another age, at another time, they would have gone to Brook Farm, or joined the Peace Corps.[56]

A number of young activists found the Junior Republic an ideal outlet for their liberal, and even radical, impulses. Although founded on the rock of political and economic orthodoxy, the Republic not only liberated its young citizens from the corrupting influences of the city and factory, but more importantly for the radicals, it implicitly repudiated the role of the family, the church, and the school in rearing and edu-

[56] Willard E. Hotchkiss to Mrs. William R. George, July 1, 1941. The search for relevance, wholeness, meaningfulness, and experience by students in the 1890's has been discussed variously in: Bremner, *From the Depths,* 61–66; Lasch, *The New Radicalism in America, passim;* Frederick Rudolph, *The American College and University* (New York, 1962), 366–368; George E. Peterson, *The New England College in the Age of the University* (Amherst, Mass., 1964), 172–195.

cating youth. It is little wonder that George's experiment was mistaken for a utopian community. George's emphasis on youth, his frank acceptance of sex and race (the Junior Republic was coeducational and integrated), and his insistence that the Republic was in no way an institution contributed to his radical image. The Republic motto, "Nothing without Labor," promised abolition of privilege and monopoly. Within the youth community there was no unmerited suffering or poverty, no unearned stigma or handicap.[57] One editor compared George to Sir Thomas More; more balanced appraisals matched George with Edward Bellamy and declared that the Junior Republic was a model communistic utopia.[58]

Unwittingly, the Junior Republic promoted its own utopian image. Adopting a utopian literary convention, literature describing the work of the Junior Republic was almost always written as a dialogue between a doubting observer and a Republic guide. Like other utopians, George took great delight in comparing the serenity of his model community with the chaos and anarchy of the outside world. If the visitor objected that George's society demanded more of human reason than could be expected, George answered that the Republic did not govern by reason alone, but laid hold of the basic instincts and drives of human nature. Thus *The Junior Republic* can legitimately be read as a utopian critique of the Progressive Era.[59]

[57] For a general statement of these principles, see George's *Junior Republic Principles and Bulletins*, 1–5, and his "Remarks before the City Club of Los Angeles," Los Angeles *Examiner*, March 14, 1908.

[58] "A Modern Utopia," editorial in the New York *Weekly Witness*, Sept. 25, 1895. St. Louis *Globe-Democrat*, Jan. 29, 1910; Harriet Bishop Waters, "The George Junior Republic," *General Federation Bulletin*, n.d., c. 1908; Harriet Gillespie, "A Miniature Republic," *Christian Endeavor World*, XII (Feb. 17, 1898), 414.

[59] An informative analysis of literary utopias can be found in

Although the George Junior Republic was a conservative institution concerned with inculcating traditional American values upon delinquent and dependent children, it also served young radicals as a kind of "social laboratory." Neither fact excludes the other. Americans have generally underestimated the strength of their own radical tradition. Searching for radicalism in economic and political precincts, and finding little there, they have concluded that America has provided especially sterile ground for radical movements. If American radicalism is broadly understood as the revolt against social institutions, however, its extent becomes more evident.[60] The church, family, sex, race relations, schools, and penal institutions, for example, have been traditional targets for radical criticism. But in both ante-bellum America and the Progressive Era, the identity of the radical program has been lost in the general olio of reform.[61] No rigid ideological definition of Progressive reform can be made, and to the question "Were the Progressives conservative or liberal?" we must answer that they were both, at one and the same time.

At its inception, the George Junior Republic attracted, for various reasons and on various terms, a mixed bag of radicals and socialists, businessmen and conservatives, social gospelers and evangelists, students, feminists, professors, publicists, and politicians. From their varying backgrounds, occupations, and ideologies they brought to the Junior Republic a wide variety of expectations. Caught up in the excitement and fervor of a common cause, allied in their devotion to a single leader, and unified by the use of a common rhetoric, the supporters of the George Junior Republic supposed they were marching

---

Northrop Frye, "Varieties of Literary Utopias," in Frank Manuel, ed., *Utopias and Utopian Thought* (Boston, 1966), 25–49.

[60] See, for example, Lasch, *The New Radicalism in America, passim.*

[61] David B. Davis, ed., *Ante-bellum Reform* (New York, 1967), 9.

toward the same historical goals. So close and intimate were the personal interrelationships among the supporters of the institution that incompatible beliefs were seemingly fused by the bonds of common labor and sacrifice. This bit of self-deception, perhaps, was necessary, but it should not deceive us. Despite the fact that neat divisions among Junior Republic advocates are almost impossible to discern, one should not conclude that the George Junior Republic created its own Progressive consensus. Indeed, because it both reflected and blurred all shades of ideology and commitment, the George Junior Republic produced its own microcosmic version of the stormy Progressive Era.

II

WILLIAM R. GEORGE:
THE MAKING OF A REFORMER

———————— William R. George was the linchpin that held together the delicate alliance of reformers who gathered at Freeville. He was instinctively liked by almost everyone he met, and could quickly earn the confidence and good fellowship of even the most casual stranger. His friends remembered him as a hearty extrovert who had a keen sense for the needs of others.

Dr. Willard Hotchkiss recalled, "During that first winter at the Republic, when everyone was trying to keep warm in the remodeled barns that housed us, 'Daddy' always seemed to come around at times when I was about ready to pack my grip and go. Totally oblivious to my discouragement and my nostalgia for other scenes, he would proceed to unfold marvelous projects and to put me squarely in the midst of them." [1] George protested that Republic principles, and not personality, should explain the success of his work. Most observers

[1] Willard E. Hotchkiss to Mrs. William R. George, July 1, 1941. Hotchkiss was a teacher at the Junior Republic, dean of the School of Commerce at Northwestern University, president of the Armour Institute at Pittsburgh, and dean of the Graduate School of Business at Stanford University.

insisted, however, that George himself was largely responsible for the ascendancy of the Junior Republic.[2]

George was also a generous, gregarious, open man who rarely turned down a request for a favor or an invitation to speak. Yet the long list of his speaking engagements testifies that his appeal was based on more than simple good fellowship. When Graham Taylor invited George to speak before the Chicago School of Civics and Philanthropy, Julia Lathrop arranged for a reception at Hull House. Thereafter, George was a regular guest at Hull House and the Chicago Commons whenever he was in the Midwest.[3] His lectures at the University of Wisconsin in 1910 were so successful that E. A. Ross invited him to return to give a series of four more in the fall of 1911. Only after Ross and his old friend John R. Commons insisted that George come did he fit the engagement into his schedule.[4] In the first six months of 1913, George attended twenty-five dinners and gave sixty-seven lectures to approximately 30,000 people.[5]

In 1902, he joined the New York State Child Labor Committee, endorsing the principles of his fellow members Florence Kelly, Herbert Lehman, Owen R. Lovejoy, and Frances Perkins. By 1908 he had become a member of the Board of Trustees of the International Juvenile Court Society, headed by Ben B. Lindsey, and a member of the Committee of One Hundred of the American Health League which included, among others, Jane Addams, Charles Eliot, Judge Lindsey, Josiah Strong, and Booker T. Washington.[6] Two

[2] Theodore Roosevelt, "The Junior Republic," *The Outlook*, C (Jan. 20, 1912), 119.

[3] Graham Taylor to George, Sept. 19, 1909. See George, Diary, 1906–1912.

[4] E. A. Ross to George, Dec. 19, 1911.

[5] Mrs. William R. George to Lyman Beecher Stowe, May 27, 1913.

[6] George to the Secretary of the New York State Child Labor

years later, George refused to review Judge Lindsey's book, *The Beast,* which attacked child labor, on the grounds that he was too good a friend of Lindsey's to be impartial.[7]

As the Progressive Era moved into a climactic phase, William George appeared in the front ranks of the reformers. In many ways he, too, might be considered an almost "archetypal Progressive." At forty-six he was only a few years older than the "average" for Progressives. He was unquestionably middle-class, and though born in the country, became a small businessman in New York City, manufacturing jewelry boxes. His reform activities began with his work at the Five Points Mission in New York City and ended with the establishment of the Junior Republic. Never wealthy, George had the reputation of being moderately successful. A Rotarian and a Republican, like most other Progressives he was only mildly tolerant of organized labor, and had remained politically conservative through the nineties, supporting McKinley in the national elections and the Good Government League in New York City. He was intensely proud of his Northern European ancestry and his New England heritage. His religious antecedents, while evangelical, were respectable for the "Burned-Over District." Lastly, he was intensely individualistic,

Committee, Dec. 19, 1903; to Ben B. Lindsey, March 3, 1908; to the Secretary of the Committee of One Hundred, April 6, 1908. George also became a member of the Reform Bureau (June 1897), the board of trustees of the Industrial Christian Alliance (May 1898), the board of directors of the Federated Boy's Clubs (Jan. 1909), the Committee on the Care of Children, Tenth New York State Conference of Charities and Correction (Nov. 1909). Finally, in December of 1909, he declined an invitation to join the American Institute of Criminal Law and Criminology because he was "busted completely" (George to Edwin Keedy, Dec. 15, 1909).

[7] George to E. W. Kennerer of Cornell University, July 13, 1910. Judge Lindsey's house was a regular stop for George whenever he passed through Denver.

throughout his life remaining suspicious of organized, "professional" reform.[8]

George might well have been mistaken for a Mugwump. His family were displaced agriculturalists who had fled the farm for the city, and the Georges undoubtedly suffered in the 1870's and 1880's from a loss of status. But George did not enter reform in reaction or revolt against the plutocracy of the "new wealth." As his contemporaries were beginning to flock to the state agricultural colleges and universities, George found the reform movement to be his primary means of social mobility. Though never guilty of exploitation, George found a vocation and career within the Progressive movement which provided him material as well as spiritual well-being. By 1912 he could be considered a typical middle-class Progressive precisely because the reform movement had provided the means to respectability. Others may have used

---

[8] My composite picture of the "archetypal Progressive" is again drawn from George Mowry, *The California Progressives* (Berkeley, 1951), 86–102; Richard Hofstadter, *The Age of Reform* (New York, 1955), 143–145; Mowry, *The Era of Theodore Roosevelt, 1900–1912* (New York, 1958), 85–105. In addition, see Alfred D. Chandler, Jr., "The Origins of Progressive Leadership," in Elting E. Morison, ed., *The Letters of Theodore Roosevelt*, VIII (Cambridge, Mass., 1954), 1462–1465.

George was descended from Welsh, English, Scotch-Irish, and Dutch stock. Most of his family were farmers, though at least one ancestor was a blacksmith. His mother was a descendant of John Davenport, the founder of the New Haven Colony, and his father counted among his ancestors a circuit-riding Methodist by the name of James Kelsey. Great-great-grandfather Howe reportedly fought at Bunker Hill. When great-grandfather George moved from New Jersey to Tompkins County just prior to the War of 1812, he established the Georges as one of the pioneering families in the area (Mrs. William R. George, "William R. George," MS, 1899; George, "Notes on the Biography of William R. George," MS, June 6, 1934).

reform to defend their middle-class status; George used reform to attain it.[9]

[9] See Hofstadter, *Age of Reform*, 135–148; Mowry, *California Progressives*, 89–102; Mowry, *The Era of Theodore Roosevelt*, 85–105, for explication of the "status revolution" thesis. Both Hofstadter and Mowry have made only careful and tentative claims for their thesis. Like Alfred Chandler, Jr., they have confined their generalizations to a "large and strategic section of Progressive leadership," admitting that many other adherents to Progressivism came from "a heterogeneous public whose various segments responded to various needs" (Hofstadter, *Age of Reform*, 135). Almost anyone, Hofstadter contends, can "at sometime and on some issue, be called 'Progressive.'" There were numerous "one-interest and one-issue people" who worked only for the promotion of their reform, remaining indifferent to all others. Remaining flexible, Hofstadter would prefer to define Progressives as that group of optimistic Mugwumps, along with their academic, journalistic, clerical, and female allies, who sought Jeffersonian (liberal) reforms through Hamiltonian (political) means (Hofstadter, *The Progressive Movement, 1900–1915* [Englewood Cliffs, N.J., 1963], 3–8).

However supple and comprehensive this version of the "status revolution" thesis may be, it is still not completely satisfactory. Many individuals whose reform credentials cannot be questioned would still have to be considered exceptions to the mainstream of Progressive involvement. Politically oriented Progressives, such as Al Smith and Raymond Robbins who rose to political power during the Progressive Era, can hardly be classed as "Mugwump" types. Nonpolitical reformers, whom Hofstadter would class among the "allies" of Progressive reform, such as Jacob Riis, John R. Commons, and William R. George, found in reform a ladder to middle-class respectability. For this group, status revolution works in reverse. See Oscar Handlin, *Al Smith and His America* (Boston, 1958); Hugh G. Camitta, "Raymond Robbins: A Study of a Progressive, 1901–1917" (senior honors thesis, Williams College, 1965); John R. Commons, *Myself* (New York, 1934); Roy Lubove, *The Progressives and the Slums: Tenement House Reform in New York City, 1890–1917* (Pittsburgh, 1962), 49–80.

For recent criticisms of the "status revolution" thesis, see J. Joseph Huthmacher, "Urban Liberalism and the Age of Reform," *Mississippi Valley Historical Review*, XLIX (Sept. 1962), 231–241; Jack Tager,

It would be misleading, however, to conclude that George's reform activity was entirely a product of his material ambition. By the end of the nineteenth century, urbanization, industrialization, and immigration had profoundly altered the fabric of American civilization. William R. George was among the thousands of anxious Americans troubled by the changes that had taken place in American society and institutions. Like most reformers, he believed that the new technological, economic, and political developments had rapidly weakened America's traditional means of social adjustment. Unlike the Social Darwinists, George optimistically believed that individual will and effort could bring the new forces under control once old methods of social control had been altered and new methods devised. George shared the Progressive faith that the individual was not helpless before the impersonal forces of the new order and the reformer's belief that each citizen had a personal responsibility for correcting and ameliorating abuses resulting from America's industrial revolution.

George, a latter-day perfectionist, failed to recognize the radical implications of his own experiment.[10] He assumed that nothing stood in the way of human progress but man's in-

---

"Progressives, Conservatives, and the Theory of Status Revolution," *Mid-America*, XLVIII (July 1966), 162–175; Geoffrey Blodgett, *The Gentle Reformers: Massachusetts Democrats in the Cleveland Era* (Cambridge, Mass., 1966), 19–47; David P. Thelen, "Social Tensions and the Origins of Progressivism," *Journal of American History*, LVI (Sept. 1969), 325–341.

[10] John L. Thomas, "Romantic Reform in America, 1815–1865," *American Quarterly*, XVII (Winter 1965), 656–681. Thomas has alerted me to the radical inclination of romantic reform. Although Thomas maintains that romantic perfectionist reform expired after the Civil War, George and his friends may provide at least one link between ante-bellum and Progressive reform.

ability to take advantage of his God-given opportunities. Like
many other nineteenth-century reformers, however, and despite his affinities with "utopians," he persistently denounced
what he termed the "utopian fallacy," which held that youth
should be raised and nurtured in an utopian environment.[11]
Were the world a utopia, George admitted, such a contention
would be sound.[12] "[But] the plan of this Republic," he declared, "is not so much to form a Utopia, as it is to have youth
adjust themselves to the questions as they really exist under
the laws of our country at the present time." [13] George professed no greater aim than to Americanize the New Immigrants and to reclaim displaced native Americans. He criticized Bellamy's utopia because it denied citizens economic
responsibility, while exacting from them a conformity which
reduced them to mere dependents. Ironically, George leveled
similar charges against the family.[14]

George's conservatism revealed itself in still other ways. A
history buff, he believed that the "heroic age" of American
history was in the past. Contrary to utopian communitarians,
George did not regard his vision as the harbinger of a "new
era" of fraternal love and cooperation. In an address before
the Society of Mayflower Descendants in the Commonwealth
of Pennsylvania, George declared that the Junior Republic's
purpose was to recapitulate American history as well as American institutions. The Americanizing influences of the frontier
were reintroduced in the program of sacrifice, hard work,
and plain living required of each new Republic citizen. The

[11] See Frank Manuel, "Toward a Psychological History of Utopias,"
in Manuel, ed., *Utopias and Utopian Thought* (Boston, 1966), 69–98.

[12] George and Stowe, *Citizens Made and Remade* (New York,
1912), 211.

[13] George, MS, c. 1903; New York *Times*, May 5, 1897.

[14] George, "History in Brief of Things from the Time of the
Founding of the Junior Republic to the Years 1930–1931," MS, 1931.

ideal of the Junior Republic was to fulfill American history, not repudiate it.[15]

There can be no doubt that George was a reformer. But he was also a conservative. Not once in forty years of reform activity did he call for the alteration of America's basic political, economic, or social institutions. He favored women's suffrage and direct democracy but did not work actively for either. With Osborne, he cheerfully accepted the contributions of Rockefeller and Carnegie, and toward the end of his career he actively supported the interests of the National Association of Manufacturers. His belief that most American institutions were sound and beneficent was fundamental to George's conservatism. It was individual Americans, incapacitated by immigration and rural dislocation, who were out of phase with industrial developments. If Progressives were alarmed by the growing presence of poverty in the midst of plenty, George assumed that poverty resulted from the inability of the individual to take full advantage of American opportunities.[16]

[15] George, "The Junior Republic," address delivered to the Society of Mayflower Descendants in the Commonwealth of Pennsylvania, Nov. 22, 1909, pamphlet (Philadelphia, 1910).

[16] According to Robert Bremner's *From the Depths: The Discovery of Poverty in America* (New York, 1956), George's view of poverty contrasts sharply with the "new view" of poverty held by most Progressives. The belief, common to ante-bellum reformers, that individuals were responsible for their own impoverishment was largely abandoned by Progressives, Bremner asserts. In its place, the Progressives adopted a "new view" of poverty which assumed social, rather than individual, factors as the major cause of poverty. I have no argument with Bremner's description of the "old" and "new" views of poverty, nor do I doubt that the shift from one to the other took place much as he has demonstrated. I am not as confident as Bremner, however, that the new view of poverty was held universally by Progressives, or that the old view of poverty passed so completely into oblivion.

George's disclaimers of radical design apparently achieved their purpose. From the editors of the *Yale Review* came assurances that the George Junior Republic was "not socialistic or otherwise utopian, [but] rests upon a frank acceptance of present conditions." The Junior Republic promoted nothing more radical than "individual responsibility, industrial independence, thrift, business sagacity, respect for law, acquaintance with the forms of civil government, sympathy and patriotism." [17] Jacob Riis echoed this sentiment. "I believe in it," he wrote, "as a practical effort to fit the boy to things that are, rather than to such as might be in a millennium he nor we will live to see." [18]

It is not surprising that in his lifetime William R. George was compared with Jacob Riis and Booker T. Washington.[19] Riis and Washington not only held out the promise of Americanization to the immigrant and the Negro, but through their own careers they provided an inspiring example of what their people could actually accomplish. George similarly reaffirmed the Horatio Alger myth for the native born. Although he did not literally rise from rags to riches, his lack of formal education and material advantage gave him the aura of being a "self-made man." In an era oppressed by the grim sordidness of urbanization and industrialization, there was an epic quality

[17] William F. Blackman, "The George Junior Republic," *Yale Review*, V (Aug. 1896), 212–213.

[18] Jacob Riis, "Introduction," MS, George Junior Republic Papers.

[19] Ellery Sedgwick, editor for D. Appleton and Company, enthusiatically described George's book, *The Junior Republic*, as "the most genuine record of a work which I have read since 'Up from Slavery'" (Sedgwick to George, March 13, 1908). Another reviewer compared it to *The Making of an American* and *Up from Slavery* (Redlands, Calif., *Daily Review*, March 19, 1911). George was personally acquainted with Washington, having been introduced by Thomas Mott Osborne. As we shall see in the next chapter, Riis provided George crucial inspiration and assistance in the early days of the Republic.

about George's heroic struggle to build a new society on the rural landscape.[20]

The history of the George Junior Republic, then, is both the story of the personality and vision of William R. George and of the values and attitudes of an age which accepted him as one of its own. Yet the social, economic, and psychological factors which carried him to the apex of the reform movement also contributed to his ultimate downfall. George's dilemma is a familiar one. For a moment he stood at the center of history and thought that it was for all eternity. Like his Puritan ancestors, George endowed his life history with redemptive and inspirational value. He never tired of telling it,[21] and like so many others, could not accept the fact that his biography became increasingly irrelevant as history passed him by. To bring George's personal crisis and tragedy into sharper focus, we must begin by recounting his steps into the Progressive movement.[22]

[20] Two apostles of self-help, Lyman Abbott (*How to Succeed;* New York, 1882) and Wilbur F. Crafts (*Successful Men of Today and What They Say of Success;* New York, 1883), were ardent supporters of the Junior Republic (Crafts to George, Jan. 1897); see also Irvin G. Wyllie, *The Self-made Man in America: The Myth of Rags to Riches* (New York, 1966), 59.

[21] George published three books, all of which were largely autobiographical: *The Junior Republic* (1910), *Citizens Made and Remade* (with Lyman Beecher Stowe, 1912), and *The Adult Minor* (1937). He also kept a regular diary from 1905 until his death. At least five versions of an unfinished autobiography can be found in his papers.

[22] The story has an epic quality about it. Occasionally the reader may want to form his own judgments about what is fact and what is fiction. Reality, myth, and illusion are not always well defined in the context of George's rich fantasy life. The fantasy itself is richly revealing, and no attempt has been made to expunge it completely from the history. The difficulty, if not impossibility, of discovering what actually happened is reflected in the following letter from Lyman Beecher Stowe, who was helping George write his second book, to George: "There are presumably some minor in-

The Republic football team on the Miller Athletic Field, about 1905. Jane Hope Cottage and New York Cottage are in the background.

The Furniture Shop, about 1910, where furniture was made for the Republic cottages and for sale. The chair bears the GJR insignia.

The Printing Office in the early 1900's.

Members of the Junior Republic police force, about 1896.

i

On June 4, 1866, William R. George was born on the farm in West Dryden, New York, that his great-grandfather had settled over one hundred years before. He was the only child of John F. and Eleanor Baker George, and loneliness was the one sorrow of his early youth. A ninety-year-old great-grand-mother held him spellbound with stories of the Revolutionary War, but he had few friends and constantly longed for the companionship of a brother or sister.[23] Though he loved his mother "almost to the point of distraction" and "suffered mental tortures whenever she was ill," he occasionally wished she would become just sick enough so that a sympathetic doctor would bring her a baby.[24]

George's relationship to his father is unclear. Though he professed deep devotion for both parents, little mention of his father is found in any of his extensive memoirs and papers. John F. George has been described as "quiet, unassuming, humorous, and industrious."[25] George's mother, on the other hand, clearly dominated his life until his marriage. She was not just his mother, he wrote, she was his pal, his "chum,"

---

accuracies which you will please correct. There are, however, I imagine some inaccuracies which I hope you will let pass so long as the general impression is truthful. Remember, we are not writing a history or a biography of yourself, but merely interpreting the work. Truth in details can and should be subordinated and even sacrificed when necessary to truth of impression which must be a bit colored to penetrate the brain of the ordinary reader. There is a kind of prose license as well as poetic license" (Dec. 30, 1911).

[23] George to Mrs. Wade, April 24, 1911. George had male cousins whom he rarely mentioned.

[24] George to his daughters (Eleanor, Esther, and Edith), 1922; George to Mrs. Mary H. Wade, April 24, 1911.

[25] Jacob G. Smith, " 'Daddy' George," introduction to George, *The Adult Minor* (New York, 1937), xiii.

and for this reason he claimed he did not really miss having friends. There were four boys in the neighborhood his own age, but George seldom played with them. Though he remembered liking them well enough, he found none of them as companionable as his mother.[26]

Eleanor B. George, determined that her son have the proper religious instruction, required him to spend many hours memorizing verses from the Bible. When he was five years old, he became a life member of the West Dryden Juvenile Missionary Society of the Methodist Episcopal Church. The three-dollar membership fee presumably was paid by his father, who was secretary of the unit. Most of the religious leadership in the George family came from William's maternal grandfather, R. T. Baker, who was licensed as a local preacher by the Methodist Church.[27]

George's education was typical of that given country children of his day. He attended the district school which was located nearby in a primitive, one-room school house. There were no grades in the school, and the pupils were most often taught by a young local girl who had just been graduated from the same school. Nor surprisingly, there was very little system of instruction. Most teachers simply allowed the students, especially the older boys, to study whatever they liked best. As a result George was largely self-educated. He disliked mathematics intensely, and since no teacher bothered to have him master arithmetical tables, even as an adult he often used his fingers as aids in calculating simple problems.

Although he professed to be a serious student of geography and history, George was often more intent on creating a world of his own fantasy than in mastering the one in which he lived. Instead of studying McNally's *Geography*, he drew maps of imaginary continents that suited his fancy. He filled

[26] George to Mrs. Wade, April 24, 1911.   [27] *Ibid.*

the maps with mountains, rivers, lakes, seas, gulfs, bays, valleys, and plains, and then strategically placed cities and towns on the landscape connecting them with turnpikes, canals, and railroads. After giving place names to all his creation, he fixed national boundaries and then plunged the countries into war. Occasionally he even drew pictures and wrote short biographies of the national heroes connected with governments of his imaginary countries.[28]

George's fantasy life was further encouraged by the fact that his father did not regularly require him to help with the chores. Thus, when most boys his age were working on farms, young George was allowed to roam loose and alone over the field and wood. Often he armed himself with a wooden knife and revolver, and tearing across the valleys or dodging from tree to tree, he extended his "paper wars" to fighting mock battles across the undulating terrain of central New York.[29]

In addition to playing his lonely games and fighting mock wars, young Will George read insatiably. His mother taught him to read at an early age, and he did not remember a time when he could not read at least the simplest works. On many an afternoon he was seen shambling down a dusty road with a volume of *Youth's Companion* or *Oliver Optic* under his arm. Fascinated with adventure stories, he devoured the columns of *Youth's Companion*, reading the accounts of "The Lost Trail," "Left on Labrador," and "Indian Pete." He liked best, however, books and stories that dealt with the triumphs of poor youths and the salvation of the unfortunate. He avidly read the famous American story writers, Horatio Alger and William Makepiece Thayer, who made most popular the "rags to riches" theme.[30] The book which had the greatest

[28] *Ibid.*   [29] *Ibid.*

[30] George to his daughters, 1922; George, "Notes on the Biography of William R. George," MS, June 6, 1934.

impression on him was *Robinson Crusoe*, which he rated next to the Bible as the most influential book he ever read. Through Defoe, George claimed to have learned that no man can be a society unto himself. Living alone, Crusoe could commune with God, but he could not share the spiritual fellowship with man. He could daydream, "twiddle his thumbs or toss rocks in the ocean," but lacked human companionship. Wealth was impossible, for he could only barter with himself. And patriotism and civic duty could hardly have any meaning at all. George understood that when Friday entered into Crusoe's life, social isolation and loneliness ceased. Through Friday, Crusoe found fulfillment of man's four basic social instincts; spiritual, recreative, economic, and civic. Thus, Crusoe became a kind of new Adam, creating a new and utopian social order—utopian not in the sense that it repudiated the values of the past, but that it swept away the encumbrances preventing their fulfillment.[31]

Laying his books aside, the lonely young idealist cast his eyes on the hills of West Dryden and built imaginary towns and cities on the ground over which he had often fought battles. Populating his cities with imaginary citizens, he created imaginary histories of success and conquest. Nor did he always confine his imaginary histories to his make-believe cities on the hills. He loved to create hypothetical careers for the very lads with whom he had so little real contact. One was to be a famous lawyer, another a great general, still another a governor or even President. It is interesting to note that although he remembered dreaming of fame, success, and con-

---

[31] George, undated MS, and *The Adult Minor*, 161. Of course, one must be careful in attaching undue importance to an adult's memory of the significant events of his youth. The full significance that the mature George attributed to Robinson Crusoe may have been only dimly perceived by the boy.

quest for others, George never reported doing so for himself.[32] George's flights into fantasy, rather like young Thomas Mott Osborne's, almost always focused on the activities and accomplishments of others.

One of the most memorable events of his youth was a sleigh trip to Corning, New York, in the year 1879. There, at the railroad station where his father had come to receive some farm implements, he saw a sight he would never forget. While he was standing on the platform, a trainload of immigrants bound for homes in the west pulled into the station. In great wonder and excitement, the shy country lad gazed upon more children than he had ever seen before, all of them foreigners. His feelings were ambivalent: on the one hand, he felt pangs of anxiety as he contemplated this great horde of immigrants that was flooding the country; on the other hand, as he regarded the hopeful faces, he extended a silent welcome to all the future American citizens. He later recalled that he watched in tears as the train resumed its westward course.

When the train moved on I watched till it was out of sight and then walked away seriously pondering the future of those immigrants. Would the natives be good to them when they arrived in their new homes? Would their friends back in the old country follow them to this land of freedom which I was certain was the one and only place for the oppressed? Then as I walked away I found myself imagining marvelous careers for those prospective citizens in their new American homes.[33]

The very next year, young William George was to encounter the immigrants first hand. It was not in the west, however, but in New York City that this took place. Like thousands of his generation, George's father finally tired of

[32] George to his daughters, 1922; George, "Notes on the Biography of William R. George," MS, June 6, 1934.
[33] George to his daughters, June 1922.

what seemed to be the endless and fruitless toil of farming, and in the spring of 1880, he moved his family into neighboring Ithaca where he studied shorthand and became a court reporter. For a short time Will George attended the old Ithaca Academy. But although Ithaca was only five miles from the old homestead, George soon complained of city life and was overjoyed when his father, unable to support his family on a clerk's salary, moved back to the farm. The respite was short lived, however. Bursting into the farm house on an unusually hot day during the harvest, John F. George dramatically announced to his brother that he was through with farming and was determined to quit for good and move his family to New York City.[34]

In November of 1880, John F. George, his wife Eleanor, and their fourteen-year-old son Will, like millions of their countrymen, turned their backs on rural America and embarked for the city where with other immigrants, both native and foreign, they were traumatically cast into the maelstrom of industrial society.[35] George's first impression of New York City was probably little different from that of other country boys. "The shoreline and buildings that we were approaching," he wrote of his first crossing of the Hudson River, "had no skyscraper skyline as today, but it was big enough to surprise a country lad who had only seen buildings approximating the size of an oversized haystack."[36] At first he thought the harbor was jammed with battleships and was greatly embarrassed to discover that they were only ferryboats. When he walked ashore on Manhattan Island he was fascinated by

[34] "Alvord Baker," Oral History Interview 150, p. 9 (Collection of Regional History and University Archives, Cornell University).

[35] George, *The Junior Republic* (New York, 1910), 1; George, "Autobiography," MS, Oct. 1, 1935.

[36] George, "Autobiography," MS, Oct. 1, 1935.

the cobblestone streets and the great bustle of the city. He was amazed at the size of a huge beer wagon that rumbled by. The rag pickers and tramps he saw on all sides puzzled him. In his first few hours in the city he explored the docks, chased a horse-drawn fire engine, watched a policeman drag a middle-aged man to the station house, and stood transfixed watching the elevated trains.[37]

Despite his initial excitement over the city, George could not reconcile himself to his new urban environment. He felt choked and stifled by the city and longed for the days when he had roamed freely around the countryside or lounged in the fields reading and dreaming of clean, bright worlds. He pled with his parents to be allowed to return to his old country home. His depression became so acute that he could not attend the public school. Twice he enrolled in a neighborhood school, but found he could not keep his mind on his studies. The transition from the comparative anarchy of his one-room country school to the relatively disciplined regime of the city school may have been too difficult for George. His father gave him English lessons at home, and his mother valiantly tried to teach him mathematics. Unable to roam freely as before, George again turned to his books to escape his melancholia, spending long hours reading history and Emerson's *Essays*.[38]

Finally, his parents became so alarmed at their child's depression that, in the spring of 1881, they allowed him to return to West Dryden to live with his grandparents. After his arrival, George wrote his mother and father: "I put on my old clothes and went out dores and commenced knealing summersalts (or at least tried to) and shouted and sung and felt as though I was 'going-up'." [39] On visiting their old home,

[37] *Ibid.*   [38] George, "Autobiography," MS, Oct. 9, 1935.
[39] George to his parents, May 29, 1881.

George broke down and cried. Again he wrote his parents, wishing more than anything else that they could all move back to West Dryden. How nice it would be, the boy lamented, if they "could put on our old clothes and work around like we used to." [40]

For the next eight years, George alternated living in the city with brief, but frequent, hegiras to his old home in the country. By degrees George adjusted to his urban surroundings, but by the fall of 1883 he had still not completely reconciled himself to the city. Once again he returned to West Dryden, supposedly to help his grandfather with the harvest, but more importantly to settle his nerves. To his great surprise, he found that his few adventures in the city had dulled his enthusiasm for farm work. He quickly reverted to reading and daydreaming to pass the time, and at last, weary of the dull country life, he returned to New York City in October 1883, determined to find a regular job. [41]

There was little available for the unskilled and under-educated youth. George was not unmindful of his good fortune when he found a position as delivery boy and bill collector for the publishing house of Ford, Howard, and Hulbert. The job was therapeutic for the boy. His mother reported that Will's fits of depression were greatly alleviated by his work. He could hardly endure it when he was forced to sit still for some time. His job with Ford, Howard, and Hulbert kept him walking the streets most of the day, and after only a few weeks he almost entirely forgot his depression. [42]

George's new job was ideal for him. Involving no set routine, he was free to work his own hours. Besides paying six

[40] George to his parents, April 9, 1882.
[41] George to his daughters, 1922.
[42] Mrs. Eleanor Baker George to Mrs. J. B. George, Oct. 21, 1883.

dollars a week, the publishers furnished George carfare which enabled him to travel to all parts of the city and, to his great delight, allowed him to meet all kinds of people.[43] As he became acquainted with the city, he was more and more fascinated by the life he found surging around him. He discovered the public and Y.M.C.A. libraries, the book stores on Nassau Street, and Liggett's Book Store on Chambers Street, and spent part of every day at one of them. In addition he began to roam again, often exploring the city blocks from his home on 104th Street all the way to the Battery.

As he wandered alone through the city, George again took refuge in his make-believe world. He dreamed about the future of the city and began to construct imaginary histories of the families he saw living in various flats along the route of his walks. His favorite pastime was to walk in the poorest sections of town observing the conditions of the people, and then in his mind reconstructing their lives. His curiosity became inextinguishable and he desired to know not only the neighborhood, but the antecedents of all its residents, the size of each family, the economic, political, religious, and cultural status of all its members. He was especially interested in ascertaining the number of children in each family. Having few companions of his own, he made friends, in his imagination, of all in the neighborhood. As he had done in West Dryden, he took great delight in proposing marvelous careers for them.[44]

The similarities between George's anonymous walks through the city and Thomas Mott Osborne's masquerades are striking. In many ways both were "marginal men" caught

[43] George, "Notes," undated MS; Mrs. William R. George, "William R. George," MS, 1899.

[44] George to his daughters, 1922; George, "Autobiography," MS, Oct. 1, 1935.

between two cultures and not really able to identify fully with either.[45] After his move to New York City, George became torn between the secure but restricted world of his childhood and the confusing, frightening, but exciting world of his adolescence. Since he was not fully accepted by either world, George became insecure, moody, hypersensitive, excessively self-conscious, and extremely nervous.

During this period, as well as later, George may have been suffering from neurasthenia.[46] Though he was physically robust and unusually strong, he constantly complained of fatigue, headaches, and other aches and pains. He had difficulty in concentrating on minute or routine details. This, coupled with his general listlessness, may explain his difficulty in school. He napped often, yet frequently awoke "tired." Nevertheless, his fatigue was selective, for he was able to devote long hours to reading and exploring New York. In all probability his crises were due not to physical overwork but rather to the emotional strain of adjusting to city life. It is possible that George, unable to cope successfully with his new environment, unconsciously found in neurasthenia a convenient cover for his complete discouragement.[47]

[45] For a recent discussion of the concept of "marginality," see Milton M. Gordon, *Assimilation in American Life* (New York, 1964), 56.

[46] Neurasthenia, or the asthenic reaction, is not included in the latest American Psychiatric Association *Manual*, but the term was useful for describing a frequently observed neurotic reaction (James C. Coleman, *Abnormal Psychology and Modern Life* [Chicago, 1956], 174). Another historian who has found his subjects plagued with neurasthenia is Christopher Lasch, *The New Radicalism in America* (New York, 1965), 18, 38, 61, 115. Of course, there are dangers of the historian "playing" psychoanalyst; some of these are noted in Bruce Mazlish, ed., *Psychoanalysis and History* (Englewood Cliffs, N.J., 1963), 1–19.

[47] These neurasthenic symptoms do not necessarily prove that George was neurotic. Dr. Robert Kleck of the Psychology Depart-

It would be a mistake, however, to attribute George's obvious emotional problems solely to the traumatic shock of moving from the country into the city. He had always been a dutiful child, well behaved and extremely anxious to please his mother. Eleanor George, who has been described as "imperative, persistent, with dominating and unyielding loyalty," believed her son to be divinely called to the Methodist ministry and determined that he should prepare for college or divinity school.[48] His inability to live up to her expectations may have contributed further to George's feelings of worthlessness and failure. In retrospect, George did not remember acting as selfishly and egocentrically as other children. Rather, he remembered himself as the super-idealist, always ready to give, to sacrifice for the sake of others. George shared with his mother the idea that he had some special mission in life. But though unselfish and hyperethical to the point of self-righteousness, George was haunted by his aggressive impulses and hostility. He was always afraid of doing something that would hurt his mother or make her ashamed of him.[49]

George realized that there were two aspects to his per-

---

ment of Dartmouth College, in consultation with the author, would only state that it was his guess that George was neurasthenic. See also Coleman, *Abnormal Psychology and Modern Life*, 181–184.

[48] Smith, " 'Daddy' George," xiii. Smith relates that an injury sustained while jumping off the Third Avenue streetcar ended George's studies. However, this account appears in none of George's own memoirs, and though I do not doubt the fact of the injury, I am inclined to believe it served as an excuse rather than a reason for discontinuing school. R. W. Chamberlain (*There Is No Truce: A Life of Thomas Mott Osborne* [New York, 1935], 222) reports that George rebelled against the set regimen of preparatory school and college. See George's own comment on this in *The Junior Republic*, 2.

[49] For a discussion of the hypervectoral neurasthenic see Benjamin Wolman, *Handbook of Clinical Psychology* (New York, 1965), 1001, 1132–1133.

sonality that he was never able to understand. He remembered: "the deeply sentimental, imaginative, idealistic, peace-loving, religious side . . . and then there is the somewhat pugnacious side." [50] His pugnacity and aggressive impulses were manifested in two ways: One was his passion for boxing; he once watched "Gentleman" Jim Corbett defeat John L. Sullivan and was never able to express the thrill he experienced that day. Secondly, he had always had a strongly militarist bent. The soldier's life fascinated him, and at one time, longing for a career in the United States Army, he hoped for a chance to attend West Point. The nearest outlet for his military instincts was the National Guard. Accordingly, on reaching his eighteenth birthday, he joined Company H of the Twenty-second Regiment, New York State National Guard. He never rose high in the ranks but did become drill sergeant. His military "career" was brief, but, like his love of boxing, it was to prove important in shaping his life work. [51]

Aggressive and adventuresome as he was, George still could not hold a permanent job. For a time he alternated between periods of menial employment, serious illness and melancholia, and convalescence in West Dryden. Finally, at the encouragement of his father, George went into business for himself manufacturing jewelry cases and firearms boxes. His father set George up in business, and when his son met with some financial difficulties, came to his rescue. Eleanor George continued to worry about her son's health. She secretly wished he would sell out, for she feared George was hurting his lungs working at his bench. [52]

[50] George to his daughters, 1922.

[51] George, *The Junior Republic*, 2–3; "Notes on My Life," MS, 1935–1936; and letter to his daughters, 1922.

[52] Eleanor Baker George to Mrs. J. B. George, Feb. 19, 1890; anonymous letter to the editor, *American Magazine*, June 14, 1910;

George proved to be a poor entrepreneur, although his family, like Osborne's, remembers him as an excellent business-man—when he put his mind to it. But increasingly he found the business world tedious and dull. His trade never flourished, but since he continued to live at home with his parents, his small income proved adequate for his limited material needs. Gradually, he spent less and less time at his bench, until, in the spring of 1890, he was spending one-half of his time in social work. By 1895 he had turned over the entire business to an assistant. Throughout his life, George enjoyed the public reputation of being a successful businessman who had sacrificed his financial security for the sake of reform. George and his fellow Progressives probably found the myth necessary, but it should be noted that reform was the only real vocation that George ever enjoyed.[53]

ii

Rather inauspiciously, George drifted into reform. In 1888, much to his mother's relief, he was "converted" to the social gospel. In that year he was overwhelmed by a wave of religious enthusiasm that swept through the Methodist Church when the congregation was visited by an itinerant revivalist. Now convinced that he was called to be an evangelist, minister, or missionary, George became quite active in his church, becoming assistant superintendent of the Sunday school. In 1892, at twenty-six years of age, he was licensed as an exhorter of the Methodist Episcopal Church in New York City.

George, "Notes," undated MS; Mrs. William R. George, "William R. George," MS, 1899. See also George's notebook for Dec. 5, 1886, to Dec. 1, 1887.

[53] Lyman Beecher Stowe, "Mr. George Studies the Street Boy at Close Range," *Citizens Made and Remade*, 3; George, "William R. 'Daddy' George," MS, 1930, and "Notes on the Biography of William R. George," MS, June 6, 1934.

Soon thereafter he became involved in the Christian Endeavor movement. He was the first president of the New York City Junior Christian Endeavor Union and vice-president of the senior group. George actively engaged in the organization of new societies in New York State and other sections of the country. In 1890, he attended the national meeting of the Young Peoples' Society of Christian Endeavor in Cincinnati and rose on the floor of the convention to dedicate his life publicly to the service of the children of New York City. By 1892, he was on the arrangements committee for the inter-national convention of Christian Endeavor to be held that year in New York.[54] As Jacob Smith, first president of the George Junior Republic, has written:

He indulged his love of country by enlisting in the Twenty-second Regiment of the National Guard of New York and served his Master by becoming an exhorter, a Sunday school superintendent, a leader in Christian Endeavor. Early photographs reveal him in the uniform of his regiment, with sergeant's chev-rons, and in civilian clothes with the Christian Endeavor pin in his lapel. He was a patriot and a Christian.[55]

Before 1890 most social work in New York City was done by the church. Charity relief was generally unorganized and uncoordinated, often independent and individual. Beginning in 1882 the New York Charity Organization Society (COS), founded by Josephine Shaw Lowell, sought to infuse high standards of integrity, competence, and efficiency into the many independent relief agencies. In addition, the COS sought to coordinate the work of competing social agencies and to expose the frauds of impostors. The COS was not a relief

[54] George to Carlton M. Sherwood, Oct. 7, 1920; to Bernard Clauson, Aug. 8, 1910; untitled MS, 1918; "Autobiography," MS, Nov. 5, 1928.
[55] Jacob G. Smith, " 'Daddy' George," xii.

agency itself but acted as a clearinghouse for such charities as the Salvation Army, the Children's Aid Society, the Society for the Prevention of Cruelty to Children (SPCC), the Association for Improving the Condition of the Poor (AICP), the Y.M.C.A., orphanages, and a few boys' clubs and settlement houses. Many of the older agencies, however, were reluctant to cooperate with the COS, and as a result the COS came to rely principally on "friendly visiting" of the poor.[56] "Friendly visiting" eventually became the major weapon of the COS for combating the effects of urban poverty. The unpaid visitors, working under the supervision of a trained, professional social worker, were to bring encouragement, counseling, and sympathy into the lives of the destitute.[57] However, many friendly visitors like William R. George were semi-independent and remained autonomous, much to the distress of the COS.

Shortly after his "conversion" to the social gospel in 1888, George began his visiting and charity work under the auspices of the Methodist Church of the Savior in Harlem. This church served an economically and socially mixed congregation of Irish Protestants and old-stock Americans. As assistant superintendent of the Sunday school, George organized children's outing clubs to visit museums and other points of general interest chosen for their usefulness in social and cultural uplift. In addition, George introduced his Sunday school class to the activities of the Five Points Mission.[58]

Through the Christian Endeavor Society George came to

[56] Robert Bremner, *American Philanthropy* (Chicago, 1960), 98–99; Bremner, *From the Depths*, 51–53; Roy Lubove, *The Professional Altruist: The Emergence of Social Work as a Career, 1880–1930* (Cambridge, Mass., 1965), 1–22.

[57] Lubove, *The Professional Altruist*, 12–14; Bremner, *American Philanthropy*, 99.

[58] George, MS, Nov. 5, 1928.

work closely with the children of the Mission, visiting their homes and including them on his outings with the Sunday school. The Five Points area had long been recognized as America's original and worst slum. Charles Dickens, on his first visit to America in 1842, had noted the vile character of the Five Points district years before Jacob Riis "rediscovered" it while describing how the other half lived.[59] The Five Points, located a scant block and a half from the infamous Mulberry Bend, was one of the roughest sections in New York before the establishment of the Five Points Mission. In 1852, the Ladies Missionary Society of the Methodist Episcopal Church purchased the old brewery which had stood at the Five Points since 1792 and converted the site into the celebrated Five Points Mission, known officially as the Five Points House of Industry.[60]

His work among the Mission youth provided George with invaluable experience as well as a source of children when he began his Fresh Air work. But George found Christian Endeavor and the church too narrow and stifling. The Endeavor Movement tended to limit his contacts exclusively to Protestants, while the church seemed intolerant and repressive. Too

[59] Charles Dickens, *American Notes* (New York, 1842), 35–37; Jacob Riis, *How the Other Half Lives* (1900; reprint ed., New York: Hill and Wang, 1957), 41–42; Bremner, *From the Depths*, 5.

[60] New York *Tribune*, April 9, 1916; Wilbur F. Crafts, "A Day at the Boys' Republic," *Christian Endeavor World*, XII (Feb. 17, 1898), 415–416. The Five Points House of Industry became one of the best known and most successful missions in New York. For an excellent description of the Old Brewery at Five Points which harbored Murderer's Alley and the Den of Thieves, see Herbert Asbury, *The Gangs of New York* (New York, 1927), 13–16. For the story of the reclamation of Five Points, see [The Ladies Mission Society] *The Old Brewery and the New Mission Home at Five Points* (New York, 1854), *passim;* and William F. Barnard, *Forty Years at the Five Points* (New York, 1893), *passim.*

often, George believed, the church was more concerned with defining creeds and behavior than with meliorating poverty and misery. The Mission was preoccupied with combating vice and gave insufficient attention to having fun. A lonely young man, starved for companionship, George found greater satisfaction in breaking the church's prohibitions than advocating them. He loved a good fight, supervised or not, and though he didn't drink, he especially enjoyed the boisterous camaraderie of his regiment.[61] Anxious to prove that he was no sissy, George developed his own boxing talents, and thereafter took the stance of a moral, clean-cut, but tough Christian.

Rejecting the church's restricted program, George gradually moved into more independent activities. He was attracted by the Children's Aid Society and the SPCC, but his aversion to a supervisor's discipline caused him to reject any formal commitment to these agencies. He elected to become a freelance social worker, unpaid but unencumbered by the routine and regulations of the established societies. In keeping with the character of his solitary reveries, George was carried into social work by his own whim coupled with considerable zeal to reform the world in his own way. This fierce independence was always to be one of George's strengths, but it was also his major handicap. At a time when the COS was attempting to direct the major currents of social reform, William R. George conspicuously remained autonomous.[62]

George continued to live with his parents in an apartment on the upper east side of Manhattan. Here, with his mother's blessing, George engaged in his own version of settlement work and friendly visiting. In a nearby vacant lot he organized

[61] George, MS, Nov. 5, 1928.
[62] George, MS, May 26, 1928; Lubove, *The Professional Altruist*, 49–52.

and umpired baseball games for mission youth. In the evenings he would invite about a half dozen Italian or Irish youths to his home to hear Bible stories, look at picture books, and sing around the piano. Eleanor George, delighted with her son's interest in moral reform, was relieved to discover that she "could not tell who was happier, Will or the children." [63]

Usually George encountered no trouble during his wanderings around New York City. But there was one notable exception. One day while walking alone through Harlem, George encountered eleven members of the infamous Duffyville Gang, which dominated the ward controlled by the "boodle" alderman Michael Duffy. He was deep within their territory and was mistaken for a member of a rival gang. Though he had had some "words" with various members of the gang before, up to this time he had never encountered more than one tough at a time. As the eleven closed in, George successfully appealed to their sense of honor, asking that he be allowed to fight them fairly—one at a time—beginning with Logan, the leader of the gang. The battle was hard fought on both sides, and when George was eventually knocked down, he got immediately to his feet, ready to take on the next comer. But none of the remaining ten stepped forward to resume the fight. As a result, George so earned the respect of the gang that from then on he was able to wander freely through Duffyville territory without fear of being molested. This enabled him to become intimately acquainted with that section of Harlem and, at the same time, to begin to win the confidence of the New York street gangs which eventually were to become the nucleus of his Fresh Air camp. [64]

[63] Eleanor B. George to Mrs. Joel George, Dec. 22, 1890; Stowe, in *Citizens Made and Remade*, 3; George, MS, Nov. 5, 1928.

[64] George, "Autobiography," MS, Oct. 9, 1935, and MS of Nov. 5, 1928. There are several versions of this encounter, all similar with but minor variations.

Under the auspices of the Five Points Mission, George had founded several outing clubs. After his scrape with the Duffyville Gang, George began to direct most of his attention toward the street "arab," using his outing clubs as the nucleus of his activities. George hoped that if he could include the gang within the activities of the outing clubs, the gang members under his close supervision would be influenced by the behavior of the Mission children. But first he had to get into the gang.

Unlike the Mission children, the Duffyville Gang did not respond to George's invitation to play baseball. Noting that most of the members read the crime headlines before they read the baseball scores, George then posed as a police reporter. He met with immediate success, gaining the confidence of the gang and free access to their two hideouts, a shanty behind a factory and a den beneath a pier. In this respect George's experience was very similar to that of Jacob Riis, who had also found gangs receptive when they learned he was from the papers. George believed that the bravado of the gangs was fostered by the detailed newspaper accounts of their crimes and escapades. He opposed such publicity, for he believed that it fed the gangs' passion for recognition. If the papers eliminated crime news, George contended later, a motive and stimulation of delinquency would be removed.[65]

But George recognized that the press played only a minor role in fostering juvenile delinquency. Indolence, incompetence, intemperance, and idleness were the major causes of human misery, he believed. Of the four, idleness was by far the most serious. Long, hot summer vacations made idlers of many boys in a city where there was virtually nothing to do. Only a very few found relief from the heat and boredom through

[65] George, MS, May 26, 1928, and letter to Mark O. Prentiss, Nov. 6, 1926; Stowe, in *Citizens Made and Remade*, 28; Riis, *How the Other Half Lives*, 164.

the Fresh Air outings. Most boys drifted into mischief and trouble. The street child soon learned that the games he wanted to play usually collided with rights of property and the maintenance of public order and peace. Hardly had he learned to run before he discovered that most of his street games were illegal, and that having fun and breaking the law were one and the same thing. Most boys soon concluded that the policeman was his natural enemy.[66]

If police officials tended to view the street gangs as bands of potential desperados and cutthroats, most of the reformers of the 1890's viewed them as unfortunate products of environment and instinct. Riis described the average boy as "just a little steam-engine with the steam always up." "Play is the only safety valve the child has," Riis continued. "If his landlord runs him out of what yard he might have, and the police keep him off the streets, he is bound to explode. When he does, when he throws mud and stones, and shows us the side of him which the gutter developed, we are shocked, and marvel much what our boys are coming to."[67] The tenements prevented the slum child from developing the normal mental, physical, and moral faculties that most children acquire from healthy play. As a consequence they were inclined to break windows, ring doorbells, steal, and generally harass those in the neighborhood they didn't like.[68]

The formation of the gang itself was seen to be as natural as human nature. Every normal boy was believed to participate in three primary social groups: the family, the neighborhood, and

[66] William R. George, MS, Nov. 5, 1928; Jacob Riis, "The Making of Thieves in New York," *The Century*, XLIX (Nov. 1894), 115; Russell Sage Foundation, *Boyhood and Lawlessness* (New York, 1914), 12.
[67] Riis, *The Battle with the Slum* (New York, 1902), 234.
[68] Robert Hunter, *Poverty* (1907; reprint ed., New York: Harper Torchbooks, 1965), 196–197.

the play group. With the deterioration of the family and the neighborhood by the urban slums, the story of the gang began. Denied his normal outlets for instinctive association, the slum "kid" had no other choice than to run with the pack. Robbed of home and childhood, with every prop knocked from under him, the children of the poor were transformed into the "dangerous classes" of New York. They became the homeless boys, the street-wandering girls, the city "arabs," the street "rats" who were bred in the filth of the slum. They slept anywhere and lived by petty theft or street jobs. Frequently luckless children were sent to the reformatory where contact with older and more experienced youth confirmed them in a life of crime.[69]

Few Progressives believed that the boy gangs were intrinsically corrupt. The crimes of the gang were nothing more than tragically misdirected boyhood adventure and mischief.[70] The Russell Sage Foundation reflected that "nothing could be more persuasive and uplifting in the boy's life than the gang's development when given proper scope and direction." [71] Boys' Clubs and Fresh Air outings were believed to be proper ways to deal with the gangs, for they could direct the boys' energies into socially acceptable activities. The gang, after all, was not without its inherent virtues; it fostered cooperation and loyalty, furnished an outlet for the genius of organization, and, in its own way, provided for a measure of self-government.

[69] J. Adams Puffer, *The Boy and His Gang* (Boston, 1912), 7; Riis, *Battle with the Slum*, 236–237; Russell Sage Foundation, *Boyhood and Lawlessness*, 39–54 and *passim*; Riis, *How the Other Half Lives*, 136; Edith Abbott, *Some Pioneers in Social Welfare* (Chicago, 1937), 129; Charles Loring Brace, *The Dangerous Classes of New York* (New York, 1880), *passim*; Jane Addams, *The Spirit of Youth and the City Streets* (New York, 1909), *passim*.

[70] Riis, *Battle with the Slum*, 250–255.

[71] Russell Sage Foundation, *Boyhood and Lawlessness*, 40.

The gang member's sense of justice, while rude, was often well developed. He was usually fiercely independent, placing a premium on freedom and self-reliance. These were the strong handles, Jacob Riis argued, "by which those who know how can catch the boy and make him useful." [72]

Only a few adults, J. Adams Puffer wrote, can see the world through the boys' eyes, and fewer still are at home in his world. Those men who were most successful in handling boys, men like Judge Ben B. Lindsey and William R. George, were men who appealed most powerfully to the basic boyish impulses.[73] George had begun his work with the boy gangs by organizing military drill teams in connection with his outing clubs. The drills, at first, were his only means of combating "that ugly monster, idleness." He noted that children wearied of play just as often as they wearied of work. His own experience as drill sergeant for the Twenty-second Regiment convinced him that marching not only consumed a good deal of excess energy, but provided an elementary basis for social control. Eventually George organized six military companies, with the headquarters company at the Five Points Mission and others scattered throughout Manhattan, including one in Greenwich Village.[74]

George's militarism was not at all at odds with Progressive social thought of the 1890's. When Jacob Riis was asked if he thought military drill and military spirit might not endanger the democratic institutions of the country, he replied, "No my anxious friend, I do not. Let them march; and if with a gun, better still. Often enough it is the choice of the gun on the

[72] Riis, *How the Other Half Lives*, 148, and *The Children of the Poor* (New York, 1902), 215.

[73] Puffer, *The Boy and His Gang*, 1, 143.

[74] Mrs. William R. George, "William R. George," MS, 1899; George, MS, Nov. 5, 1928.

shoulder, or, by and by, the stripes on the back in the lock-step gang." [75] According to Riis, the gang was simply the boys' club run wild. Nothing would cut the ground out from under the gang so much as the boys' club organized into military units. Nothing was as beneficial as "drill of some sort." Indeed, Riis speculated, the real solution to the child problem during the long summer vacation might be to organize all the school children into a great military body. "The man who first organizes them into an army, and marches them off to the mountains to camp under military rule in July or August, will come near to solving the problem, I think, by making truant-schools superfluous and by clearing our police courts of child thieves." [76]

As early as 1890, George had begun to combine his outing activities with independent Fresh Air work, taking a small company of his Mission children to the old homestead near Freeville to drill and march for two weeks. Each year thereafter this Fresh Air camp in Freeville expanded in direct proportion to the growth of his military clubs in New York. George secured an abandoned Methodist church in the city which he turned into a hangout for his Duffyville Gang. But as he reflected on his social work of the past three years, George became disheartened. He realized that the Mission did not hold the key to child-saving. The Mission could hand out food, clothing, and a place to sleep to those who professed conversion, but it did not really save the poor. Instead it pauperized them and thereby added to their degradation. In addition, many of the original Duffyville Gang with whom he worked had been sent to jail or to the reformatory. George had become their friend and earned their confidence, but he had not succeeded in reforming them. He decided he needed

[75] Riis, *Battle with the Slum*, 255.
[76] Riis, "The Making of Thieves in New York," 115.

a new departure and sought a hangout which would free him from all supervision by the church. When he found a friend who would pay the rent on the old loft above Kennedy's distillery on 11th Street, George decided to concentrate all his energies on one of the toughest districts of Manhattan's lower east side.[77]

The neighborhood into which George moved was dominated by the Graveyard Gang, a group considerably tougher than the old Duffyville Gang. The inner circle of the Graveyard Gang was composed of the "Sons of Arrest." Only members who had a police record were eligible for this select group, and the member with the largest number of arrests was the leader of the entire gang. George conceived an audacious scheme of gaining entry into the "Sons of Arrest" and of eventually securing control of the gang, turning their natural energy and loyalty into helpful and constructive paths. After outfitting the three-room loft as a club room with games, a small library, and a little furniture, he set out to make friends with some of the members of the gang and induce them to hang out at the club room rather than on the street corners. While reconnoitering the area George was unexpectedly set upon by the Graveyard Gang. He stood them off single-handed until the police arrived to rescue him, exhibiting a fearlessness, endurance, and strength that soon became well known in the area.[78]

[77] Stowe, *Citizens Made and Remade*, 6; George, MS, Nov. 5, 1928. A picture of the block in which the loft was located can be seen in the original edition of Riis, *How the Other Half Lives* (New York, 1900), 163.

[78] Lyman Beecher Stowe, "What To Do with a Boy," *World's Work*, XXVI (June 1913), 190–195. Curiously, this incident closely paralleled an experience of Jacob Riis, another lonely wanderer through the slums, who ran into the Why-os Gang early one morning and escaped with his life only by the timely interference of the precinct captain and his detective; Riis, *The Making of an American* (1901; reprint ed., New York: Harper Torch books, 1966), 238–240.

George's first recruit to the new club was a member of the Graveyard Gang who called himself "Badger." He cornered the youth alone one evening and promised Badger his freedom if he could fight his way past. George then proceeded to administer a sound thrashing to the boy. Intimidated or converted, Badger joined the club. As more and more members were "recruited," George's reputation as a boxer spread throughout the district. His recruits, of course, boasted that no one could beat him. Disgruntled members of the Graveyard Gang, fearing the threat that George was presenting to their organization, arranged for George to meet their champion, a huge brute who had aspirations of becoming a prize fighter. George accepted the challenge on the condition that the fight take place in a locked room with no one but the fighters present. It was agreed that the fight would last until one of the men conceded defeat. Whether George converted the erstwhile prize fighter to the club is unknown, but his victory brought him undisputed leadership in the gang.[79]

In the fall of 1894, George and his gang were swept up in the excitement of New York municipal reform. Originally organized on a semimilitary basis with boxing, baseball, outings, reading, and drilling the main activities of the group, George knew his club would be a valuable asset to any political campaign. Throughout the 1890's civic and religious organi-

[79] Stowe, "What To Do with a Boy"; George Witten, "He Turned Bad Eggs into Good Citizens," *Success Magazine*, XI (April 1927), 46–47, 94–95. There is an air of unreality surrounding the stories of George's pacification of the Duffyville and Graveyard gangs, but there has always been great skepticism regarding such exploits. Possibly this is because we insist that gangs are tougher and more remote than they actually are. Certainly they choose for themselves ominous names. From the Fresh Air records we know that the boys with whom George worked were from twelve to eighteen years old, mostly from Irish, Italian, and other New Immigrant stock. George was in his mid-twenties, a prime period for successful street work, we have subsequently learned.

zations had bent every effort to defeat Richard Croker's Tammany machine. The Reverend Charles H. Parkhurst, minister of the Madison Square Presbyterian Church, denounced the Tammany-controlled police department from his pulpit on February 14, 1892. Parkhurst, in disguise, had toured the New York underworld alone and collected evidence proving that the police department sanctioned vice and illegal practices. It soon became apparent that the root of the corruption lay much deeper. The Lexow Committee, formed in 1894 to investigate Parkhurst's charges, revealed that the police had been guilty of extortion, blackmail, and bribery. The police scandals of 1894 convinced members of the Good Government Clubs formed in 1892 that the election of 1894 would offer a propitious opportunity for the overthrow of Tammany. Reform organizations multiplied, and by the fall of 1894 the Good Government Clubs, the Citizen's Union, the Society for the Prevention of Crime, the Committee of Seventy, the Citizen's Association, and the City Club had all appointed committees to work for the defeat of the Tammany machine. The Christian Endeavor Society also lined up behind city reform efforts, urging its members to work for the election of good men and the adoption of good laws. That summer, with the ardent support of Theodore Roosevelt, all the dissident organizations agreed on one of New York's first fusion candidates for mayor, William L. Strong, bank president and a man of highest character.[80]

[80] Clifford W. Patton, *The Battle for Municipal Reform: Mobilization and Attack* (Washington, D.C., 1940), 34–39; Wallace S. Sayre and Herbert Kaufman, *Governing New York City* (New York, 1960), 12–15; Charles H. Parkhurst, *Our Fight with Tammany* (New York, 1895), *passim*; Richard Welling, *As the Twig Is Bent* (New York, 1942), 57–73. For the relation of the campaign of 1894 to New York reform politics, see Theodore Lowi, *At the Pleasure of the Mayor* (New York, 1964), *passim*; Roy V. Peel, *The Political Clubs of New York* (New York, 1935), 13–44.

George joined a Good Government Club and volunteered his little band to assist in the election campaign. The Progressives had long recognized the political importance of boys' gangs in slum neighborhoods. Ward heelers and party bosses were often recruited from such gangs, and the power of the machine in some districts depended upon the strength of the gang, which duplicated in miniature the structure of Tammany Hall. When George offered his gang on the side of Good Government, the reformers were only too happy to accept. In addition to doorbell ringing, the gang carefully went over the voting lists, checking to make sure that each registrant was a bona fide voter. On election day, the whole club was sworn in as "Parkhurst Cops," George serving as a poll watcher and the rest of the gang serving as spotters. When a suspected repeater appeared at the polling place, George would assign two spotters to tail him for the rest of the day to make sure he didn't vote again elsewhere.[81]

Soon after he won the election, Mayor Strong appointed Theodore Roosevelt as police commissioner. Roosevelt devoted himself to the reformation of the police department and to the enforcement of laws against gambling and vice. As part of his program he made the "Parkhurst Cops" an adjunct of the police department. Early in his crusade against urban vice, Dr. Parkhurst had founded the City Vigilance League, an organization whose main business had been to watch saloons

[81] George, MS, Nov. 5, 1928, and "The George Junior Republic," MS, 1916; Witten, "He Turned Bad Eggs into Good Citizens," *passim;* Welling, *As the Twig Is Bent,* 66; Parkhurst, *Our Fight with Tammany,* 264–265. For a discussion of the relationship of gangs to machine politics, see Allen Davis, "Settlement Workers in Politics, 1890–1914," *Review of Politics,* XXVI (Oct. 1964), 507–517; and Oscar Handlin, *The Uprooted* (Boston, 1952), 209–210. For two excellent contemporary accounts of the same subject in Boston, see Robert Woods, *Americans in Process* (Boston, 1902), 147 ff., and *The City Wilderness* (Boston, 1899), 140–145.

and hotels in order to report violations of regulatory laws. Roosevelt adopted the "vigilante" principle and rewarded volunteers with appointments as unsalaried and un-uniformed special police officers with the power of arrest. George offered the services of his gang to the police department, and with Roosevelt's blessing the "Law and Order Gang" was founded.[82]

The formation of the Law and Order Gang climaxed George's work with the boys' gangs of the city. Now whenever he caught a lawbreaker, George took him to the loft above the distillery rather than turning the culprit over to the police. After administering his usual initiation, a boxing match, George promised to teach the boy to fight (literally) for law and order. In this manner, George hoped to recruit all the toughs of the neighborhood. He divided the Law and Order Gang into the craps squad and the policy squad. Using spotters and informers to locate crap games, the craps squad broke up every game it could find in the district, resorting to violence whenever necessary. The policy squad was no less thorough in its activities. This squad was allowed to observe the police raids on all the policy shops they "fingered." [83]

George dreamed of establishing Law and Order Gangs in all parts of the city, converting every neighborhood gang from law-breaking to law-enforcing. He pictured himself as

[82] Patton, *The Battle for Municipal Reform*, 39; Frederic C. Howe, *The Confessions of a Reformer* (New York, 1925), 50–55; Charles H. Parkhurst, *My Forty Years in New York* (New York, 1923), *passim*; George, "Daddy George Biography," MS, 1930, and MS, Nov. 5, 1928.

[83] Welling, *As the Twig Is Bent*, 147; George to Mark O. Prentiss (organizer of National Crime Commission), Aug. 25, 1925, and to Jacob Smith, Dec. 21, 1911. Lyman Beecher Stowe, in *Citizens Made and Remade*, 7–19, has a slightly different version of the founding of the Law and Order Gang. But Stowe is given to hyperbole and is highly unreliable.

commander-in-chief, leaving a trusted lieutenant in charge of each conquered territory and, with a team of battle-tested, hard-core regulars, advancing to each new battlefield. Much to his credit, however, George recognized that the tenuous loyalty of his band was directed toward himself and not toward the principle of right. His followers were not committed to the law, but responded to more primitive instincts. Their loyalty was to their gang and to their leader, who in this case just happened to lead them on the side of the police rather than against their traditional enemy. George had the elemental charisma of leadership, courage, and brute strength. But he knew that in his absence his organization would collapse and his gang would revert to its old ways. In all his relations with young people, George had played the role of the "boss." Though he had many trusted followers and would occasionally delegate responsibility to them and follow their advice, George kept absolute control in his own hands. He realized that most of his followers liked him for a regular fellow. At the same time he knew that they feared him.[84]

George's disappointment in his Law and Order Gang was similar to the disappointment of the city reformers with the administration of William Strong. Just as George discovered that civic responsibility meant little to his street "arabs," the Good Government Clubs discovered that many of their followers had joined for reasons of ambition or novelty. One ardent Good Government reformer, Richard Welling, observed that after the election it became "plain that public spirit was lacking to carry forward the Good Government Clubs between elections and that many . . . had no interest in politics except for what they could get out of it." As ten thousand members of the Good Government Clubs clamored for political appointment, Welling came to the same conclusion as

[84] George to Stowe, Jan. 10, 1912.

William George: the city had failed to instill in its inhabitants the common American virtues of self-government, self-reliance, and responsibility.[85]

The failure of Americanism in the city, many Progressive reformers believed, was not due to any inherent defects in the city population, but rather to the debilitating effects of the urban environment. Among conservative Progressives, however, the solution to the urban problems was not Edward Bellamy's Boston of the year 2000. The country had no need of utopianism, socialism, communism, communitarianism, or any other form of collectivism. What Americans needed was a revitalization of the old agrarian values which the expansive boom of the city threatened to crush. Trapped in their new cities, Americans forgot that their virtue sprang from the soil of the land. The country had always provided the training ground for self-government and self-reliance. In rural America, a lad was brought up under the close supervision of the extended family, learned respect for hard work, love of country, reverence for nature, and fear of God. The city, in contrast, with its dirt, disease, and overcrowding, stifled the tenement-dweller's ambition and calloused his moral and esthetic sensibilities. Moreover, the blight of the cities seemed to be gradually consuming rural America. Could the nation survive, a generation wondered, if the rural sources that fed the city were destroyed? [86]

[85] Welling, *As the Twig Is Bent*, 146, and MS, Jan. 8, 1941; New York *World Telegram*, May 5, 1936.

[86] Roy Lubove, *The Progressives and the Slums*, 50–61. Lubove, from whom the above draws heavily, has written one of the most penetrating analyses of a conservative reformer in ch. 3: "Jacob Riis: Portrait of a Reformer." The literature on the impact of urbanism, immigration, and industrialization on rural Amerca is vast. Robert Bremner, *From the Depths*, 309–345, provides an exhaustive bibliography on this subject. See also Henry Jacob Silverman, "American

At the heart of the whole problem, most early Progressives were convinced, was the immigrant. Every major social, economic, and political problem of the 1890's was traced directly to him. Though the immigrants were not entirely responsible for political bossism, criminal gangs, and overcrowding, they provided the basis for it all. In addition, the New Immigrants showed a disconcerting immunity to Americanization. Their old-world ties and clannishness seemed to cut them off from traditional American values. Crowded together in the slums, packed together in the dumbbell tenements, the immigrants clung to the vestiges of their old-world culture in the midst of social disintegration. Not only did the New Immigrant carefully preserve his mother tongue but, worst of all, many continued to revere the institutions of their homeland while despising the habits of old-stock Americans. Because of his ignorance of American institutions and because he was not schooled in self-government and self-support, the New Immigrant naturally became the victim of political machines, poverty, filth, and degradation. "In an intensely nationalistic decade," Roy Lubove noted, "the shadow of the new immigrant seemed to cover the land with the darkness of un-Americanism." [87]

Lubove has demonstrated that the urban reformers of the 1890's are incomprehensible apart from this context. Men like Jacob Riis and William R. George acted as interpreters for American Society, helping to guide America's transition from

---

Social Reformers in the Late Nineteenth and Early Twentieth Centuries" (Ph.D. diss., University of Pennsylvania, 1964).

[87] Lubove, *The Progressives and the Slums*, 50–51, 55, 72. See also Oscar Handlin, *The Uprooted, passim;* John Higham, *Strangers in the Land* (New York, 1965), 68–105; Bremner, *From the Depths*, 10. For a recent critique of the Handlin thesis, see Rudolph J. Vecoli, "Contradini *in* Chicago: A Critique of *The Uprooted*," *Journal of American History*, LI (Dec. 1964), 404–417.

an agrarian to an industrial society. Both men loved rural America and both had been shocked by the worst of the urban slums.[88] Together, George and Riis inspected the tenements and sweat shops of "Jewtown." [89] They also devoted much of their spare time to the work of settlement houses and "friendly visiting." Each had hoped that these agencies would provide a key to urban reform. The settlement house, founded as a neighborhood center, was modeled after the village meeting house, town hall, or country store. Through the settlement house, primary social relationships that were common to the small town and village could be established in the city. "Friendly visiting," as the Charity Organization Society called it, by rendering aid and advice to the urban poor, also attempted to re-establish the patterns of social control known in the village. By reproducing the social institutions of rural and small-town America in the big city, settlement workers and friendly visitors hoped they could facilitate the Americanization of the immigant.[90]

But the urban poor could not use these resources for counseling and advice as their country cousins had. New York was not a small town. Riis and George became more and more convinced that the attempt to recreate the social structure of

[88] For an interesting expansion of this theme with respect to other Progressives, see Wayne E. Fuller, "The Rural Roots of the Progressive Leaders," *Agricultural History*, XLII (Jan. 1968), 1–13.

[89] George, MS, 1935.

[90] Lubove, *The Professional Altruist*, 12–14; Higham, *Strangers in the Land*, 237–240; Gordon, *Assimilation in American Life*, 99. The best contemporary accounts of social settlement work are: Jane Addams, *Twenty Years at Hull House* (New York, 1910); Lillian Wald, *The House on Henry Street* (New York, 1915); and Robert Woods, and A. J. Kennedy, eds., *Handbook of Settlements* (New York, 1910). Mary Richmond, *Friendly Visiting among the Poor* (New York, 1906), written as a handbook for charity workers, contains an excellent description of friendly visiting.

the village in unstable and poverty-ridden tenement neighborhoods was futile. They agreed that the children of the poor were the key to neighborhood reconstruction and Americanization of the immigant. Only as the children of the tenements were schooled in the duties of being Americans would there be hope that the slum could be eliminated. Since the children themselves were products of their slum environment, it was desirable to remove them to more wholesome environments in which they could mature.[91]

Such was the aim of the "placing-out" and Fresh Air programs. Some reformers even contended that excursions and outings into the country were absolutely necessary for the reclamation of city children. For example, Joseph Lee wrote: "No other form of teaching could be more appropriate to the summer or could meet more acutely the needs of the city child. Every healthy boy or girl at a certain age (as Froebel and Stevenson . . . have taught us) likes to explore, to dig in the ground for treasures, to climb a tree and discover a new world." [92] Depriving the city child of the opportunity to experience the country would have the effect of stunting his mental and spiritual development. Gangs, after all, were only city boys deprived of their "tribal industries"—hunting, fishing, building and sailing rafts, going to ponds or into the woods, building huts and playing Indians.[93]

The experiment of placing New York City children in rural homes had begun in 1853 when Charles Loring Brace founded his Children's Aid Society (CAS). The CAS held religious meetings, established workshops and industrial schools, and

---

[91] Riis, *How the Other Half Lives*, 140; Joseph Lee, *Constructive and Preventive Philanthropy* (New York, 1906), 117, 185; Bremner, *From the Depths*, 212; Lubove, *The Progressives and the Slums*, 71.

[92] Lee, *Preventive and Constructive Philanthropy*, 117.

[93] Puffer, *The Boy and His Gang*, 43.

provided lodging houses for the poor, homeless children of the city. The most important project of the CAS, however, was finding foster homes in the country for vagrant children. It was Brace's ambition to drain New York City of destitute children by providing them with homes in the country. His plan appealed to all practical men. Because of the demand for unpaid farm labor, Brace found it fairly easy to obtain homes for his children in return for work. Brace did not question the desirability of such a plan, assuming that the best antidote for idleness was hard work. In the spirit of "rugged individualism," Brace believed that the Christian home, and especially the farmer's home, was better than any institution in raising up dependent children.[94]

It soon became obvious that no more than a fraction of New York's "dangerous classes" could be colonized in rural America. Although placing-out, as it was generally called, continued to be favored whenever possible, it was all too apparent that there were not enough homes for eligible children. Furthermore, most farmers wanted only "good" children and refused to accept those children whom the program would most help. A few reformers criticized the placing-out system as exploitative, but many more believed it was inadequate.[95]

[94] Brace, *The Dangerous Classes of New York*, 225-270; Emma Brace, *The Life and Letters of Charles Loring Brace* (New York, 1894), *passim;* Children's Aid Society, *The Children's Aid Society of New York: Its History, Plan, and Results* (New York, 1893), *passim;* Bremner, *American Philanthropy*, 63, and *From the Depths*, 39; Abbott, *Some Pioneers in Social Welfare*, 128-136.

[95] Robert Hunter (*Poverty*, 256) noted that work on the farm protected children from the evils of the factory, mine, and mill. Jacob Riis also highly praised Brace in *Children of the Poor*, 187. Hardly a session of the Conference of Charities and Corrections was held without some reformer suggesting an extension of the placing-out system. For a criticism of the system, see the report of the Secretary of the State Board of Charities of New York, Robert W. Hebberd,

An alternative to placing-out was found in the Fresh Air movement, established by the New York *Tribune* in 1877. The Fresh Air Fund began simply by providing a two-week vacation with a rural family for needy children. Gradually the program grew and by the 1880's generous supporters, wishing to make the country vacation available to more children, invited groups of fifteen or twenty to their homes. Eventually unoccupied buildings, unused hotels, and hospitals were procured to house even more children. One large home operated by the AICP on Coney Island taught housekeeping, sewing, cooking, carpentry, and gave lessons in sanitation and hygiene. In addition, expeditions were organized for gathering shells, seaweed, and rocks and making collections of the flora and fauna of the surrounding fields and woods. Another home, operated in conjunction with the People's Seaside Home, catered exclusively to crippled children. By 1895 there were thirty-seven Fresh Air agencies distributed among twenty-four cities in thirteen states.[96] The expansion of the Fresh Air program ultimately led to the establishment of permanent Fresh Air vacation camps, of which the George Junior Republic was the first.

By 1890 summer vacation camps had been established by the school systems of Switzerland and Paris, with the cost to poor students defrayed by school authorities. Most American vacation camps and summer schools, however, were established for the children of the rich and moderately well-to-do.

"Placing Out Children: Dangers of Careless Methods," Conference of Charities and Corrections, *Proceedings* (Cincinnati, 1899), 171–188. Interestingly, Hebberd was one of the chief critics of the George Junior Republic as well.

[96] New York *Tribune*, Aug. 8, 1948; Walter S. Ufford, *Fresh Air Charity in the United States* (New York, 1897), 11–12, 56; George C. Bennett, "Up to Date Fresh Air Work," *Advocate and Family Guardian*, LXIII (Jan. 15, 1879), 19.

The tenement child was absolutely excluded from them. Thus when George set up his Fresh Air camp at Freeville, Albert Shaw, editor of the *Review of Reviews*, declared, "It is not to Switzerland or France that we must now look for the best model of a vacation camp, but to our own country. The most attractive and promising experiment in this direction that has ever been tried is known as the George Junior Republic, and it belongs to New York City." [97] However exciting the propects seemed to Albert Shaw, in 1890 the idea of settling slum children on rural farms still reflected four old assumptions: (1.) that the tenets of American democracy could only be taught and learned in a rural environment; (2.) that individuals, not institutions, were in need of reform; (3.) that gradual reform, through the rehabilitation of children, and not precipitous change was necessary; (4.) that colonization and removal (such as was proposed for the Negro and accomplished with the Indian), and not basic economic and political reform, provided the best solution to the immigrant problem.

iii

George founded his Fresh Air camp quite by accident. One spring evening in 1890, while he sat at his desk planning his summer vacation, a story in the New York *Evening World* caught his eye. It told of a street gamin who dared to ignore the signs to keep off the grass and went to pick a bright orange flower growing in the middle of the park's lawn. The risk was for nothing, however, for the flower turned out to be an orange peel. George was struck by the pathos of the story.

[97] Albert Shaw, "Vacation Camps and Boys' Republics," *Review of Reviews*, XIII (May 1896), 572–576. See also E. A. Kirkpatrick, "Continuous Sessions of Schools," *Ibid.*, XVI (Aug. 1897), 190–191, and William H. Tolman, "Vacation Schools in New York," *Ibid.*, 191–192.

Like Riis, he was an agrarian romantic. George and Riis agreed that one of the worst evils of slums was that they denied street children the redemptive powers of nature. "Take into a tenement block a handful of flowers from the fields," Riis wrote in *How the Other Half Lives*, "and watch the brightened faces, the sudden abandonment of play and fight that go ever hand in hand where there is no elbow-room, the wild entreaty for 'posies,' the eager love with which the little messengers of peace are shielded, once possessed." [98] George shared Riis's belief in the regenerative power of nature.

George attributed his own superiority over his street gangs to his country breeding. Despite his own difficulty in adjusting to urban life, George maintained that the country boy stood a far better chance of achieving success in the city than did the city-bred boy. George was always physically stronger than any of his followers, and he recognized the value of his regular country vacation as a purifier and a preparation for his return to the city. "Why not," he asked himself, "take a lot of them up to the country with you this summer?" [99]

From Willard Parsons, manager of the *Tribune* Fresh Air Fund, George learned that the Fund would provide transportation if George could find farmers who would take care of the children. He then conceived a daring plan, radically different from usual Fresh Air programs. Most Fresh Air chari-

[98] Riis, *How the Other Half Lives*, 135. Riis was an enthusiastic admirer of Charles Loring Brace and the *Tribune* Fresh Air Fund. He supported all manner of summer excursions sponsored by churches, missions, charities, and settlements. For example, Riis' rapturous description of the road to a farm school run by the CAS ("One Way Out," *The Century*, LI [Dec. 1895], 303–308) contrasts strikingly with the "realism" of such books as *How the Other Half Lives* and *Children of the Poor*.

[99] George, *The Junior Republic*, 4–7, and MS, Oct. 12, 1935; George, "The Junior Republic," address to the Society of Mayflower Descendants in the Commonwealth of Pennsylvania, Nov. 22, 1909.

ties made no provision for older children or for boys who had gotten into trouble with the law. The great majority of the better class of older boys was able to find work in the city, leaving only less desirable children as possible recipients of Fresh Air philanthropy. Most Italian and Jewish children could find no rural hosts at all.[100] The larger boys and the foreign youth were considered a dangerous threat to the well-ordered tranquillity of the Fresh Air outing. Though most fresh air charities set a minimum standard of moral excellence for their charges, George set a standard of "moral badness" for his group. The tougher the boy, the better the chance he would have to enjoy two weeks in Freeville.[101] The youngsters who flocked to Freeville came from the lowest classes of the city. The plan, George confided, was to take "the worst foreign element, regardless of religious belief, children of the pauper element, and even those who have committed crimes or have been incarcerated for some time during their short lives, the average age about thirteen, and put them through a course of training at the camp." [102]

The Fresh Air camp was conducted in much the same way as George's outing clubs and the Law and Order Gang. The Freeville encampment not only provided the children fresh air, but also instilled in them middle-class morality and discipline. Many of the children had no concept of right or wrong, self-control or cleanliness, George believed. He wanted to give them religious instruction and to teach them the mainstays of society: patriotism, self-government, hygiene,

[100] Lee, *Constructive and Preventive Philanthropy*, 171; Riis, *How the Other Half Lives*, 49.

[101] Ufford, *Fresh Air Charity in the United States*, 58–59.

[102] Rochester *Democrat and Chronicle*, clipping in George Junior Republic scrapbook, dated 1894; "The End of the Century: An Epitome of Things of Current Interest—The George Junior Republic," *The Argosy*, XXI (Jan. 1896), 301–305.

and industry. If nothing else, he hoped that two weeks in the country observing the good rural folk and sharing their table and entertainments would "succeed in making the tenement-house child thoroughly discontented with his lot." [103]

It is possible that George gave his charges little opportunity to become discontented. The Fresh Air children, like the Law and Order Gang, were disciplined "autocratically, but beneficently." George was not alone among reformers who discovered that military drill provided a rudimentary basis for social control. But George did not confine himself to organizing drill teams. He founded a military company which engaged in military maneuvers and exercises among the hills of West Dryden. George personally led his little army over the same terrain he had conquered in the solitary war games of his youth. Observers reported that the "Freeville Cadets" received a military education equal to that given by the best and most expensive military schools.[104]

On his first excursion in 1890 (known as the "Pioneer Year" in Junior Republic history), George took twenty-two youngsters and six helpers with him to Freeville. The girls were housed with various farmers, and the boys were put up in an abandoned farm house. Local farmers generously supplied food and clothing and whatever else seemed necessary. As the work grew in later years, the churches of the surrounding communities formally organized to aid the camp. Women from the missions of New York volunteered to help out for the summer. Some families spent two-week vacations

[103] Riis, *The Children of the Poor*, 161; Rochester *Democrat and Chronicle* clipping, 1894; George, "Purpose of the Fresh-Air Camp," MS, 1891.

[104] Mary Gay Humphreys, "The Smallest Republic in the World," *McClure's Magazine*, IX (July 1897), 735–746; Lyman Abbott, "A Republic in a Republic," *The Outlook*, LXXXVIII (Feb. 15, 1908), 351–354.

at the camp assisting George, and a few schoolteachers devoted their entire summer to the Fresh Air work.[105]

As the fame of George's experiment spread it was inevitable that his work should be compared to that of Charles Loring Brace.[106] The successful operation of the Fresh Air camp gave promise that even the toughest child might become manageable. The superintendent of the Five Points Mission, Dr. A. K. Sandford, praised the discipline and order that were maintained in every department of the camp and was thrilled by the reverence the children displayed toward the flag and the national anthem. But he was even more thrilled by the fervor of their religious meetings, which exceeded the excitement of the flag-drill.[107] The *Christian Herald* was quick to stress, however, that the Fresh Air camp was not just an evangelistic work, but was an ingenious plan of education for neglected youth. The camp freed children from the vice, idleness, poverty, and fear that degraded their lives in the slums.[108] The work was often discouraging, and more often thankless, but no observer failed to note the remarkable transformation of the children who attended the camp. When the Fresh Air children returned to New York in September 1895, the New York *World* marveled:

The parents and other relatives of one hundred and thirty typical New York boys . . . scarcely recognized in the sunburned, manly bearing, bright-eyed young soldiers the shiftless, ill-behaved and slouchy youths from whom they parted July 7 last. The boys

[105] George, *The Junior Republic*, 11–18; Smith, "'Daddy' George," xv–xviii; Ufford, *Fresh Air Charity in the United States*, 57.

[106] Theodore Cuyler, "The Junior Republic," George Junior Republic scrapbook, Sept. 3, 1896.

[107] A. K. Sandford, "A Trip to Freeville," in George Junior Republic, *Our Work* (Freeville, N.Y., 1897).

[108] "A Child Republic in Tents," *Christian Herald*, XVIII (Sept. 4, 1895), 573.

wore white leggings, red sashes and soldier caps, and carried wooden guns to distinguish them from other boys. . . . Although very little concerning it has found its way into print, the George Industrial Camp [its official name before it became the George Junior Republic in 1895] . . . has proved itself to be a most remarkable institution for the improvement of city boys.[109]

For George, the success of his Fresh Air work was literally a dream come true. Having spent so many hours in youthful reverie creating make-believe histories of immigrants and delinquents, he could at last shape the destinies of countless real children. Walking alone through his encampment at night George reflected upon his many solitary walks through those same Dryden hills and through the streets of New York. Returning to his bed, he dropped upon his pillow and, with the utmost feeling of contentment and exhilaration, "put [himself] to sleep planning careers for each individual arab in the crowd." [110]

[109] New York *World*, Sept. 4, 1895. For further praise of the Fresh Air work see: Auburn *Advertiser*, Aug. 5, 1898; New York *World*, Sept. 7, 1895. George himself described the work in "The Youth's Republic at Freeville," *Christian City*, VII (Sept. 25, 1895), 3; this account closely parallels that found in *The Junior Republic*.

[110] George, MS, 1905–1906.

III

"A VILLAGE LIKE ANY OTHER"

──────── By the end of the summer of 1895 William R. George had decided to give up his work with the Law and Order Gang in New York City and devote himself exclusively to the expansion of his Fresh Air work and to the establishment of his newly named Junior Republic. Complex motives lay behind his decision. The resolve to abandon city work in favor of a permanent rural settlement was prompted both by conscious choice and uncontrollable circumstance. The establishment of the Junior Republic was purposeful, yet fortuitous; its success was fed by frustration and failure. George was hard hit by the depression of 1893, and as his jewelry-box business declined, he found more and more time to devote to benevolent activities. Thus, economic depression, rather than a loss of social status, seems to have provoked his initial venture into Progressive reform.[1]

In 1895, contributions to his Fresh Air work in Freeville provided George with housing, food, and some small expenses. Having no reason to return to New York at the end of the season, and not wanting further to burden his parents, he stayed behind in camp to fend for himself. It would not be

[1] There is no direct evidence that George lost his business as a result of the depression, but there is ample evidence that he was a poor business manager (see below, 131 ff.).

accurate to charge that George exploited the Junior Republic for personal gain. Though the Republic provided a comfortable living, he never became wealthy. Having once served him as an emotional sanctuary, Freeville in 1895 provided the young man an economic refuge and offered him another chance to reaffirm his faith in America's economic system.[2]

George did not remain in Freeville simply because he found economic security in the Junior Republic, however. As social work became more and more professionalized during the 1890's, George's anti-institutional and unorthodox methods brought him into conflict with the Charity Organization Society. Despite his studied independence from the COS, George at first cooperated with the Society. The COS divided New York into several districts. In each district social workers, ministers, doctors, and others interested in social work were asked to form a committee to investigate the various cases brought to the attention of the COS.[3] Because his work with the Fresh Air children took him into the homes of their families, George was asked to join the COS committee for District Three. George valued this association with fellow social workers since he found the COS a source of Fresh Air children which completely freed him from dependence on the missions.[4]

In the summer of 1892, the "Pilgrim Year" at the Fresh Air camp, most of the children George took to Freeville had been referred to him through his friends on the COS. Among the Fresh Air children were three boys whom George determined to care for on their return to New York City. At first

[2] George's observations on how best to save oneself in an economic depression may be found in his MS of Sept. 22–24, 1932.

[3] Roy Lubove, *The Professional Altruist: The Emergence of Social Work as a Career, 1880–1930* (Cambridge, Mass., 1965), 22 ff.

[4] George, "Statement about the State Board of Charities and Its Secretary, Robert W. Hebberd," MS, 1914.

George's parents objected to the scheme, his father arguing that the household could not carry the additional expense of raising three boys. George appealed to his mother, promising to help support the boys if they were allowed to move into the family's apartment. After Eleanor George yielded, John George readily consented to the scheme.

With his jewelry-box business already on the skids, George was hardly in a position to contribute significantly to the household. Rationalizing that the boys would lose their self-respect if they did not contribute to their own support, George arranged for them to learn a "clean and useful occupation." From his friends and relatives in Freeville George obtained eggs and butter to be peddled in the city.

The scheme seemed to work to everyone's advantage. The Freeville farmers, already beginning to feel the agricultural pinch that preceded the depression of 1893, welcomed the New York City outlet. George's neighbors in the city were delighted to have a cheap source of fresh eggs and butter. The three boys, with their pushcarts, were able to occupy their spare hours with a useful service and, at the same time, they learned the joys and responsibilities of earning their own money. The fact that they were dealing in wholesome farm goods appeared to mitigate the grim reality that they were involved in a street trade. George maintained he had no desire to sell goods at a profit in excess of the amount needed to cover the actual cost of food, laundry, clothing, and rent for his boys.

As the enterprise prospered, George printed a circular explaining the nature of his work with the boys. To allay any questions concerning his motives, he reminded the boys' customers that he was the President of the Junior Christian Endeavor Societies of New York, superintendent of a Sunday

school, director of a Fresh Air camp, and member of the
Third District Committee of the COS. One of the circulars
fell into the hands of Robert W. Hebberd, then an investigator for the Society. The COS, among other reasons, had
been founded to expose as cheats and frauds the large number
of bogus reformers engaged in "charity" work for their own
profit and aggrandizement. Upon reading George's circular,
Hebberd's suspicions were immediately aroused. Hebberd informed Paul U. Kellogg, who undertook a personal investigation of the matter, interviewed George, and asked for an audit
of George's books. Though no irregularities were found, Kellogg was concerned that the egg and butter trade might reflect on the reputation of the infant Charity Organization
Society. Seeking to protect itself, the COS offered George
three alternatives. He could give up his scheme entirely, he
could form a board of trustees to oversee the finances of his
project, or he could sever all connection with the COS. Unwilling to abandon his work, and even more unwilling to
place himself under the direct supervision of the COS, George
chose to resign his position on the committee for District
Three. Thereupon, the COS, admitting that George was personally honest, reluctantly declared George irregular in his
methods and thus not to be fully trusted.[5] The lesson George
learned was a lasting one. Official supervision, whether it
came from his own trustees, the State Board of Charities, or

[5] There are several versions of this incident. Most vary only on
the issue of whether George quit or was thrown out of the COS.
Neither George nor Lyman Beecher Stowe criticized the COS for
its decision; both agreed that, under the circumstances, the COS had
little choice. Stowe and George, *Citizens Made and Remade* (New
York, 1912), 3–6; George, "Statement about the State Board of
Charities"; George, MSS, Nov. 5, 1928, and 1918; Jacob G. Smith
to Mrs. William R. George, March 16, 1950.

the federal government, never set well with him. He always asserted that this incident first alerted him to the dangers of official inquisitors on the city, state, and national levels.[6]

The effect of the COS censure was not immediately evident. George continued his Fresh Air work and founded the Law and Order Gang after his troubles with Hebberd and Kellogg. Yet, when his efforts to pacify New York City through the Law and Order Gang failed, his separation from the missions and his alienation from the COS left George with few prospects in the city. If Freeville provided him an emotional and economic refuge, it also supplied a new field for his reform activities. Comfortable in the material contributions of his friends and neighbors, safe from the lingering taint of censure, secure among his beloved hills of West Dryden, George launched his Junior Republic, hardly suspecting that, in time, it too would produce a tangle of discord, jealousy, and opposition.

The immediate success of the George Junior Republic can hardly be explained in terms of George's personal difficulties. Though a consideration of the economic, emotional, and professional motives behind the founding of the Junior Republic contributes to our understanding of the mind of the reformer, it is in no way decisive in explaining why a generation of reformers became excited over the Republic experiment. It was not George's problems that attracted the nation's attention to his venture in Freeville. Rather, it was because the George Junior Republic embodied within its vision the fundamentals of the Progressive faith that George's contemporaries looked upon him as a major figure in the Age of Reform. Most Progressives considered George a man with a mission and would have been profoundly shocked at any suggestion that Republic rhetoric was merely altruistic rationalization. Thus an

[6] George, MS, 1918.

analysis of the "official" explanation of the founding of the Junior Republic will best illuminate how many Progressives consciously viewed themselves and how they wanted to be remembered.

i

Believing that he failed to regenerate the members of his Law and Order Gang and his Fresh Air children, George gradually came to the conclusion that he was doing them more harm than good. Since he shared the conservative Progressive's attitude toward poverty, George feared that his social work was actually pauperizing the children. Along with most Progressives by 1895, George rejected the notion that poverty reflected moral weakness and deficiency among the poor. Though a conservative reformer, he was willing to concede that most victims of poverty were not entirely responsible for their plight. William R. George would have joined with such liberals as Henry George, Edward Bellamy, and Henry Demarest Lloyd in rejecting the notion that society's failures had no one to blame but themselves.[7] Men like Jacob Riis, William George, and Robert Hunter conceded that the slum environment of America's cities was a major cause of poverty in the United States. They were all environmentalists in this broad sense.

Nevertheless, George and his friends retained many of the attitudes toward poverty associated with Americans of the ante-bellum period.[8] Extreme caution was needed in dealing with the poor. One of the great dangers of his work in Har-

[7] Robert H Bremner, *From the Depths: The Discovery of Poverty in the United States* (New York, 1956), 16–30.

[8] Alice Felt Tyler, *Freedom's Ferment* (Minneapolis, 1944), 291–294; Charles C. Cole, *The Social Ideas of the Northern Evangelists* (New York, 1954), 186–187; Bremner, *American Philanthropy* (Chicago, 1960), 60.

lem, George discovered, was that those he tried to help, believing him to be rich, continually tried to take advantage of him. "The quickest way to secure an open enemy or backbiter," he observed, "was to give them some very special assistance." [9] Instead of being grateful for what they had received, many would become bitter over what they could not have. George had observed this phenomenon at the missions where unfortunates were content to live on their dole, never attempting to earn for themselves.

He was horrified when he discovered the same tendency in his own work. Fathers of boys he befriended suddenly began "losing" their jobs. Often they appealed to George for a barrel of potatoes or an extra suit of clothing while they looked for work. In many cases George learned that the fathers had not lost their jobs at all, but were merely scheming to get "something for nothing." [10] In the Fresh Air camp he observed a similar tendency. Though they were learning how to sing many Christian and patriotic hymns, the children were robbed of their self-respect by the charity that was lavished on them. As more and more generous contributions of food and clothing poured into the camp, the Fresh Air children began to claim the goods as a matter of right. They showed no hint of gratitude, no sign of responsibility. Good clothing was often destroyed so that the child might claim a better suit from a later shipment. Clothing that was much too large was worn back to the city and given to an indolent father or mother. The children returned from each summer outing healthier, stronger, happier, and better clothed. But they also measured the success of their summer solely in terms of the amount of "loot" they took back to the city. Angered by their

[9] George, MS, Nov. 5, 1928.
[10] George, *The Junior Republic* (New York, 1910), 16.

incessant demands for goods, George finally challenged a crowd of ragamuffins, "Can you tell me any reason in the wide world why these people should give you anything? Haven't you had a whole summer of good food and good times with good health thrown in? What right have you to expect anything more?" A little Italian girl with flashing black eyes supplied the answer when she immediately snapped back, "What do you tink we come fur enyway?" [11]

George suppressed the temptation to abandon his Fresh Air work as a failure. The camp provided an important outlet for charitable impulses in upstate New York. More importantly, George realized that most of his children came from homes where desperate poverty had denied them needed food, clothing, and country air. Nor could he hold them responsible for the dependency he had so insidiously cultivated. His problem, then, was to get the needed material goods into their possession without destroying their self-reliance and self-respect. [12]

The obvious solution to his problem was work. Work was regarded as the universal specific for social ills. Theodore Roosevelt declared before the Conference of Charities and Corrections in 1877 that "able-bodied tramps and paupers must work." Another speaker in 1880 advocated that the able-bodied be given the choice between work and starvation. [13] Charles Loring Brace had made farm work the keystone to his placing-out system. Both Homer Folks and Robert Hunter believed work beneficial for city youth, and Jacob Riis had

[11] George and Stowe, *Citizens Made and Remade*, 38–39; George, *The Junior Republic*, 17.

[12] Mary Wagner Fisher, "Daddy's Boys," *Rural New Yorker*, LVIII (June 24, 1899), 1.

[13] Frank Bruno, Jr., and Lewis Towley, *Trends in Social Work, 1874–1956* (New York, 1957), 72–73.

praised the work of the Kensico Farm School established by the Children's Aid Society as "one way out" of slum problems.[14]

George agreed that work was the only means by which the poor could establish their worthiness. But like other conservative reformers', his attitude toward poverty was mixed, and he did not let environment or heredity, as he understood them, serve as excuses for the failure of will. According to George, a "strong-willed" individual could rise above both environment and heredity. The volitions of a strong-willed person, he argued, were stronger than his inherited tendencies. "He may at his pleasure rise above them, fall below them, or follow them." Only with the "weak-willed" was heredity and environment a large, and perhaps determining factor.[15] Work consequently was the ultimate molder and exerciser of character and will. George believed that once the slum child was liberated from the influence of the tenement, he became responsible for his own success or failure. "Our self-made men," he argued in 1897, "seem to give unanimous testimony, that if you would achieve success, *you must fight for it yourself.*" [16]

In 1894, George ended the dole at his summer camp. He shocked one supporter who was accustomed to donating croquet sets each summer by requesting a contribution of picks and shovels instead. Resolving that no child would ever

[14] Folks, "The Care of Delinquent Children," Conference of Charities and Corrections, *Proceedings*, 1891, 136–144; Robert Hunter, *Poverty* (1907; reprint ed., New York: Harper Torchbooks, 1965), 256; Riis, "One Way Out," *The Century*, LI (Dec. 1895), 303–308.

[15] George and Stowe, *Citizens Made and Remade*, 154–155.

[16] MS, Jan. 1, 1897. Lubove, *The Professional Altruist*, 8–9, comments on reform attitudes toward work and poverty; as does Bremner, *American Philanthropy, passim*. See below, 263–267 for further discussion of George's attitudes toward will.

again be pauperized by his hand, George launched his program of "Nothing without Labor." Upon arriving in camp that summer, the Fresh Air children displayed the familiar characteristics of greed, irresponsibility, lawlessness, and ingratitude. To their astonishment, George announced that instead of playing games that summer, they would work on a nearby road. At first the response was encouraging. More boys than could be supplied with picks and shovels volunteered to work. Soon the novelty waned, and within four days the work stopped. George noted that during the days of industry the camp was cheerful and content, but with idleness, discontent and grumbling returned. On the fifth day of camp the first shipment of clothing arrived, and with it the first test of George's new scheme. In response to the demands that he pass out the clothing, George pointed to the picks and shovels and announced that clothing would be distributed only to those who earned it. The proclamation was met with howls of protest, but eventually the camp acquiesced rather than risk returning to the city empty-handed.[17] From then on, clothing was not distributed unless it was earned.

The willingness with which the campers accepted the work scheme did not deceive George into thinking that their characters had been reformed in any way. His experience with the Law and Order Gang had taught him that most children were extremely pragmatic and capable of adjusting profitably to almost any regime. George agreed with Puffer and Riis that the character of children was universally the same, most children sharing similar standards, desires, and ambitions. Children desired to get as much as they could with as little effort of muscle or brain as possible. Thus, the children of the poor were especially victimized by political clubs, Sunday

[17] George, *The Junior Republic*, 19–35; George and Stowe, *Citizens Made and Remade*, 42–47.

schools, and other charitable organizations that exploited their need for material goods. These children soon learned that the most greedy, the most hypocritical, the most devious, and the most improvident got the most favors, clothes, and food. Under his new regime, George merely reversed the rules. "Nothing without Labor" dictated that the most industrious, honest, and provident would receive the most of the material pleasures. It was politic, George urged, to be good. Understanding that he could not expect an immediate change of heart, George appealed to the child's basic motives in order to secure proper behavior and to begin right habits.[18]

The principle of self-support was relatively easy to establish. Not only did the campers respond to it with little trouble, but the adult supporters of the Fresh Air camp accepted it eagerly. Most of the children were employed in farm work or household industries. In many cases, Fresh Air children worked in the fields beside the children of camp patrons. Central New Yorkers believed the myth of the self-made man (John D. Rockefeller himself had been born a scant twenty-five miles away), and self-reliance was second only to patriotism as an article of their secular faith. Work, coupled with fresh air, only enhanced the urban waif's chance for social and moral regeneration. Besides, work was even more effective than drill and games as a means of social control.

The Junior Republic had had a long history of troubled relations with the citizens of Freeville and Dryden.[19] The Fresh Air camp itself was established because local residents refused to take George's "bad boys" into their homes. No

[18] George and Stowe, *Citizens Made and Remade*, 48–49.

[19] It should be pointed out that difficulties with local authorities have generally been outweighed by the amicable relationship between the George Junior Republic and the Freeville community.

doubt the situation was aggravated by George's insistence on bringing the worst possible type of delinquent to Freeville. Local farmers bitterly complained that their orchards were robbed, their crops were decimated, and their chicken coops were plundered. Ruffians roamed the countryside, and decent folk were afraid to let their children out alone.

Within the camp, matters were not much more satisfactory. The camp was plagued with rowdyism and often by malicious mischief. George hardly dared to go to town, for without his strong-arm assistance camp counselors found it hard to maintain order. Corporal punishment was his first solution to the problem. He established a "whipping bee" in the chapel tent where each morning he administered stripes for transgressions of the day before. One morning he flogged thirty-two boys.[20]

Two discoveries ultimately led George to abandon corporal punishment. First, he observed that the daily whipping bees were becoming one of the chief entertainments of the camp. Each session was well attended by campers, who obviously looked upon the proceedings as a kind of Roman circus. This, coupled with the fact that the floggings in no way served as a deterrent to mischief (the numbers of daily floggings remained fairly constant), convinced George that his punishments were not effective. Second, industrious children, who wanted to enjoy the material status of their labor, began to demand effective protection of their newly acquired property.

The establishment of self-government at the Fresh Air camp and the subsequent founding of the Junior Republic were not the result of a theoretical or moral rejection of corporal punishment. Rather, self-government slowly evolved from a desperate search for an effective means of social con-

[20] George, *The Junior Republic*, 38–42.

trol. Whippings were only the institutionalized version of the beatings George administered to the recalcitrant members of his Law and Order Gang. Had corporal punishment proven effective, there is no doubt George would have continued it. After meeting with several youths to establish codes for the protection of personal property, he noted that the regulations made by the children's community were the only rules regularly respected and obeyed. Labor had created property and property had created law. Given a stake in society, the children's concern for law and order no longer stemmed from personal loyalty to George. Rather they were motivated by the basic desire to protect their own self-interest.[21] Selfish as the original civic motive might be, it was the beginning of self-government. George agreed with E. A. Ross that few persons acted purely from disinterest.[22] The definition of self-interest was the first and essential step in defining the community interest. Once the children were enlisted into the ranks of the world's workers they quickly forgot their irresponsible and lawless point of view. When it became evident that the good and the prudent lie in the same direction, moral regeneration began.[23]

When the Fresh Air children entrained for New York at the end of the summer of 1894, George remained behind in Freeville to relax and ponder the meaning of his discovery. Never before had his children departed so cheerful and contented. Never before had they marched off so full of pride and gratitude for their new clothes. Never before had they expressed a desire to return again the next year. George recalled their sweat and toil in the fields and on the roads. He

[21] George and Stowe, *Citizens Made and Remade*, 51–52; George, MS, 1903.

[22] E. A. Ross, *Sin and Society* (Boston, 1907).

[23] George and Stowe, *Citizens Made and Remade*, 220–227.

remembered their ardent demand for law and order and their inspiring triumph in securing conformity to their own rules. He had observed such incidents of "self-government" among his boys' gangs of the city, though he had usually passed it off as interesting play. Now George realized that what he had witnessed that summer had not been play at all. Instead, he had been privileged to observe in the "wilderness" of up-state New York the re-enactment of an American rite—the formation of a community. Liberated by the country, up-lifted by the church, and disciplined by work, the immigrant children from the city had discovered for themselves the es-sence of American democracy.

George thrilled on reflecting that his children had thrown off the comfortable tyranny of his own gentle, but absolute, rule in favor of the awesome responsibility of self-govern-ment. How wrong he had been to preach patriotism and yet neglect the very fundamentals of the American government! How foolish he had been to believe he could Americanize his foreign children with the militaristic-autocratic methods of the old country! The answer to civic and social responsibility was *participation*. There was no other solution, George con-cluded. Yet he did not believe this revelation to be particu-larly surprising since it was the same principle which secured civic tranquillity in the American Republic. Why, George wondered, should the principle work differently for chil-dren? [24]

Daydreaming in front of his uncle's woodshed, George slowly formulated a plan for the next summer's camp. If children could work for their clothing, they could work for luxuries and for food and other necessities. Work, of course, was scarce during the depression years. George resolved that

[24] George, *The Junior Republic*, 55–63; George, *The Adult Minor* (New York, 1937), 61.

any kind of "make work" might do. Road-building on the camp grounds, ditch-digging for sewer pipes, carting rocks from fields for stone fences were a few of his projects. Each child would be paid in currency issued by a bank in the name of a citizens' government. The government would be modeled on that of the United States. The citizens would make their own laws through a legislature; administer them through an executive; and enforce them with a police force, a court system, and a jail. Besides the bank, there would be need of a post office, possibly a government-operated store, and other agencies under the control of the campers. Once enrolled in the camp, each citizen would be allowed to enjoy the fruits of his own labor, either prospering or starving as he chose.

Suddenly George was jolted from his reveries by the very familiarity of his scheme. He recognized that the dream not only was similar to the reveries of his boyhood but mirrored the essential structure of the United States government. It was, he later wrote, "Our Glorious Republic in miniature—a Junior Republic—and I recall shouting at the top of my voice, 'I have it—I have it—I have it'; and like a school boy I ran as fast as my legs could carry me, and told my mother. I felt it to have been a God-given idea." [25]

The "revelation" of the Republic principle was thus described in the manner of an evangelical religious conversion which George had so often witnessed but had never experienced. His redemptive scheme came as a flash of inspiration after years of frustrating and fruitless toil. God had at last shown him how his Junior Republic could serve, among others, as a primary means for Americanization of the New Immigrant. At last he could build a real city, or in this case a village, upon the hill. No longer would he have to create imaginary states with imaginary histories. His inhabitants

[25] *The Junior Republic*, 64.

would be real persons for whom he could create real success stories. As in the Horatio Alger novels, George as the great benefactor could bring the poor out of the cities into the country, and through the principles of "Nothing without Labor" and self-government make or remake citizens for the United States. Like the Puritan fathers, George believed he had an "errand into the wilderness." His was to found his City on the Hill (a "village just like any other village," he called it), which could not be hid from public view and which preserved its missionary tasks by protecting and transmitting the essentials of American democracy.[26] For George, the Junior Republic principle was as much an article of faith as it was a method of social control and correction. Throughout his career, he was often more concerned with protecting the purity of his ideal than with working out practical solutions to adverse criticism. George would entertain almost any critical suggestion, as long as it could be reconciled to his Republic creed.

ii

In the late fall of 1894, George hurried back to New York City to tell his friends of the new project. To all who would listen, George explained how he planned to establish a Junior Republic modeled on the plan of a "village conducted just exactly the same as a village of grown-ups," wherein the "citizens" would be self-governing and would work and live according to their individual abilities. All citizens would be equal before the Republic's laws, each receiving "Nothing

[26] George, "History in Brief of Things from the Time of the Founding of the Junior Republic to the Years 1930–1931," MS, 1931; George, "The Junior Republic," address to the Society of Mayflower Descendants in the Commonwealth of Pennsylvania, Nov. 22, 1909, pamphlet (Philadelphia, 1910).

without Labor" and each determining his own standard of living according to his ambition, intelligence, and ability.

At first, few paid much attention to the scheme. Although "radical" institutional experiments for reform of destitute and problem children were comparatively rare in nineteenth-century America,[27] the country did not lack discipline for its youth. Most discipline was not imposed by the state, but rather was imparted through the church, school, and, most important, "by a way of life close to nature and subject to nature's iron laws."[28] Almost every boy or girl who lived in the country was disciplined by the endless round of chores that was required on every farm and in most villages (George, of course, was an exception to this rule). The establishment of the Junior Republic was important not only because it successfully reintroduced familiar patterns of work discipline,[29] but because it sought to introduce its citizens to the inescapable responsibilities and obligations of membership in a self-governing and self-regulating rural community. The George Junior Republic was designed to check the dissipation of social responsibility which came with industrialism and urbanization in the nineteenth century. In the classic pattern of countless American organizations, the Junior Republic attempted "to give the appearance of stability to an unstable society, to create order out of disorder, to substitute new loyalties for those which had been dissipated and new conventions for those which had been lost, to enlarge horizons and inflate opportunities."[30]

[27] For a discussion of the Boston House of Reformation and the New York House of Refuge, see below, 243–249.

[28] Henry Steele Commager, *The American Mind* (New Haven, 1950), 21.

[29] The Berkshire Industrial Farm, founded in 1885, for example, antedated the George Junior Republic in this respect.

[30] Commager, *The American Mind*, 22.

George's friends, however, were skeptical of the self-governing principle, especially as it applied to slum youth and delinquents. One social worker went so far as to inform George that his scheme was like a machine she had seen in Japan, remarkable for its mechanism and design, but having one serious defect—it wouldn't work. Most social workers acknowledged that the self-government theory was plausible, but they believed that slum youth were too irresponsible and immature for any such plan to be possible.

One day, quite discouraged, George wandered into police headquarters on Mulberry Street where, in the first-floor corridor, he ran into his friend Jacob Riis. George told Riis of his plans to establish self-government and "Nothing without Labor" principles at the Fresh Air camp. Riis enthusiastically grasped George's arm and piloted him upstairs to place his proposition before the police commissioner. In the office of Theodore Roosevelt, George repeated his story, fearing that Roosevelt would react with the skepticism of his friends. Instead, according to George, "Mr. Roosevelt brought his hand down upon my shoulder with a resounding whack, and exclaimed, 'By George, I know it will work.' " [31] With the support and encouragement of Riis and Roosevelt, the establishment of the Junior Republic moved quickly toward reality.[32]

[31] George, "Roosevelt Story," MS, April 1933. Allen Davis has noted that during his years as police commissioner Roosevelt provided much encouragement and inspiration for social workers in New York City by supporting a large number of worthy reforms; this earned him their loyalty, as it did that of William George (" 'Theodore Roosevelt—Social Worker,' A Note," *Mid-America*, XLVIII [Jan. 1966], 58–62).

[32] George, "The Junior Republic," address to the Society of Mayflower Descendants in the Commonwealth of Pennsylvania, Nov. 22, 1909.

On July 10, 1895, since known as "Founder's Day," a train-load of 144 boys and girls from New York's toughest districts and a handful of volunteer adult workers arrived in Freeville to found the George Junior Republic. The details of the evolution of the Junior Republic into a full-fledged self-governing community are vague. Junior Republic history is steeped in heroic romanticism and clouded by Lyman Beecher Stowe's dictum that "truth in details can . . . be . . . sacrificed when necessary to truth of impression." [33] George claimed to have wanted to introduce absolute self-government immediately. But nervous assistants, remembering their difficulties of past summers, talked George into assuming the office of president, much against his better judgment. Indeed, in the original Junior Republic, all the administrative officers, including the chief justice, chief of police, president of the bank, civil service examiners, and members of the board of health, were adults. Republic citizens were appointed as administrative assistants and served as the Republic legislature. Members of the old Law and Order Gang, because of their training in "law enforcement," supplied the manpower for the police force and held most of the offices open to citizens. Adults controlled the economy of the Republic; George as president let all work contracts to adult helpers, who in turn employed the Republic citizens. The George Junior Republic, as it was founded in 1895, was a republic in name and form only.[34]

As soon as practical, however, George directed that the government be turned over to the citizens. During the first

[33] Lyman Beecher Stowe to George, Dec. 30, 1911.

[34] George, *The Junior Republic*, 67–69; George and Stowe, *Citizens Made and Remade*, 67–69; John R. Commons, "The Junior Republic, I," *American Journal of Sociology*, III (Nov. 1897), 281–296.

summer, boys were allowed to assume all but the top administrative offices. By the time the summer citizens left in
the fall of 1895, George, as president, was the only adult
within the Republic government. By the end of the summer
the program had been such a success that George decided to
abandon all his New York work and stay in Freeville to establish the Junior Republic on a permanent basis. Since the farm
upon which the Republic was founded had been rented for
the whole year, George saw little point in returning to a bleak
and jobless life in New York City.[35]

Announcing to the assembled citizenry his plan to establish
a year-round Junior Republic, George called for volunteers
to serve as pioneers in the venture. He assured them that the
house would keep them comfortable throughout the winter,
that there were plenty of cooking utensils, blankets, and other
furnishings, and that the bumper potato and tomato crop
from the Republic gardens would keep them safely through
till spring. It would be pioneering with a vengeance, he
warned, and only a select few could be honored. All firewood
needed to be gathered and cut by hand, and water would have
to be hauled from a spring located at the base of a steep hill.
In midwinter, the whole party might become snowbound for
days. George did not add that, in addition to these hardships,
he had but $100 to meet expenses for the entire company
throughout the ten months ahead. His call brought forth
twenty-five volunteers, but on asking permission from their
parents, the number was reduced to fifteen. As the day of
departure for the summer citizens drew near, uneasiness was
evident among the fifteen. One by one, faint-hearted fellows
came forward to ask to be excused; one had a sick grandmother, two more felt their education would be better served

[35] George and Stowe, *Citizens Made and Remade*, 66; George,
The Junior Republic, 99.

in New York City schools. At last only five boys remained to join the permanent Republic. Of these, three stayed behind out of personal loyalty to George, and only two purportedly understood the larger significance of the experiment.[36]

The winter of 1895–1896 was unusually severe in Freeville and proved to be a "sternly excellent preparation for self-government for the pioneer citizens of the Junior Republic." The religiously oriented among George's followers immediately saw the parallel between the first winter of the Junior Republic and the "starving time" of the Puritan fathers. But George himself believed the experience was more appropriately analogous to Washington at Valley Forge. George was not only the "Father of his Country" [37] who had been deserted by the "sunshine" patriots, but "just as Washington and his men . . . fought cold and hunger and privation in bringing the Big Republic into being," so George and his little band suffered cold, hunger, and privation in "giving birth to the Junior Republic." [38] Significantly, Republic literature gives no hint that the deprivations were anything but self-imposed. Thus comparing themselves to the Puritans and the Patriots who, for the sake of their ideals, voluntarily submitted to the ultimate tests of self-reliance, the George Junior Republic struggled through the depression of 1893.

More candidly, George was willing to admit that in such circumstances "self-reliance became a necessity rather than a virtue." [39] The hardships that the camp faced were real. Boys woke up in the morning to discover that snow had sifted down on their beds through the roof above. At times they

[36] George, *The Junior Republic*, 99–102; George and Stowe, *Citizens Made and Remade*, 66–67.

[37] He was known to all the citizens as "Daddy" George.

[38] George and Stowe, *Citizens Made and Remade*, 66–67.   [39] *Ibid.*

had to walk the three miles to school in temperatures as low as thirty degrees below zero. By mid-February George became expert at treating chilblains. They survived on a monotonous diet of "poor man's soup" until "Mama" Griswold (Mrs. Sarah Griffen Griswold), who had the unusual talent of making appetizing meals out of almost nothing, came to cook for them.[40]

According to Republic legend, it was at this time that George stepped down as president and the community became entirely self-governing, electing "Jakey" Smith first citizen president.[41] During Smith's administration the Junior Republic quadrupled in population, boasting a total of twenty citizens by spring. Naturally, George was extremely pleased with his little experiment.

The hard winter had been a necessary conditioning for self-government, George rationalized. His environmentalism did not simply stress the competitive struggle for the survival of the fittest, though he believed under natural circumstances individuals would differentiate themselves. The winter experience had not culled the "unfit" from the pioneer Re-

[40] George, *The Junior Republic*, 103; Kathleen Smith, MS on George Junior Republic, 6.

[41] Jacob Smith was one of the boys who had lived with the Georges in New York City and had helped George peddle his eggs and butter. Smith undoubtedly was one of the two who supposedly understood the deeper significance of the work. He was elected the first citizen judge before his selection as president. He later graduated from Cornell and Harvard Law School, and served as a trustee for the Junior Republic. According to Commons ("The Junior Republic, I"), complete self-government was not established until 1897. Commons, however, was more concerned with *de facto* functioning than *de jure* organization. Stowe observed ("What To Do with a Boy," *World's Work* XXVI [June 1913], 190–195) that Smith was elected President on George's recommendation. When George suggested Smith's re-election, however, the citizens, rejecting "boss" rule, elected Smith's opponent.

public, George pointed out, but had "fitted out" the young Republic with a hard core of reliable and malleable leaders. All youth needed an intensive exposure to hardship to keep the race from going soft and becoming too dependent. "The majority of the youth of the human race," George wrote, "are fond of getting on with as little personal effort of muscle or brain as is possible." This predisposition was not limited to slum children, he stressed. "No matter what their social status may be, the inclination [of youth] is to lean upon a prop of some character." [42]

"The starving time" which symbolically re-enacted the nation's conquest of the frontier, George recognized, had not only created the necessary group self-consciousness which cemented the pioneers' devotion to the Junior Republic principle, but it had served as a kind of initiation and purification rite prior to the adoption of full self-government responsibilities. The young citizens, proud of their victory, developed the *esprit* of first-generation settlers. When he later founded other Junior Republics, George attempted to re-create this experience by sending out small groups of "pioneer citizens" to establish Republics under conditions similar to those prevailing in Freeville in 1895–1896. In the Junior Republic itself, George unconsciously institutionalized the "starving time" through the agency of the jail. Almost every citizen found himself in jail soon after his arrival at the Junior Republic. There he was privileged to endure almost the same privations and purification endured by the heroic little band of founders. As the conditioning process was the same, George unwittingly found a "rite of passage" that transmitted Republic zeal to the second-generation citizens.

At first George attempted to model the government of the Junior Republic exactly on that of the United States. The

[42] George, MS, Jan. 1, 1897.

Republic government included a president and his cabinet, a two-house congress, a judicial system, a written constitution, a code of laws, and so forth. But when the summer citizens returned in 1896 this system proved too cumbersome, and the Republic adopted the town-meeting form of government, using the laws and constitution of the State of New York in cases not covered by Republic law. Ultimately, the only adults who served in the government were the members of the Executive Committee of the George Junior Republic Association, who became the Junior Republic Supreme Court. Thomas Mott Osborne, chairman of the Executive Committee, served as Chief Justice. As previously indicated, the Supreme Court was established at the instigation of the citizens of the Republic who requested it as a buffer against the harsh verdicts of their own courts.[43]

Political democracy was relatively easy to establish at Freeville, meeting little resistance from the public, Republic workers, or citizens. The establishment of economic democracy, on the other hand, proved to be the Republic's most difficult problem in the early days. Even the most radical experiments with juvenile self-government in the nineteenth century at the Boston House of Reformation and the New York House of Refuge did not include an economic feature.[44] But George insisted that the democratic structure of the Junior Republic should be paralleled by a capitalist economy also duplicating that of the United States. It would do no good, he warned, to teach the immigrants self-government without teaching them self-support.[45] George wanted each new citizen to learn that

[43] George and Stowe, *Citizens Made and Remade*, 94; Rudolph W. Chamberlain, *There Is No Truce: A Life of Thomas Mott Osborne* (New York, 1935), 225–226.

[44] Orlando F. Lewis, "Inmate Self-government a Century Ago," *The Delinquent*, VIII (Jan. 1918), 9–14.

[45] George, "The George Junior Republic," *Silver Cross*, Feb. 1896, 8–12.

in the Junior Republic idleness meant hunger, but that ambition earned wealth, prestige, and advancement.

Ideally, each child was free to work at whatever job he chose. Wages would be determined by the basic supply and demand of labor. Like Bellamy, George believed that the least desirable jobs in the Junior Republic eventually would pay the highest wages. The citizen workers were free to quit their jobs at any time and look for different work within the Republic. Of course, workers could be fired by their employers, and without a letter of recommendation from his former boss, the lazy, slothful, or irresponsible worker could not secure another satisfactory position.[46]

"Nothing without Labor" was often taken to mean "work or starve," but this was never literally true. George, like other Progressives, wasted little sympathy on vagrants, paupers, tramps, and other indigents.[47] Before a lazy citizen had much of a chance to become hungry he was popped into jail. It was never a crime to be poor in the Republic, but it was always a crime not to work. "Bad habits willfully exercised," George declared, "[must] meet with a natural result." Each child had to learn that only a fair amount of industry produced comfort in the Junior Republic. "Thrift and economy [are the creators] of wealth, character, confidence and self-respect," George reminded his citizens.[48]

Yet, even with the hotel, stores, restaurant, currency, jail,

[46] Thomas Mott Osborne, address before the National Conference of Charities and Corrections, Washington, D.C., May 13, 1901; George, *The Junior Republic*, 238–242; Howard Jones, *Reluctant Rebels* (New York, 1960), 16–17; Commons, "The Junior Republic, I," 286–287.

[47] See Roy Lubove's "Introduction to the Torchbook Edition," of Jacob A. Riis, *The Making of an American* (1901; reprint ed., New York: Harper Torchbooks, 1966), xv–xvi; Bruno and Towley, *Trends in Social Work*, 72–73.

[48] George, MS, Jan. 1, 1897.

and so forth, a natural economy was almost impossible to establish in the Republic. Since George owned all the land and property, ran all the stores, hotels, and restaurants, and employed all the citizens, he was the sole source of wealth and the only real capitalist in the Republic. Only a few high-ranking Republic officers were not totally dependent on George for their incomes. As the largest taxpayer in the Republic, George effectively held the power of the purse over the government.[49]

During the summer of 1896, George decided to take steps to extend economic democracy. Keeping the Republic farm, which employed by far the majority of citizens, under his own control, George proposed that citizens gradually be granted licenses to operate Republic hotels, restaurants, stores, and other services not essential to the maintenance of the Republic physical plant. At first only a few franchises were let through competitive bidding at public auctions. Citizens were also encouraged to obtain licenses from the government to operate their own businesses. Initially, the responsibilities were not large; the operation of a hotel, for example, might include nothing more than changing the sheets and sweeping the floors of the sleeping rooms. But George hoped that such small steps might eventually provide the basis for a real Republic economy.

At first the results were gratifying. An immigrant boy by the name of Jimmie came to the Republic unable to speak a word of English. But since he had worked in New York City sweatshops he became the Republic tailor and was so successful that in time he became one of the Republic's "millionaires." Another lad who had a special interest in nature studies ran a successful museum. Another opened a shoe repair shop. An especially enterprising citizen, the son of a union leader,

49 Commons, "The Junior Republic, I," 286–287.

undertook a construction contract to dig a sewer ditch, but went broke when his employees struck for higher wages. Girls found a ready market for candy and sandwiches. The Republic even began to develop a professional class as children who passed the Republic bar examination found their talents as defense lawyers in great demand.[50]

Soon after the arrival of the summer citizens in 1896, however, the Republic faced a severe political and economic crisis. It became immediately apparent that the Republic had developed two classes of citizens: the patrician winter (year-round) inhabitants and the plebeian summer transients. Although outnumbered 160 to 20, the winter residents held all the political offices and most of the profitable contracts and comfortable accommodations. They had formed a highly cohesive "People's Party," led by the conservative citizen president, Jacob Smith, and supported by most of the permanent adult helpers who welcomed the stability of the Smith administration. Tensions mounted, however, when some of the summer volunteers encouraged the summer citizens to form an opposition party.

Identifying themselves with Bryan Democrats, the summer citizens formed the "Free Tin Party" under the leadership of Jimmy Dolan. It is difficult to know whether or not the move was aimed directly at George, though the rhetoric of the Free Tin Party could not have been better calculated to infuriate him. After what is reported to have been one of the most colorful, hard-fought, and bitter campaigns in Republic history, Dolan and the Free Tin Party were triumphantly swept into office.[51] The Free Tin Party, which

[50] George, *The Adult Minor*, 14–28; Commons, "The Junior Republic, I," 281–296.

[51] George, *The Junior Republic*, 105–137; Commons, "The Junior Republic, I." 281–296; Chamberlain, *There Is No Truce*, 225. The Free Tin Party was so-called because at this time Republic money consisted of tin tokens.

had campaigned on a platform of "high wages, plenty of work, and prosperity," immediately launched a large-scale program of government spending: repairing roads, building sidewalks and drains, laying out parks. The contracts for the projects were let to party stalwarts who used their patronage to secure party regularity. They paid their workers the comparatively high wage of fifty cents a day, foremen often receiving as much as a dollar. Even at this rate, they were often able to make a profit of $150 on a $200 contract. Soon, the political chieftains of the Free Tin Party became "millionaires," living in the best hotels without any need of work. The high wages they paid depreciated the currency, pushing the cost of luxuries beyond the reach of the common citizens.[52]

The politicians were not the only source of trouble in the summer of 1896. Some shrewd boys began importing apples, candy, and other merchandise, underselling the merchants who had purchased the same items on contract from the government. The "government" merchants demanded that a 35 per cent tariff be levied to protect their infant businesses. The irregular merchants countered by charging that government monopoly, not free enterprise, would result from such a tariff. The tariff was passed, but not before further ill will was created. Republic officers shortly discovered they had smuggling and a black market to cope with.[53]

Another crisis developed when it was revealed that a citizen had bought up most of the shoes in the Republic during the warm summer months. At the approach of fall and harvest when the demand for shoes increased, the boy resold the shoes to the improvident citizenry at greatly increased prices. An investigation disclosed that such speculation had become common and that many of the speculators were becoming rich

[52] Commons, "The Junior Republic, I," 289.
[53] Commons, "The Junior Republic, II," *American Journal of Sociology,* III (Jan. 1898), 435.

by Republic standards. A "millionaire-class of idle rich," strutting around the village in their gay clothes, became a feature of the community. George was horrified to see some of the more intelligent and unscrupulous citizens quit regular labor and yet live extravagantly on the profits from their fat government contracts and investments.[54]

It is evident that George had almost let affairs get out of control. Aided by volunteers who believed the summer children had been reduced to second-class citizens, older summer citizens were quick to seize on the weaknesses of the Junior Republic scheme. The major shortcoming, of course, had been George's great reluctance to intervene in the affairs of the government or economy. With George maintaining a strict "hands-off" policy, it did not take the older boys long to figure out how to use the system to their greatest advantage.

By 1896 it was evident that laissez faire, even in the George Junior Republic, was intolerable. When the summer citizens departed in 1896 the power of the Free Tin Party departed with them. Immediately the People's Party, now entirely made up of winter citizens, took control of the government. A delegation of citizens then approached George, requesting him to confiscate all money in the Republic treasury, take possession of all hotels, industries, and shops, and manage the Republic economy in the name of the Republic Association.[55]

[54] Walter Haviland, "The George Junior Republic," *Guilford Collegian*, XIII (Dec. 1900), 35–40; Commons, "The Junior Republic, II," 440–441.

[55] George, *The Junior Republic*, 132; Chamberlain, *There Is No Truce*, 225. Though it cannot be proven, it is probable that a petition was arranged by George and the Association. Commons avoided the fiction of self-government and stated flatly: "In 1897 Mr. George took the matter in hand and returned to his policy of 1895" ("The Junior Republic, I," 289). Washington Gladden earlier had recommended an abandonment of strict *laissez faire* with regard

George was not dissatisfied by this arrangement, for it allowed him the face-saving inference that an irresponsible fiscal policy had failed in the Junior Republic, just as it must also fail in the greater Republic. Most importantly, however, as manager of all industries, George was able to regulate the rise of "millionaires." He discontinued letting contracts on a strictly competitive basis, and instead awarded them to those he felt to be most deserving. Thus he could protect the honest and industrious from the depredations of the merely shrewd and unscrupulous.[56]

In a companion move, the government passed a law declaring that a citizen must have at least one month's residence to qualify for public office. This meant that the summer citizens on their return in 1897 would be barred from immediately regaining control of the government. Since most of the leaders of the summer party were thrown into jail during the first four weeks of their return, they were also ineligible for election during the second month of their stay. As a result, the summer citizens, who made up three-fourths of the population, were permanently excluded from control of the Republic government or economy.

iii

Most observers agreed that the summer citizens presented the greatest obstacle to the working of the Junior Republic scheme. John R. Commons, for example, felt it was apparent that a boy needed the year-round care of the Republic in order to receive its full benefits. Two months' summer

---

to the Republic economy. Such an economy was much too complex for children, he warned, and only led to speculation, inflation, smuggling, and other dishonesty ("The Junior Republic at Freeville," *The Outlook*, LIV [Oct. 31, 1896], 780–782).

[56] Commons, "The Junior Republic, I," 290.

residence was simply not enough time to deal with the problems of the misbehaving, apathetic, or lazy child. Many of the
summer visitors spent their two-month stay in the Republic
in jail, working on the rockpile. Most citizens, George noted,
first entered into Republic life with enthusiasm. However, a
relapse was almost inevitable, and by the time the summer
citizen repented and began to reap some of the benefits of his
reformed life, it was time for him to go home. Boys who remained throughout the year, on the other hand, had an opportunity to become model citizens and enjoy the full benefits
of Republic citizenship.[57]

Washington Gladden concurred with Commons on this
issue, stressing that the summer term was too short; if campers
were to remain at the Junior Republic only temporarily, he
felt, it would be better to extend their stay to four or six
months. Gladden spent a day and a half in Freeville closely
inspecting all aspects of the Republic and confessed that it was
far "easier to criticize than to create," in appraising George's
work. "But because this thing is so essentially good," he continued, "one does not wish to see its success imperiled by
remediable errors." [58]

Gladden had further suggestions: He thought the Republic
Association should fix the minimum age of citizens at twelve,
for the younger campers did not fully profit from the regime.
The presence of girls in the camp bothered Gladden and he
recommended they not be included in the Republic. George
should be relieved of all business duties so that he could devote
his full time to the social problems of the Republic. The number of visitors allowed to roam the grounds should be limited,
for they often hampered the operation of the Republic.

[57] Commons, "The Junior Republic, I," 294; George, MS, Jan. 1,
1897.
[58] Gladden, "The Junior Republic at Freeville," 780–782.

Ironically, Gladden's friendly criticism exacerbated the existing discontent among summer workers and precipitated dissension and revolt within the Republic Association, which ultimately led to a brief, but spectacular, public scandal that almost wrecked the experiment. Gladden's criticism of the summer program was resented by some members of the Republic Association who actually opposed the year-round program and were distressed at what they believed was an assault on the original purpose of the Fresh Air camp. They charged that keeping children the year round, to which they had never given their full approval, was gradually taking precedence over the summer excursions. Not only were the increased costs of the winter program hurting the summer work, but George himself was believed to be undermining the Fresh Air project by his obvious preference for the permanent citizens and his persecution of the summer people. It was George, the dissidents contended, who instigated the reforms that made second-class citizens of the summer group. Though the reforms were supposedly directed against Republic monopoly, it was noted that one of George's favorites, a permanent citizen, was still police chief, inspector, lawyer, and proprietor of a hotel and a clothing and grocery store. Furthermore, with the permissive indulgence and encouragement of George, the Republic government had zealously arrested, tried, convicted, and sentenced (thus disenfranchising) those among the summer citizens who challenged the established leadership. George's critics within the Association further charged that the winter program itself had serious deficiencies. The children were not adequately schooled, nor were they properly clothed, fed, or housed.[59] But most of all, various board members became disturbed by George's inability to accept criti-

[59] George, Notebook, 1897; William C. Orton to Mrs. William R. George, July 1897.

cism. William C. Orton, the treasurer of the Association, complained that George mistook honest suggestions offered in the spirit of help as attempts to take over administration of the Republic.[60]

To aid in the management of the Republic, the Association appointed a business manager, J. D. Merriman, as George's assistant during the summer of 1897, the last year citizens and volunteers came from New York City for a two-month outing. Hardly had the train from New York arrived when friction developed between the permanent staff and citizens and the summer volunteers and visitors. The two programs greatly strained the limited budget and facilities of the Republic Association. Each group accused the other of extravagance. George was dismayed, for example, when Merriman ordered sixty dollars' worth of pots and pans for the summer boarding house. By the end of August the Republic Association was $1,500 in debt and needed an additional $5,000 to meet the expenses of the coming year.[61] "The whole season," George reported, "was a period of misunderstanding and disappointments, which I feel might have been avoided if each party could have fully appreciated the other's point of view." [62] The Board of Trustees voted to discontinue the summer work after George reported that the summer citizens, helpers, and business manager had left the whole Republic in a shambles.[63]

Piqued by George's accusations, Merriman submitted his own report. The jail, Merriman contended, had been so infested with vermin that fumigation had been necessary. The

[60] Orton to Mrs. George, July 1897.
[61] Anon., "Special Appeal in Behalf of the George Junior Republic," MS, 1897.
[62] George, *The Junior Republic*, 158.
[63] Mrs. William R. George to Dr. E. A. Foote, Oct. 4, 1897.

buildings had needed extensive remodeling and repairing. There had been no adequate eating facilities until Mrs. Rogers (one of the trustees most critical of George) had generously provided a temporary dining building. Head lice were common among tenants at the Waldorf and Savoy hotels. The outhouses had been allowed to become filthy and smelly. Despite all this, Merriman conceded, the citizens were generally free from sickness. Mrs. Rogers, for her part, claimed that George was cruel and rough with the boys.[64]

A small group of Junior Republic supporters, believing that the summer program was worth continuing, decided at this time to discontinue their association with George and launch their own project called the Industrial Colony Association of New York City, which subsequently established a republic on a farm at Gardner in Ulster County.[65]

Upon the departure of most of the dissenters at the end of the summer, the whole affair might have been forgotten had not a Rochester paper seized the opportunity to boost circulation with a series of muckraking exposés. Learning of the dissatisfaction in Freeville, the Rochester *Herald* asked, "Did you ever see a beautiful design marred in the execution? A painting, for example, exquisite in theme, but faulty in development . . . botched and bungled; well begun and then a retrogression almost fatal to the desired good results? At Freeville, Tompkins County, New York, there exists just such a state of affairs; and it goes by the name of the George Junior Republic." [66]

Relying on the reports of three visitors to the Republic

[64] J. D. Merriman, "Report of the Business Manager of the George Junior Republic for the Summer of 1897," MS; George to T. M. Osborne, April 16, 1898.

[65] New York *Sun*, Aug. 14, 1897.

[66] Rochester *Herald*, Aug. 14, 1897.

from Rochester and the investigation of its own reporter, the *Herald* echoed the criticism of the dissident trustees. The *Herald* claimed to be sympathetic to the Republic principle and idea; it was only "the development of that idea at Free-ville, as exemplified by the George Junior Republic, [that had] become a matter of just and unanswerable criticism." [67] Like Mrs. Rogers and Merriman, the *Herald* was most disturbed by the dirt and disorganization: it reported six boys confined to the same jail cell with rough pine boards for bunks, insufficient blankets, and a small, inaccessible overhead window as the only source of light; in another cell a boy served a three-week sentence in solitary confinement for stealing cherries. To compound matters, the jailer, who had all the keys for the cells, could not be found. A large barn, which might have been a comfortable dormitory, had not been cleaned of refuse and manure before the boys were moved in. The beds were exceptionally dirty, as though the boys had slept with their boots on. Everywhere there seemed to be lack of standards in cleanliness, order, and workmanship. Drainage ditches were crooked and irregular; the garden was ungeometrical and full of weeds; the sidewalks and paths were haphazard and seldom paved, which contributed greatly to the mud and dirt that was tracked everywhere. In the dining room the tables were not neatly arranged, and many were not clean. The kitchen was disorderly and unscreened, with a large population of flies.

The *Herald* also raised doubts about the quality of instruction at the Junior Republic, contending that the high turnover of teachers and advisors introduced instability into the Republic system. The whole program, in short, lacked continuity, the *Herald* charged.

Even this criticism might have passed had not the *Herald*

[67] *Ibid.,* Aug. 16, 1897.

hammered at two very sensitive points. First, it charged that the presence of girls in the Junior Republic contributed to an immoral environment. Though boys and girls lived in separate dormitories and ate in separate dining rooms, the *Herald* reminded its readers that "still, on the playground and in other ways, there [was] an opportunity of intermingling of the sexes." Secondly, the *Herald* criticized George for business mismanagement. "Mr. George is not precisely the right man in the right place," they editorialized. "Some people even go so far as to say that Mr. George is a visionary, almost wholly devoid of the practical, definite, executive capabilities requisite to the highest success of such a scheme as the Junior Republic.[68] The *Herald* concluded its attack by lamenting that it was unfortunate the Junior Republic was not a public institution and thus could not be thoroughly investigated by the New York State Board of Charities.

As it turned out, the State Board of Charities needed no special authorization. Robert W. Hebberd, George's old foe from the Charity Organization Society, had become secretary of the State Board of Charities. Hebberd, on hearing from Rochester of the difficulties of the Junior Republic, authorized an official inquiry by the Committee on Placing Out Dependent Children. At the end of the summer, the three-member committee from the State Board of Charities visited the George Junior Republic to make their investigation. Cyrus Lathrop, an inspector for the State Board who had been a volunteer worker at the Junior Republic in 1896, warned George that Hebberd was opposed to the Junior Republic and was especially bitter against George. The forewarning, however, hardly seemed necessary after the inspectors arrived. Though they very carefully inspected the entire Republic, George was led to believe that the three men

[68] *Ibid.,* Aug. 12, 1897.

were satisfied with what they had found. A few weeks later
George was stunned to learn that the Committee on Placing
Out Dependent Children was preparing a derogatory report
which it planned to submit to the State Board of Charities
that fall.[69]

In their report,[70] Commissioners Enoch V. Stoddard and
Peter Walrath of the State Board of Charities and Harvey W.
Putnam (the three men who composed the Committee on
Placing Out Dependent Children) conceded the value of the
Junior Republic in providing a refuge for neglected and
unfortunate children during the season of greatest heat in the
city, but they felt that it lacked those features which were
essential to its ultimate success and permanence. The inspectors concluded that, without the influence of the family and
lacking in educational provisions, the Junior Republic stood
"only as an ingenious effort at temporary restraint."

The basic problem of the Junior Republic, the commissioners suggested, was George's naïveté. Their interviews with
George did not convince them that he fully comprehended
the complex nature of the problem he was confronting.
George's primary concern, as far as they could tell, was to
avoid in every way possible anything that might suggest an
institution. They found George ready, even anxious, to accept
suggestions for improving his plan if they conformed to the
simple principle, "How is it done in a republic?" "In other
words," the committee charged, "the present condition of the

[69] George, "Statement about the State Board of Charities." George
contended that the inspectors had in fact originally submitted a
favorable report, but that Hebberd refused to accept it.

[70] "The George Junior Republic," supplementary to the Report
of the Committee on Placing Out Dependent Children, Oct. 13, 1897,
Legislative Reference Library, New York State Library, Albany. See
also *Thirteenth Annual Report of the New York State Board of
Charities,* I (Albany, 1896).

George Junior Republic is a mimic form of national and municipal government, with nothing above and nothing below it."

The investigators recognized that George exerted considerable personal influence over each member of the Freeville community. They conceded that if the affectionate relation that existed between George and the citizens were fused into a "predominating home atmosphere," much of what was lacking in the Junior Republic plan would be overcome. In place of the home, however, the Republic ran a "hotel," which suggested "no kinship or relationship, but an aggregation of individuals, each bent upon his own business or occupation." As a result, discipline and control were vested, not in a "house father" or matron, but in a system of police. Though this was interesting, and often entertaining, the committee deplored "the unfortunately demoralizing influences of the Police Court. In the daily life of these children, this has already found the prominent place, and the gentler and refining influence of the home circle too little."

The investigators also noted that the Republic was extremely dirty, but desired to make no criticism as to disorder or uncleanliness in the institution. They believed that George was handicapped by the irregular and insufficient financial organization of the Republic which prevented the establishment of a system for insuring cleanliness in all departments of the Republic. George, for his part, was largely indifferent to the matter.

In conclusion, the investigators expressed little confidence that George, working alone, could grasp sufficiently the issues involved to allow him to achieve success. The reliance on unpaid, part-time help and the absence of a professional advisory board precluded the establishment of services and departments essential for the long-range success of the experiment. Without family, home, or adequate school, the George Junior Republic was simply a benevolent police state, run by an amateur social worker whose methods were unorthodox and questionable. The investigators found George personally attractive and his ambitions laudable, but they could not in good conscience give the Junior Republic a strong recommendation. "Laying aside all sentiment, and viewing it solely from the standpoint of the practical," the report concluded, "your Committee feel that it possesses none of the essentials of success."

It is not puzzling that the George Junior Republic should have drawn criticism from the press and investigation from the State Board of Charities. The State Board would have been remiss had it not investigated the charges brought by the Rochester *Herald*. Yet it did not investigate reluctantly. The financial difficulties and George's lack of administrative ability were serious shortcomings which were probably magnified in the minds of the commissioners who were distressed by the anti-institutional methods and lack of professional regularity evident at the juvenile institution. Only three years before, in 1894, the State Board had investigated the neighboring Elmira Reformatory after the local press printed sensational accusations against Warden Zebulon R. Brockway made by a paroled convict. Brockway, a critic of the solitary system of the Eastern State Penitentiary of Pennsylvania and the silent system of Auburn Prison, had aroused the suspicion of prison authorities and social workers since becoming warden at Elmira in 1876. Though Brockway was cleared of any irregularity, subsequent investigations by the State Board reflected a continuing uneasiness of that body over Brockway's innovations.[71] If the State Board of Charities had difficulty in accepting the disciplinary methods of the "Elmira system," it

[71] Zebulon R. Brockway, *Fifty Years of Prison Service* (New York, 1912), 328–339.

should not be surprising that the board was even less able to look beyond administrative difficulties to appreciate the essentials of the Junior Republic system. The administration of justice at the Republic was not only unwholesome, it was dangerous. Without adult keepers and tight security, rioting was possible. The presence of girls in the Junior Republic complicated matters. In short, the administration of the Junior Republic was especially suspect because it contradicted almost every canon of prison and institutional discipline.[72]

Ironically, just as the investigations by the State Board of Charities had enhanced the fame and renown of Zebulon Brockway as Progressives rallied to the defense of the Elmira system,[73] the investigation of the Junior Republic was turned from a potential disaster into a Republic triumph.

Prior to the attacks on the Junior Republic, knowledge of, and support for, George's work was confined largely to his friends and associates in New York City, the patrons of several Adirondack resorts visited by the Republic's Singing Quartet on their fund-raising tour, and the ladies of the missionary guilds of the Finger Lakes region. To be sure, the work of the Junior Republic had attracted the attention of many prominent New Yorkers. Precisely because of its bold innovations, Lyman Abbott, William H. Maxwell,[74] Bishop F. D. Huntington of the Protestant Episcopal Church, Thomas Mott Osborne, Charles H. Parkhurst, Jacob Riis, Albert Shaw, Josiah Strong, John R. Commons, and Theodore Roosevelt had all endorsed George's system as an enlightened solution to the problems of institutional and social control.[75]

[72] Chamberlain, *There Is No Truce,* 228.

[73] Brockway, *Fifty Years of Prison Service,* 335–336.

[74] Superintendent of Schools, New York City.

[75] In 1896, these men (with the exception of Theodore Roosevelt) formed a portion of a twenty-seven member Advisory Council organized to acquaint business, educational, and religious leaders with the work of the Junior Republic.

Unhappily, most of the financial support for the Junior Republic (as noted by the State Board of Charities), came not from these men but from small and irregular contributions of local churches and friends.[76] The adverse publicity and subsequent investigation, therefore, threatened the Republic with financial collapse as alarmed contributors withdrew their subscriptions.

When Thomas Mott Osborne became a member of the Junior Republic's Board of Trustees, secretary-treasurer William Orton had reported the treasury down to six dollars.[77] Though Republic fortunes had improved somewhat over the summer months of 1897, Osborne, determined not to let the financial condition of the Junior Republic deteriorate any more than it already had, urged the Board of Trustees to appoint a new, and smaller, Advisory Committee to investigate the various charges that had been brought against George and his management.[78] At the same time, learning from Frederick Almy that there was no chance that the State Board of Charities would amend its report before giving it to the state legislature, Osborne requested from Hebberd only that the board allow the new Republic Advisory Committee of Seven time enough to submit its own report to the legislature at the same time.[79]

Led by Thomas Mott Osborne, who was responsible for recruiting most of the members of the blue-ribbon panel, the Committee of Seven was composed of Jeremiah W. Jenks, professor of political economy at Cornell; Benjamin Ide Wheeler, another Cornell professor soon to become president

[76] "List of Subscriptions and Donations," c. 1896.

[77] Orton to George, Jan. 5, 1897.

[78] Osborne to Mrs. William R. George, Nov. 15, 1897.

[79] Osborne to Robert W. Hebberd, Secretary, State Board of Charities, Dec. 20, 1897, Osborne Papers, Syracuse University.

of the University of California; John R. Commons, then at
Syracuse University; William F. Blackman, editor of the
Yale Review; Frederick Almy, secretary of the Charity
Organization Society of Buffalo; and F. W. Richardson of
Auburn. This group became a nucleus for spreading the
"Republic Gospel" among national reformers. Jenks would
long remain a firm supporter and trustee of the Junior Re-
public after he went to Princeton. Wheeler, as president of
the University of California, helped prepare the way for the
successful Junior Republic work done in that state. John R.
Commons, after he moved to the University of Wisconsin,
discussed George's work with Richard Ely, Jane Addams, and
Graham Taylor. Blackman interested an influential Yale group
in Republic affairs; led by Irving Fisher and George Parmly
Day, this group assisted in establishing the Connecticut Junior
Republic. Richardson, a successful Auburn businessman, had
made his most important contribution to the Junior Republic
by recruiting Thomas Mott Osborne. Osborne, in his turn,
provided an incalculably valuable spiritual link to such diverse
reformers as Lucretia Mott, Homer Folks, R. W. Gilder,
Oswald Villard, Herbert Lehman, W. Cameron Forbes,
Frederick Almy, V. Everit Macy, William Lloyd Garrison,
Jr., Susan B. Anthony, and Elizabeth Cady Stanton. The
Advisory Committee of Seven, then, served not only as the
chief means for exonerating George, but also served as the
major interpreter and promoter of the Junior Republic and
its philosophy to the national Progressive moment.[80]

[80] I do not mean to imply that George enjoyed no national repu-
tation at all before the summer of 1897. Albert Shaw's *Review of
Reviews* and *Harper's Weekly* had taken note of George's work as
early as May of 1896. Washington Gladden's article on the Junior
Republic appeared in *The Outlook* on Oct. 30, 1896. Other notices of
George's work had appeared in Frank Munsey's *Argosy* as well as
Romance, The Silver Cross, the *Christian Herald,* the New York

After such powerful and dynamic personalities were attracted to the Junior Republic movement, George could not monopolize control, direction, or even the identity of his own creation. Once various reformers had made the idea their own, they brought to it a history and background only dimly understood by George himself. Discovered independently in front of a wagon shed in West Dryden, New York, the Junior Republic idea won independence from its founder when it developed a past and a history George could not share. Throughout his life, George remained the predominant personality in the history of his institution. But after 1897 he discovered that he could not monopolize or contain his basic idea, a fact which both delighted and distressed him. It is impossible to know, of course, how far anti-institutional methods and self-government principles would have been developed in the Progressive Era without the inspiration of William R. George. The historical fact remains that the George Junior Republic sharpened the Progressive recognition of anti-institutional solutions to a wide range of social problems.

World, and the New York *Journal.* But until the State Board of Charities elevated its importance by granting it an official investigation, the George Junior Republic remained essentially a local experiment, involving few people outside George's immediate circle and having practically no national consequence.

IV

THE TIME OF TROUBLES

————————— The era of the George Junior Republic's greatest growth and development spanned two seasons of turmoil and trouble. The first crisis in the summer of 1897 rallied Progressives, led by Thomas Mott Osborne, to the Junior Republic standard. The second crisis, "the time of troubles" of 1912–1914, removed the Republic from the list of Progressive experiments, and all but destroyed it after Thomas Mott Osborne resigned as president of the Board of Trustees.

The intervening history is a drama played out on two levels. On one level we shall witness the spectacular and triumphant rise of the Junior Republic movement, and the acceptance of its anti-institutional principles by innumerable reformers. The scenes shift rapidly from universities, schools, and prisons, to boys' clubs, orphanages, and the Boy Scouts. John Dewey, Nicholas Murray Butler, Stephen S. Wise, and Lillian Wald played major roles in promoting the self-government movement in American schools.[1] Wilson Gill, under the auspices of General Leonard Wood, carried Republic educational methods into Cuba, and W. Cameron Forbes, appointed governor-general of the Philippines in 1909, introduced Republic

[1] See discussion of The National Self-Government Committee, below, 197–201.

penal measures in the Ilwahig Penal Colony on Palawan Island. The Little Commonwealth, established by a Montessori group in Dorsetshire, England, was directly inspired by the George Junior Republic. The Mutual Welfare League, an inmate self-government plan established at Sing Sing and Auburn Prison by Thomas Mott Osborne, was described by Orlando F. Lewis as the most significant single contribution to Progressive penology. In 1913, E. A. Ross spoke for many Progressives when he commented on George's work: "I know of nothing that in such a small compass and in so delightful a way sheds so much light on the psychology of law breaking, of punishment, of responsibility, a number of my sociological generalizations, and put me on watch for certain kinds of facts which I hitherto little noticed." [2]

On the public level, the formation of the National Association of Junior Republics (NAJR) in 1908 certified what was already an established fact: the George Junior Republic was a pioneering institution for juvenile care whose anti-institutional experiments in education and penology brought it international recognition. Every Junior Republic, and countless organizations, institutions, and private individuals, had access to George through the NAJR offices in New York City maintained by Lyman Beecher Stowe. Thus the National Association enabled George to devote his boundless energies to assisting struggling, newly formed Republics, and to take full promotional and fund-raising advantage of his numerous speaking opportunities. Finally, as an answer to those who charged that the Freeville institution was a "one-man affair," the NAJR provided the Junior Republic movement with an appearance of professional continuity.

The other level of the drama is more private, intense, and subtle. The action revolves about the quiet, but often des-

2 E. A. Ross to Lyman Beecher Stowe, March 24, 1913.

perate, struggle for control of the Junior Republic movement. George and Osborne are the main protagonists in a story that is thick with intrigue. The two prominent upstate Progressives remained friends until 1913, but between 1897 and 1913 their ambiguous and fluctuating personal relationship determined the fate of the Junior Republic movement as certainly as did the shifting currents of public opinion.

The National Association established a tenuous *modus vivendi* between Osborne and George. Confirming that George was best employed as a Republic evangelizer and troubleshooter, George's appointment as National Director of the NAJR temporarily solved some of the Junior Republic's most pressing problems. First, the struggling institution was liberated from the management of its founder and delivered into the hands of more experienced professionals. Second, George was freed to aid and encourage other institutions without being charged with conflict of interest. But most important to the two Republic leaders, the National Association provided George with an important and independent position which, it was hoped, would not bring him into conflict with the trustees of the Freeville Junior Republic.[3]

i

So skillfully had Osborne piloted the Republic through the storms of 1897 that he became the unanimous choice for president of the Board of Trustees. He worried that he could not reconcile all his differences with George, however, and suggested that someone from New York City might be a more conciliatory choice, even if the Board had to be satisfied

[3] L. S. Levine, "Some of the Purposes of the National Association of Junior Republics and How It Is Proposed to Achieve Them," MS, 1912.

with a figurehead. But Osborne knew that no one else could effectively serve the Republic at that difficult time, and after offering the traditional protestations that he was not the man for the job, he reluctantly accepted the position.[4] Once again, he recruited Jeremiah Jenks, F. W. Richardson, and Frederick Almy to serve with him, this time on the Executive Committee of the Board of Trustees, whose first task was to put the Republic on a sound financial basis and to guard against conditions that might lead to further scandals. They all agreed that George was incapable of running the Republic by himself. "I vacillate between great admiration for George's genius and brilliant intuition, and extreme exasperation for his slipshod methods, imperfect logic and careless development," Osborne wrote. "He is gazing at the stars without seeing the dirt at his feet." [5] With the rationalization that George could be "somewhat disjointed in the handling of funds without the slightest intention on his part to be dishonest," the business affairs of the Republic were transferred to the Executive Committee.[6]

Osborne immediately moved to reconcile Mrs. Rogers and the Ladies Auxiliary in New York City. He confessed that as president he saw more clearly the force of her objections to the dirt and disorganization in the Republic. On January 8, 1898, the Executive Committee announced its decision to hire a matron, a secretary, and an assistant superintendent to help

[4] Osborne to A. G. Agnew, Dec. 20, 1897; Osborne to Frederick Almy, Dec. 27, 1897, Jan. 4, 1899; Osborne Papers, Syracuse University. Osborne to William R. George, Dec. 27, 1897, George Junior Republic Papers, Cornell University.

[5] Osborne to Miss Grace W. Minns, Nov. 11, 1899; Osborne to Miss Anna Dawes, Nov. 11, 1899; Osborne Papers.

[6] Osborne to Agnew, Dec. 20, 1897; Osborne to Almy, Dec. 27, 1897; Osborne Papers.

run the Republic.[7] To protect against overzealous citizen justice, the Executive Committee also decided to serve as the Republic Supreme Court, Osborne sitting as Chief Justice. A constitutional amendment was enacted making it a criminal offense for a Republic citizen to refuse to discharge his official duty. Lastly, all of the sleeping quarters were thoroughly cleaned, and additional clothing and bedding were issued during the coldest winter months.[8]

Osborne succeeded in reconciling Mrs. Rogers and the New York Ladies Auxiliary, but he paid a price in his relationship with George. Mrs. Rogers had accused George of being cruel, rough, and demanding with the boys, and as far as George was concerned it had been good riddance to Mrs. Rogers and her cronies. George frequently believed that his best intentions were misinterpreted by professionals or sentimentalists, and although he was piqued at Mrs. Rogers' open criticism, he dismissed her as having no understanding of his special relationship with the boys. Caring little for the financial wisdom of Obsorne's move, George saw no reason why the Board of Trustees should court the New Yorkers who had aligned themselves with his old enemy, Robert Hebberd.[9]

There was very real danger, however, that without Osborne's diplomacy vital financial assistance would have been lost, followed by the collapse of the struggling Junior Republic. If George was hurt by Osborne's "betrayal," Osborne was irritated that George could not understand the Board was acting in the Republic's best interest. The first crisis

[7] Executive Committee Minutes, Jan. 8, 1898, Osborne Papers.
[8] Osborne to Mrs. Rogers, Jan. 10, 1898; Osborne to Jeremiah Jenks, Jan. 5, 1898; Osborne Papers.
[9] George to Osborne, April 18, 1898.

between the two men reached its climax when Osborne learned that a boy, recently sent to the Republic after an operation, was forced to spend one night on the floor and another sitting in the library because no bed could be found for him. From Auburn came a blistering letter telling George that such carelessness only lent credence to Mrs. Rogers' charges. "I have no right to keep such a matter as this from the Trustees," Osborne scolded George. "Yet if I were to tell of it, they would be justified in withdrawing their support. It is so careless of your best interests—it is calculated to deprive you of your hold of the boys." [10]

George was conscious that his hold on the entire Junior Republic operation was weakening. Osborne transacted all his business with Lloyd B. Wright, the new assistant superintendent and business manager.[11] More seriously from George's point of view, Osborne won over the loyalty of several citizens. Osborne, too, liked to "pal around" with the boys, often flinging his arms around an embarrassed lad in a friendly embrace. It did not take Republic citizens long to learn that "Uncle Tom," the compassionate Chief Justice of their Supreme Court, was also the owner of the D. M. Osborne and Company who could supply jobs to needy and promising boys. In time, the number of Republic graduates working for Osborne in Auburn grew so large that an Auburn Junior Republic Club was formed.[12] George complained bitterly that Osborne undermined Republic authority by listening to complaints of malcontents, and by providing runaway and unhappy boys of temporary refuge at his home.[13]

[10] Osborne to George, April 16, 1898, Osborne Papers.
[11] See Osborne Letterbook, Jan.–Dec., 1898, Osborne Papers.
[12] Rudolph W. Chamberlain, *There Is No Truce: A Life of Thomas Mott Osborne* (New York, 1935), 230–231, 360.
[13] George to Osborne, April 16, 1898.

Osborne also undermined George's position by privately attacking George's father and wife. Osborne speculated that some of the management problems stemmed from the ambitions of Esther Brewster George, a summer volunteer whom George had married in 1896. Young Mrs. George, Osborne thought, was more concerned for the good name of her husband than she was for the welfare of the boys. "She is the reason for his loss of hold over the boys," Osborne explained to Jenks, overlooking his own role in the matter. "Under his wife's influence he has changed his attitude and got [sic] to look at the George Junior Republic as something that could be exploited to his great personal advantage." [14] Osborne proposed to loosen family control of the Republic by removing John F. George, William R. George's father, from the Board of Trustees. But always a practical strategist, Osborne abandoned the idea, admitting that the move might create more problems than it would solve.[15]

Naturally, the president of the Board of Trustees could not resist his new opportunities for secret masquerade. One day Osborne showed up at the Junior Republic disguised as an Italian organ grinder. No one, including George, suspected the identity of the visitor. After Osborne revealed himself, the citizens were naturally delighted that "Uncle Tom" had successfully deceived them, but George must have reacted to the episode somewhat apprehensively; he knew all too well that a number of times in the past Osborne had turned his innocent masquerades into clandestine investigations.[16]

The sometime organ grinder was not entirely blameless for the tension between himself and George. Osborne was often brusque and patronizing with the founder. He could match

[14] Osborne to Jeremiah Jenks, Jan. 18, 1898, Osborne Papers.
[15] Osborne to A. G. Agnew, Nov. 14, 1898, Osborne Papers.
[16] Chamberlain, *There Is No Truce*, 231–232.

George's peevishness if he thought he had been crossed, and even Osborne's best friends were annoyed by his self-righteousness. Remarkably compassionate and understanding with social outcasts, at times he was inexplicably insensitive to the most rudimentary feelings of his associates.[17]

William R. George and his family, realizing that the control of the Republic was gradually, almost inexorably, slipping from their hands, were not without resources of their own. Gerrit Smith Miller and his wife, Susan Dixwell Miller, were their chief allies in the struggle to curb Osborne's administration. For reasons that are now obscure, the Millers distrusted Osborne and his friends. Perhaps they believed Osborne was too zealously trying to put his own stamp on the work. At any rate, in the spring of 1898 the Millers purchased land adjacent to the Junior Republic on which Eleanor Baker George, George's mother, founded the Baker State of the George Junior Republic. Claiming to be associated with the Junior Republic, but actually independent of it, the Baker State provided an escape for George and his followers.

The move was blatant and obvious, and it infuriated Osborne. Avoiding a personal attack, he argued vehemently that no other Republic should be established while there was still considerable doubt concerning the success of the original institution. He would not tolerate a competing republic which served as a haven for disgruntled, schismatic groups. Fearing that the separatist threats might curtail the flexibility of his administration, limit the prospects for experimental work, and compete disastrously for uncertain financial resources, Osborne declared to Jenks, "one thing is certain. The 'Baker State' matter must be crushed at once. I shall not consent to go on with this open sore." [18]

Unsure of what had caused the friction between himself

[17] *Ibid.*, 233.
[18] Osborne to Jeremiah Jenks, Dec. 23, 1898, Osborne Papers.

and the Millers, Osborne was confident that he could move George with emotion and sentiment. Indeed, he reflected, "it seems to me the only feasible way to deal with him."[19] But if George refused to abandon the Baker State, Osborne was prepared to take the issue to the Board of Trustees and push it to the breaking point. There was no compelling need to keep George once he had founded the Republic, Osborne wrote to his friends. His experience in the implement business taught him that few inventors were capable of putting their inventions to the fullest practical use.[20] If George would not run the Republic in a proper businesslike way, it was time to replace him with someone who would.

In cooler moments, Osborne had enough sense to realize that an open attack on George would bring disaster to the Junior Republic. While pacifying George as best he could, Osborne negotiated a compromise in private talks with Gerrit Smith Miller. In return for abandoning the Baker State, Miller and George were to be elected to the Executive Committee of the Board of Trustees. Miller promised he would not follow the founder if George rejected the compromise and struck out on his own. Once Miller and Osborne agreed that George was incapable of managing his own Republic, the great threat of schism was ended.[21]

To everyone's surprise—and possibly Osborne's dismay— George cheerfully accepted the compromise. Once his position within the Republic administration was well defined and secure, George showed little interest in expansionist policies. Believing that there were not enough administrators and workers who fully understood Republic principles to staff additional Republics successfully, George was in fundamental

[19] *Ibid.*

[20] *Ibid.*; Osborne to Miss Minns and Miss Dawes, Nov. 11, 1899, Osborne Papers.

[21] Osborne to Jeremiah Jenks, Feb. 3, 1899, Osborne Papers.

accord with the Board of Trustees on this issue of Junior Republic development.[22] George cared as much for protecting the purity and orthodoxy of Republic principles as Osborne was anxious to maintain financial regularity and stability. The crisis had definitely passed by the time Osborne wrote to Dr. E. A. Foote: "At present I think it may be said that [George's] influence and personality is *most* valuable, and that we have been amply justified in not breaking with him. He is better . . . and working in more harmony with the Board than ever before since I have known the Republic." [23]

The Junior Republic idea, however, could not be monopolized in an era that was eager and ready to accept it. Despite Freeville's opposition to the establishment of additional Junior Republics, two self-governing juvenile institutions were founded shortly after the demise of the Baker State. Nellie R. Carter, wife of Philadelphia businessman William T. Carter, had given the George Junior Republic a boys' dormitory called the "Carter Cottage." But after the turmoil of 1897–1898, Mrs. Carter decided she would rather give her money to an institution more directly under her control. Accordingly, she founded the Carter Junior Republic at Redington, Pennsylvania. Making her break with Freeville as gracefully as possible, Mrs. Carter was the first to suggest that the parent Republic establish an official training school for Junior Republic administrators and helpers. The George Junior Republic made the best of the situation by sending a few citizens and helpers from Freeville to assist in founding the new institution.[24]

22 George to Albert Shaw, July 1897.
23 Osborne to Foote, Oct. 17, 1899, Osborne Papers.
24 Nellie R. Carter to Mrs. William R. George, Feb. 15, 1899. The Carter Junior Republic closed its doors in 1924, because, Mrs. Carter said, of the high cost of operation and a lack of trained personnel. She used the money to endow a chair in Child Welfare

In Washington and Baltimore, another group led by Mrs. Summerfield Baldwin and Mrs. Charles W. Fairbanks organized a Junior Republic on a 144-acre farm donated by Major John Newbold in memory of his son. Located at Annapolis Junction, Maryland, the National Junior Republic quickly attracted the attention of Washington and Baltimore society. On January 20, 1901, President William McKinley was the main speaker at a fund-raising rally sponsored by the Washington Ladies Aid Society.[25] The young daughters of several prominent Washington and Baltimore families found Republic work an ideal outlet for their restless energies. In Baltimore, the Junior Republic League under the leadership of Juliet Baldwin became one of the principal philanthropic organizations in the city.

The George Junior Republic Board of Trustees, bowing to the inevitable, accepted the accomplished facts. Short of repudiating the newly founded Junior Republics—which would have hurt all concerned—there was nothing it could do. Yet Osborne's worst fears of the consequences of unplanned expansion were confirmed when the National Junior Republic began to solicit funds in Boston, one of the prime sources of Freeville's income. Irritated that the Trustees of the Maryland Republic had trespassed on his own preserve, Osborne promised supporters of the National Republic friendly cooperation only if they restricted fund-raising to their own territory. As an ultimate threat, he was prepared to open his own Republic in Boston, thus putting the city out of bounds to both Freeville and Annapolis Junction.[26]

---

at the University of Pennsylvania (New York *Tribune*, April 27, 1924). See notes of Esther B. George, George Junior Republic Papers.

[25] Washington *Herald*, March 16, 1912.

[26] Osborne to the Rev. E. L. Hunt of Washington, D.C., Jan. 4, 1901, Osborne Papers.

The unplanned expansion of the Junior Republic movement also upset the delicate equilibrium of Osborne's relationship with George. Discovering that his position on the Executive Committee gave him little influence and still less responsibility, George could not resist the temptation to aid the new Republics. Soon he was helping to train and organize their staffs, and was soliciting funds from community clubs and service organizations in Pennsylvania and Maryland. As he warmed to his task, George envisioned the establishment of a Junior Republic in every state of the Union. While Osborne tramped the length and breadth of Massachusetts pleading for funds to sustain the Junior Republic in Freeville, George was dreaming of the establishment of a vast National Union of Junior Republics whose headquarters would be located in Washington, D.C.[27]

Osborne said nothing of George's grandiose schemes. Liberated from his hated desk in Auburn when the International Harvester Company bought him out in 1903, Osborne was at last released from the restrictions which had held his reforming zeal in check. Although the George Junior Republic was not the former manufacturer's sole interest, it benefited greatly from his increased attention. For sixteen years, the president of the Board of Trustees, skilled in parlor charades and street disguises, masked the Republic's internal rifts and tensions from the general public. Until the end, even George and the other members of the Board of Trustees were unaware of the depth of Osborne's misgivings. In retrospect it appears inevitable that the two reformers would break. On Osborne's part, there was no gradual awakening to the character of William R. George. What was most remarkable, in

[27] George, "Lecture Notes," 1898–1899; "Daddy's Prophecy," MS, Dec. 31, 1899; Osborne to George, Feb. 3, Feb. 6, March 7, 1899.

view of Osborne's early and constant assessment of the founder, was that the relationship lasted as long as it did.[28]

ii

The new century dawned on a growing but anemic George Junior Republic which seemed in danger of succumbing to two major disorders—economic malnutrition and crippling incompetency. For all its fame, the Junior Republic still reported a critical lack of cash. Officers, helpers, and employees of the Republic engaged in an almost continuous fund-raising drive. The Board of Trustees encouraged several Ladies Aid Societies, and sponsored a touring Republic chorus, and a few lecturers, including Thomas Mott Osborne. When the trustees suggested that the new business manager, Lloyd B. Wright, temporarily give up internal management of the institution in order "to work up outside enthusiasm," conditions had slipped to rock bottom.[29] By 1901, Republic income reached $18,663.38, but expenses ran to $21,415.88.[30] Throughout the next decade, the Junior Republic was apparently never out of debt, and by September 1911 the total deficit exceeded $18,000.[31]

It is difficult to know, however, just how serious were the institution's financial difficulties. There is no question that the financial burden was real, but it may not have been as oppressive as the trustees made it seem. Republic officers complained that the motto "Nothing without Labor" conveyed the false impression to prospective contributors that the Republic was

[28] Chamberlain, *There Is No Truce*, 87–100.
[29] Osborne to L. B. Wright, Sept. 2, 1898.
[30] Osborne to John D. Rockefeller, Jr., Feb. 14, 1902, Osborne Papers.
[31] Minutes of the George Junior Republic Executive Committee, Sept. 14, 1912.

self-supporting. Although the Republic did not support itself, there is no evidence that it was destitute, either. In addition to contributions from friends, the Republic enjoyed a small regular income from tuition paid by wealthy students. Osborne was always careful to suggest that the Republic was needy, but not bankrupt. In February 1902, the Board of Trustees launched a $50,000 endowment drive and quickly collected over $20,000 from such philanthropists as John D. Rockefeller, Andrew Carnegie, and Herbert Lehman.[32] Osborne candidly confessed to Rockefeller that the Republic indebtedness had decreased when measured against the growth of the institution.[33] Reassured of the Republic's financial stability, the Rockefellers contributed an additional $4,000 to build a jail and courthouse.[34] Whatever the truth of the situation, it was Osborne's strategy to create the impression that a sizable contribution to the Junior Republic was worthy and needed but would be no risk to the contributor.[35]

When the 1902 drive fell short of expectations, Osborne cautiously suggested establishing a permanent business which would employ Republic citizens and be managed by the Junior Republic Association. A self-sufficient Republic, he argued to the trustees, would be free from the competition of other Republics and from dependence on philanthropic don-

[32] Osborne to John D. Rockefeller, Jr., Feb. 20, 1902; Osborne to Andrew Carnegie, Feb. 20, 1902; Osborne to Frederick Almy, Feb. 28, 1902; Osborne to Herbert Lehman, March 27, 1902.

[33] Osborne to Rockefeller, Feb. 14, 1902, Osborne Papers.

[34] Osborne to A. G. Agnew, June 27, 1902, Osborne Papers.

[35] The George Junior Republic Account Books for the crucial years before 1903 are not available. The general impression received from the correspondence of this period is that it was not at all difficult to obtain money for buildings, improvement, and expansion. Most of this money was restricted, however, leaving the Republic critically short of funds to pay operating expenses. For example, see Osborne to John D. Rockefeller, Jr., Feb. 8, 1902, Osborne Papers.

ors. A few trustees pointed out that use of citizen labor to produce goods for profit might produce charges of "child labor." All recognized that self-sufficiency was not easily gained. Youths had been employed extensively on the Republic farm without raising suspicions that the Republic Association was exploiting its children, but the Republic farm produced very little cash surplus, and in 1901 failed completely. A Republic industry acceptable to reformers and attractive to trustees would have to provide "industrial training" for the citizens and large profits for the treasury. Unfortunately, such an industry was difficult to find.

In the early summer of 1903, Osborne discovered a windfall. Learning that the Childs' Bakery Company of Auburn, a manufacturer of chocolate and ginger wafers, was for sale for $3,000—including tools, secret processes, and good will, Osborne suggested that the Board of Trustees appropriate $4,000 and move the business to Freeville.[36] The wafer business, for which the Republic became well known locally, became the first of a group of Republic industries which eventually included a furniture shop, a print shop, a laundry, and the Republic Hotel.[37] Yet the "industrialization" at the George Junior Republic met with limited success, as suggested in a 1906 pamphlet published by the Junior Republic Association. Of recent graduates from the Junior Republic, thirty-five had become farmers, six were in the armed services, thirteen had become bookkeepers, stenographers, or salesmen, three were plumbers, and one each had become a painter,

[36] Osborne to V. Everit Macy, July 31, 1903, Osborne Papers. Minutes of the George Junior Republic Executive Committee, July 22, 1903.
[37] George, *The Junior Republic* (New York, 1910), 208–220, contains a brief description of the Republic industries. The George Junior Republic Papers are filled with interesting information, brochures, and advertisements of Republic products.

machinist, real estate agent, printer, and baker.[38] The enterprises generally prospered, but they failed to make the institution self-supporting; $25,000 a year was still collected through voluntary contributions.[39]

In 1906, the trustees launched another endowment drive. Hoping to raise $100,000, they collected over $40,000 before the depression of 1907 reduced all contributions to the institution. Once again, Osborne and the business manager depended upon the lecture circuit to raise even operational expenses. Tuition was increased on a proportional basis; the poor paid nothing, the well-to-do paid $250 a year per child, and the rich paid $500. Even with these measures, the Republic was forced to close one of its cottages.[40] The setbacks were temporary, however, and although irksome and constant, the financial problem was not the most serious issue confronting the Republic.

The George Junior Republic's major handicap—one which exacerbated its financial troubles—was its incompetent management. Osborne continued to maintain that George was completely without business sense, and utterly incapable of running the Republic by himself.[41] But a succession of six business managers in six years (1899–1905) proved no better. The problem was obvious: no business manager had the power to overrule "Daddy" George, who remained Republic superintendent. Thus the management of the Republic was no firmer than the strength of George's whims. At a time when the Republic was $4,400 in debt, Osborne was astonished

[38] These figures did not include the citizens who went on to college.

[39] "Outline of the Work of the George Junior Republic," George Junior Republic Association pamphlet (Freeville, N.Y., 1906).

[40] New York *Evening Post*, Aug. 7, 1908; Utica *Globe*, Dec. 18, 1908; Waldo Forbes to Andrew D. White, Nov. 1908, White Papers, Cornell University.

[41] Osborne to A. G. Agnew, Oct. 26, 1901; Osborne to Edith H. White, Aug. 19, 1902; Osborne Papers.

to see an unauthorized addition being added to one of the cottages.[42] George was not unmindful of administrative needs, according to Osborne, but was "so easy going and so deliciously oblivious of all financial considerations that he will promise anything if you only push hard enough." [43]

Remembering that his threatened resignation had brought about the collapse of the Baker State, Osborne once again reached for his ultimate lever to brake the Republic's financial decline. Proclaiming Republic business affairs intolerable, Osborne announced that he would not continue as president of the board unless the situation was promptly corrected. Osborne ultimately blamed himself, the Executive Committee, and overexpansion for the Republic's problems. The Republic had grown too fast without a sound administration, he contended. Since it was impossible to educate George about sound business practices, the only solution was to relieve the founder of all administrative responsibility. "I expect that we may have some rows with George before we get through," Osborne warned, "but row or no row, the thing will have to be done. . . . I blame myself very much, and I blame George, although I really think it useless to put too much blame on him, for we all knew that he was no businessman, and we ought long before this to have put the proper system into operation there." [44]

Osborne decided to ease George out of the Republic administration after the business managers had failed to balance the books, not before. Yet even then, Osborne moved indecisively. His resolve to remove George was not only tempered by fear of internal strife, but it was also dampened by genuine affection and respect for the founder. Osborne had only a

[42] Osborne to William R. George, Dec. 23, 1901, Osborne Papers.
[43] Osborne to Miss A. P. Granger, July 2, 1904, Osborne Papers.
[44] Osborne to A. G. Agnew, Nov. 8, 1901, Osborne Papers.

vague idea of George's proper relationship to the Republic, and he never intended to completely usurp George's position. Aware of his delicate problem, Osborne favored any solution which put the Republic on a sound financial basis and still allowed George to save face.

After the disastrous failure of the Republic farm in 1901, George clung to few illusions concerning his managerial ability. He became convinced that the best interests of the Republic would be served if he acted simply as "Daddy," devoting his full time to working with the Junior Republic citizens. Furthermore, George welcomed a change which allowed him to travel and speak extensively on Republic affairs. George voluntarily offered to resign as superintendent, and in return, a jubilant Osborne suggested that he be made chairman of the Executive Committee. By this arrangement, George would relinquish all control over the management of the Junior Republic to the new superintendent, but would retain indirect control over the superintendent through his position on the Executive Committee. The plan called for George to continue living at the Republic while exercising his peculiar gifts with children and "advising the superintendent on matters of Republic ideology." [45]

The arrangement seemed doomed from the beginning. Gerrit Smith Miller, the jealous guardian of George's prerogatives, objected that the plan would only humiliate George. Credence was given to Miller's charges when the Board of Trustees refused to confirm George's appointment as chairman of the Executive Committee. Instead, he was named vice-president of the George Junior Republic Association at a salary equal to that of the new superintendent, John A. Par-

[45] Osborne to Edith H. White, Aug. 19, 1902; Osborne to Mrs. Charles S. Fairchild, Oct. 2, 1902; Osborne to Jeremiah W. Jenks, Nov. 19, 1902; Osborne Papers.

ker. George was bitterly disappointed, and refused to be consoled by Osborne's distress at having been overruled by his own trustees.[46] The long-dreaded schism within Republic ranks appeared imminent. Convinced that George was on his way out, Miller could not be reconciled to the arrangement and resigned his position on the Executive Committee. George, now believing that he had been betrayed, ignored the official press release prepared by the Board of Trustees, and announced that he was resigning as superintendent in order to develop plans for additional Republics.[47] The repercussions might have been quite serious had not the situation been saved by an ironic event: John A. Parker proved to be even less competent as superintendent than George.

George had agreed to remain in Freeville to help train Parker. Probably to everyone's surprise, rather than becoming George's great rival, Parker declared himself a devoted disciple. To the great disappointment of the economy-minded trustees, Parker did not institute centralized dining, but continued the extravagantly expensive cottage system which George held so dear. Osborne also found himself pleading with Parker to fire some of the less capable helpers.[48] But like his predecessor, Parker found himself in a delicate situation, caught between the expectations of absentee trustees and the watchful supervision of the resident founder. Although Parker was vested with the full authority of the superintendent, he was neither temperamentally nor ideologically able to resist the magnetism of George's personality. Knowing that something must be done to satisfy the demands of the Board

[46] Osborne to Gerrit Smith Miller, Sept. 11; Oct. 7, 1902; Osborne to A. G. Agnew, Oct. 10, 1902; Osborne to George, Oct. 15, 1902; Osborne Papers.
[47] Osborne to A. G. Agnew, Nov. 14, 1902, Osborne Papers; New York *Herald*, Nov. 13, 1902.
[48] Osborne to John A. Parker, Dec. 19, 1902, Osborne Papers.

of Trustees, George and Parker embarked upon a campaign of strict economy. Osborne ruefully noted that the effort to reduce expenses would probably end up being the most expensive experiment of the year. Wearied and frustrated to the point of despair, Osborne, discovering that he now had to deal with two idealists, once again offered to resign. Fearing that he had become a little stale, the president of the board suggested that fresh leadership might be able to find new solutions to the Republic's financial and managerial problems. His resources were exhausted.[49]

Parker's appointment did not turn out to be totally disappointing. Although he failed as business manager, he did succeed in convincing George that someone else could safely manage the Republic. When he resigned as superintendent in 1902, George had announced his intention to aid in founding new Junior Republics, but his anxiety over the new superintendent had kept him close to Freeville. As his confidence in Parker increased, George meddled less and less in the daily routine of the Republic. In a few months Parker accomplished what Osborne had been trying to achieve for years. When Emily Buel of Litchfield bequeathed her farm to the George Junior Republic for the purpose of establishing a Junior Republic in Connecticut, the Board of Trustees, in keeping with their standing policy, accepted the gift but made no commitment to develop a new institution. At first George concurred, but as he became more confident in Parker's administration, he demanded action on the Buel bequest, and playing Osborne's game, threatened to resign and found a Connecticut Republic of his own if he did not receive assistance from the George Junior Republic Association.[50]

[49] Osborne to A. G. Agnew, June 23, 1904; Osborne to E. E. Olcott, June 23, 1904; Osborne Papers.
[50] William R. George, undated MS.

Far from being miffed at his colleague's high-handedness, Osborne also reversed himself, delighted at the unexpected opportunity to rid himself gracefully of George. "We certainly need something for George to spend his superfluous energies on," he wrote candidly to the Reverend John Hutchins.[51] Once George's interests were transferred to Litchfield, Osborne speculated, perhaps it would be possible to bring Parker under control. In fact, Osborne was willing to let both men go to Litchfield: "I am quite prepared to say that we will let Mr. Parker, our superintendent, undertake the job. He is to my mind not exactly the man we need at Freeville because he is too much like Daddy and not enough of Daddy's complement to fill the position with entire satisfaction. He works admirably with Mr. George and is filled with Mr. George's spirit." [52] After the abortive economy drive in March, he undoubtedly concluded that a fiasco in Connecticut would be far less disastrous than one in Freeville.

Thus, the Connecticut George Junior Republic at Litchfield was founded for mixed altruistic and political motives. Again the arrangement satisfied almost everyone, and this time no forces threatened to disrupt the compromise before it was given a chance to work. At first, the Litchfield Republic was to operate only in the summer, its citizens returning to Freeville for the winter months. Reviving Nellie Carter's old scheme, Osborne proposed that the winter residents be placed in a special section of the Freeville Republic which could be used as a training center for Junior Republic helpers and workers. George was to have full authority over the training center, using his talents and enthusiasm to teach proper Republic methods to prospective trustees, superintendents, and employees. Osborne thought that any sensible man

[51] March 26, 1904; also Jan. 22 and Jan. 30, 1904; Osborne Papers.
[52] Osborne to Hutchins, Feb. 4, 1904, Osborne Papers.

with a great empathy and affection for children could quickly master George's methods. If the success of the Junior Republic depended wholly on the personality of William R. George, he wrote to Ben Lindsey, "it would be a beautiful dream, but not of any practical value, because the number of children he can actually reclaim are only a few . . . in the midst of thousands." Osborne was as anxious as George to prove that the validity of the Junior Republic principle and anti-institutional methods transcended the personality of the founder.[53]

iii

At a fund-raising banquet for the George Junior Republic held at the Savoy Hotel in Denver, Colorado, Judge Ben Lindsey, the famous "children's judge," announced to an enthusiastic gathering that his juvenile court was going to found a Junior Republic just outside of Denver.[54] George, the guest of honor at the gathering, also announced the formation of a California Junior Republic by the Juvenile Court Association of Los Angeles. Soon Pittsburgh and St. Louis were also requesting Junior Republics. Lindsey favored rapid expansion of the work all over the country. In addition to calling for his own Republic and campaigning vigorously for the Pittsburgh and California cause, he assisted Judge Julian Mack who was agitating for a Junior Republic in Chicago.[55] In April of 1907 George announced that he was opening a special training colony adjacent to the Freeville Junior Repub-

[53] Osborne to Benjamin Lindsey, Aug. 17, 1904, Osborne Papers; Osborne to V. Everit Macy, Sept. 8, 1904.

[54] Denver *Post,* March 24, 1907; New York *Daily News,* March 24, 1907.

[55] L. S. Levine to George, Oct. 23, 1909; George, Diary, March 23, 1907–Feb. 1, 1908, *passim.*

lic in order to prepare "pioneer" citizens and helpers for the future Republics.[56]

In the midst of the panic of 1907, Osborne watched somewhat bitterly as potential funds and talent were drained westward. Only a week after George returned from a California trip, Osborne announced to the Executive Committee that the Junior Republic treasury was critically short of cash.[57] It was obvious to everyone that the booming Junior Republic movement needed the central planning and coordination of a national organization. With four Republics already established and several more in the planning stages, the need for some over-all direction was imperative. Furthermore, it was evident that interested people would go ahead with their own version of a "Junior Republic" if they did not get assistance from Freeville or George. When Alexander Forbes, younger brother of W. Cameron Forbes, offered to purchase land upon which a National Association of Junior Republics could operate an official training center under George's direction, there was universal enthusiasm for the plan. After organization of the National Association of Junior Republics in February 1908, George was appointed to the new position of National Director. Both Osborne and George were exceedingly satisfied with the arrangement. As National Director, George once again held a position of power and influence, and Osborne was finally freed to correctly manage the affairs of the Freeville Republic.[58]

Slightly over a decade had elapsed since the youthful, energetic free-lance reformer was censured for irregular methods by the COS. Still distrustful of professional reformers and

[56] George, Diary, April 5, 1907.   [57] George, Diary, April 13, 1907.
[58] George, Diary, June 1907–Feb. 1908, *passim;* minutes of the NAJR, May 29, 1908.

supervisors, the compulsively independent reformer, who had sacrificed his work in New York City rather than submit to a board of trustees, saw no irony in his new position as national watchdog for the Junior Republic movement. To the casual observer and to some of those present at the organizational meeting, the formation of the NAJR may have indicated that the George Junior Republic was conforming to the pressures of professionalization that affected all social reform in the second decade of the Progressive Era.[59] William R. George understood just the opposite. Convinced that trustees and professional social workers did not understand his anti-institutional methods, George wanted the National Association to provide a bulwark against the capture of the Junior Republic movement by the professionals bent upon establishing efficient, bureaucratic Republic organization. George always feared that organization would lead directly to institutionalization, the very antithesis of the Republic principle. Although George had the reformer's confidence in his own rectitude, in every other way he contradicted the popular image of the self-righteous "do-gooder." Generous to a fault, warm and compassionate, enthusiastic and trusting, George eagerly accepted all who came to him professing anti-institutional principles, rarely questioning their good intentions. It was enough that the young men and women who flocked to Freeville had sought him out, and were prepared to transform into reality his vision of a National Union of Junior Republics. He was always ill at ease among professionals and experts, however, instinctively knowing that he could not compete with their expertise. As National Director of the NAJR,

[59] Roy Lubove, *The Professional Altruist: The Emergence of Social Work as a Career, 1880–1930* (Cambridge, Mass., 1965), *passim;* Frank Bruno, Jr., and Louis Towley, *Trends in Social Work, 1874–1956* (New York, 1957), 192–206.

"Daddy" George became the guardian of the whole Junior Republic movement, and, at the same time, he obtained a position which provided the aura of professionalism without demanding qualifications and training.

The functions of the National Association were threefold: to organize and coordinate the founding of new Republics; to serve as a clearing house for Republic publicity and to assist in raising funds; and to supervise the training and indoctrination of Republic helpers, officers, and trustees. The first two tasks, George admitted, were the easiest.

The National Association of Junior Republics was greatly assisted in its work by juvenile court officers. When Ben Lindsey was asked to serve on the Board of Directors of the NAJR he wrote to George, "you may rest assured I will serve on anything you want me to serve on and count it an honor." [60] Lindsey and others discovered that the Junior Republic provided an ideal alternative to committing juvenile offenders to penal institutions. Although reformatories such as Elmira under Zebulon Brockway had segregated youthful offenders from hardened criminals, most juvenile court judges did not believe the Elmira system went far enough. Houses of refuge for juvenile delinquents rarely were regarded as much better. Convinced that juvenile crime was primarily the product of unhealthy urban environment, Lindsey advocated sending delinquents to industrial schools and industrial farms which offered educational opportunities in a healthful, invigorating setting. The George Junior Republic exactly fitted Lindsey's specifications. Not a penal institution or an orphanage, the Junior Republic provided the courts an acceptable institution for children without stigmatizing them.[61]

[60] March 7, 1908.
[61] Herbert H. Lou, *Juvenile Courts in the United States* (Chapel Hill, N.C., 1927), 19–25, 172–173; Bernard Flexner, "A Decade of the

The golden days of the Junior Republic were highlighted by George's close cooperation with the juvenile court movement. He was proud to accept a position on the Board of Directors of the International Juvenile Court Society, and counted fellow directors Lindsey, Riis, Julian Mack, and A. E. Winship among his most devoted supporters.[62] George was now in a perfect position to promote the Junior Republic among friends of the juvenile court. Judges and probation officers from all over the country began to request information of the Junior Republic. Almost as frequently, interested parties came to inspect the Junior Republic and interview George concerning the prospects of establishing a Republic for their own judicial district. Bernard Flexner, the prominent pioneering treasurer of the Juvenile Court Society, was granted a personal tour of inspection of the Freeville Republic. Judge Julian Mack, shortly after his visit to the Republic, invited George to lunch with him at Hull House following a conference of the Juvenile Court Society, and the two men discussed plans for a Junior Republic in the Chicago area.[63]

Interest in the George Junior Republic was also generated among members of the Juvenile Court Association of Los Angeles County. Curtis D. Wilbur, judge of the juvenile court, was deeply concerned with the problem of juvenile

---

Juvenile Court," National Conference of Social Work, *Proceedings*, 1910, 105–116; Eric Goldman, *Rendezvous with Destiny* (New York: 1956), 93–94; Julian Mack, "The Juvenile Court," American Bar Association Reprint (n.p., 1909), 5, 14–15.

[62] Edward W. Frost, Secretary, International Juvenile Court Society, to George, March 6, April 20, 1908.

[63] Flexner to George, n.d., 1908; George, Diary, 1906–1910, *passim*. The inquiries, visits, and invitations George received are too numerous to list. His diary is the best source of information on his activities in this period.

detention. He knew that California reformatories not only failed to reform juvenile delinquents, but that boys who spent time in those institutions often were released as hardened criminals. Wilbur shared Lindsey's analysis of urban poverty and juvenile crime.[64] Thus when he heard of the George Junior Republic from Lindsey, Wilbur became determined to investigate it. Under the sponsorship of the Juvenile Court Association, Wilbur sent Evelyn and Bessie Stoddart to investigate the juvenile community in Freeville, and instructed them to visit other child-saving institutions as well.[65]

George received the women graciously and noted the visitors in his diary, little suspecting that the two nervous sisters would be among the most important visitors in the history of the Junior Republic.[66] The Stoddarts returned to California full of missionary zeal for the Republic cause. At the instigation of the sisters, and under the auspices of the Juvenile Court Association and the Los Angeles Settlement Workers, George was invited to lecture throughout southern California.[67] On the morning of January 24, 1907, George departed from Freeville on what turned out to be a transcontinental triumph. For a month and a half, on a grand tour which took him to Chicago, San Francisco, Los Angeles, Denver, and St. Louis, George enjoyed one accolade after another. His tour was highlighted by lunch at Hull House and at the City Clubs

[64] Curtis Wilbur to M. E. Norris, in Norris, "The History of the California Junior Republic" (M.A. thesis, University of Southern California, 1930).

[65] Los Angeles *Express*, Jan. 31, 1907; Los Angeles *Examiner*, March 20, 1908; Los Angeles *Times*, Sept. 25, 1931.

[66] Bessie Stoddart's reform activities went unnoticed by George Mowry and have only recently been recognized by Allen F. Davis in *Spearheads for Reform: The Social Settlements and the Progressive Movement, 1890–1914* (New York, 1967), 81.

[67] Los Angeles *Express*, Jan. 31, 1907.

of Los Angeles and San Francisco, a reunion with his old friend Jacob Riis, a visit to Judge Wilbur's juvenile court where he was received with the ceremony befitting a visiting dignitary, and lectures at the University of Southern California, the University of Redlands, Stanford University, and the University of California. On the eve of his return, he was guest of honor at a banquet given by Benjamin Ide Wheeler, president of the University of California.[68]

His trip could not have been improved upon. Everywhere George lectured, he preached his simple yet beautiful sermon on love and compassion for the urban waif. The struggle for the cities, George reminded his audiences, would be won through the hearts and souls of the children of the poor. As in the East, the message was one the Californians were eager to hear. In a society deeply riven by political, economic, and social conflict, the Junior Republic movement provided a neutral ground upon which hostile parties could meet. Harrison Gray Otis, owner of the Los Angeles *Times*, had vilified the "goo-goos," as he called the Good Government faction of the Los Angeles City Club, yet, through lead editorials in the *Times* and generous donations of land, he joined the City Club in supporting the California Junior Republic.[69] And Hiram Johnson overlooked both Otis and the McCormick interests in giving his wholehearted support to the self-government movement in California.[70] Both George and Lindsey declared that the new Republic in California would ultimately

[68] George, Diary, Jan. 24–March 16, 1907; Norris, "History of the California Junior Republic," 12–13.

[69] Los Angeles *Times*, Feb. 17, 1907; Feb. 19, 1908; Sept. 25, 1931; Dec. 3, 1931. For Otis' reaction to the Good Government movement and reform, see George Mowry, *The California Progressives* (Berkeley, 1951), 46–56.

[70] Norris, "The History of the California Junior Republic," 13–45; Los Angeles *Times*, Feb. 17, 1907, and Sept. 25, 1931; Pasadena *Star-News*, July 14, 1931.

prove that the self-governing institution was not a one-man affair. "The world is looking over those mountains watching us today," George warned those who had gathered at Chino, eager to begin the work. They wanted to believe George, of course, and were encouraged that the California Junior Republic was hailed as the most significant advance of the Republic cause since Founder's Day at Freeville on July 10, 1895.[71]

Between 1908 and 1914, the Junior Republic movement almost boomed out of control. In western Pennsylvania, Pittsburgh lawyer and Assistant District Attorney Leonard S. Levine was an active leader in the Pittsburgh Juvenile Court Association and the boys' club movement. Reading of George's work at Freeville, Levine experimented with self-government methods in his boys' club. He was so successful that Andrew Carnegie and Julian Mack, among others, encouraged him to found a full-fledged Junior Republic. Simultaneously, Dr. Morgan Barnes, then at the Thatcher School in Ojai, California, heard George lecture the faculty and student body on the George Junior Republic. Barnes immediately became convinced that his native Grove City, Pennsylvania, would be an ideal site for a Junior Republic. George introduced Levine and Barnes to one another, and with the assistance of the Allegheny and Mercer County Juvenile Court Association, land was obtained in Grove City, sixty miles north of Pittsburgh in Mercer County. The Western Pennsylvania George Junior Republic formally opened in December of 1909.[72]

[71] A. E. Winship, "The California Junior Republic," *Journal of Education*, LXXV (June 6, 1912), 625–626; Los Angeles *Times*, March 17, 1908; Los Angeles *Examiner*, March 20, 1908; Los Angeles *Express*, March 20, 1908; Ithaca *Daily News*, March 6, 1908; Evelyn Stoddart to Mrs. William R. George, March 31, 1908.

[72] "Personal Reminiscences of Leonard S. Levine," as quoted in a letter from Mrs. Joseph B. Wolbarsht (his daughter) to the author,

During his tenure as National Director of the NAJR, George assisted in founding three more Republics; the New Jersey Junior Republic, the short-lived Strawbridge-Brophy Junior Republic, and the Little Commonwealth in Dorsetshire, England.[73] The New Jersey Republic had the enthusiastic support of the Federated Women's Clubs of New Jersey. While their husbands were being reviled by Woodrow Wilson as opponents of New Jersey political Progressivism, the Women's Clubs of Orange donated buildings and farm animals to the new Republic at Flemington Junction. The Lehigh Valley Railroad, also under attack by the Progressives, donated the land for the children's institution. The Freeville Republic was overcrowded and short of funds at this time, and it was hoped that another Republic closer to New York City would accommodate the overflow from that area, as well as attracting additional contributions. The New Jersey Junior Republic's Advisory Board included such notable citizens as Governor J. Franklin Fort (1908–1911); former Governor Edward C. Stokes (1905–1908); George Jay Gould, son of Jay Gould; Wallace M. Scudder, publisher of the Newark *Evening News;* Hamilton W. Mabie, associate editor of *The Outlook;* Mayor Charles J. Fiske of Plainfield; Mayor H. Otto Witten of Jersey City; State Civil Service Commissioner

---

June 12, 1965; "Scrapbook of the WPGJR," Papers of the WPGJR, Cornell University; E. E. Stephenson, "Interesting Chats with Interesting People—Leonard S. Levine," *The Spectator,* V (Jan. 5, 1912), 9; *Bulletin of the DeWitt Historical Society of Tompkins County,* March, 1960; Benjamin Lindsey to Kate Fowler, April 17, 1912; L. S. Levine to George, Oct. 23, 1909; George, Diary, 1906–1910, *passim.*

[73] The Strawbridge-Brophy Junior Republic founded at Morristown, N.J., had an uncertain fate. Intended as a home for girls of questionable morality, it apparently did not survive the troubles of 1914. The Little Commonwealth will be discussed extensively below, 210–221.

Willis Fletcher Johnson; Senator Joseph S. Frelinghuysen; and the Reverend Harry Emerson Fosdick.[74]

George found his third task as National Director—to train and indoctrinate Republic offices and staff—almost impossible. Over and over again, he lamented that it was one thing to stir up interest and found a Junior Republic, and it was quite another task to keep it in good running order. The Junior Republic cause had public interest "to burn," George noted. Nor was there any problem securing boys and girls to be citizens of the New Republics. Every Junior Republic admissions office was swamped with applicants. "My great problem," George wrote to Lindsey, "is not to get people interested or to get the little commonwealths started, but . . . it is to get the right sort of men to run them after they get underway." [75] On the same theme, he chastised his own National Association:

Strange as it may seem, the principal problem does not lie with the boys and girls whom we are attempting to aid through the agency of self-government. The real problem comes from some of the adults officially connected with the Junior Republic organization, and others with no official connection, who are supposedly friends of the movement, but are in reality millstones hanging about the neck of the self-government cause.[76]

George was handicapped by not fully understanding his own problem, and by using an unsophisticated rhetoric which further clouded the issue. He continually professed that the

[74] George to Katherine Porter, Feb. 14, 1911; George to L. S. Levine, Dec. 28, 1908; Newark *Sunday Call*, May 1, 1910, and May 25, 1913.
[75] George to Lindsey, June 13, 1910; George, "Report to the NAJR," Dec. 8, 1909.
[76] George, "Report to the NAJR," Minutes of the NAJR, Nov. 18, 1912.

basic principle of the Junior Republic was the principle of American democracy. Accordingly, each Republic ought to be conducted as if it were a small village in the American Republic with only one major difference: the citizens of the Junior Republic voted and held public responsibility at the age of sixteen rather than twenty-one. The problems of the Junior Republic, he contended, were similar to the problems of the American Republic. In both cases there were impatient businessmen, intellectuals, managers, and professionals who did not trust the democratic process. At the training center, George taught that the best way to run a Junior Republic was not to run it at all. His basic lesson was *how not to manage* a Junior Republic.[77] The Junior Republic plan was so simple and so obvious that few reformers trusted it to work by itself. No reformer, once he became a member of the Board of Trustees or involved in Republic management, could resist the temptation to reform. No innovator, once attracted to the model communities and granted a position on the advisory council, could eschew innovation. No manager, called to oversee the deployment of Republic resources, could fail to manage. Yet in each, George found a subtle perversion of the Republic creed. Experiments which deviated from the normal mode of village life threatened to "institutionalize" the Republics, he warned.[78]

George demanded the impossible from his superintendents. Even Osborne, one of the most orthodox advocates of absolute self-government, could not resist the temptation to experiment with the composition of Republic citizenry and the methods of Republic instruction. As the growth in public

[77] George, *Junior Republic Principles and Bulletins* (Freeville, N.Y., 1941), v–vii, 5–11; George, "Report to the NAJR," Dec. 8, 1909; "A Plan of Cooperation between the NAJR and the George Junior Republic," Minutes of the NAJR.

[78] George, "Report to the NAJR," Oct., 1910; George to Paul Seely, Nov. 11, 1909.

high schools removed more and more "normal" citizens from the Republic, and the increase in the number of commitments and referrals from the juvenile courts added to the delinquent population, it became increasingly difficult to maintain meaningful self-government. The Republic was not a normal village, and all, including George, realized it. Thus, George's rhetoric made it possible to dismiss him as unrealistic, romantic, sentimental, nostalgic, and possibly somewhat reactionary. In time, George's association with the political right wing vindicated the suspicions of his earlier opponents, but in 1911 he was merely groping for a defense of his unorthodox, anti-institutional methods.

In specific issues George was sure of himself. He adamantly opposed separate houses for the superintendent and the school principal which would be off limits to students. The residence principle was as important to the Junior Republic as it was to the social settlement. Just as the eager young social workers who went to the settlements shared in the lives of the people, so the helpers at the Junior Republic were intimately involved in the daily affairs of the institution. No distinction was made between "staff children" and citizens. All youths under twenty-one, whatever their position in the Republic, were subject to the same laws and jurisdiction. Gradually, however, the Junior Republic became more dependent on full-time adult employees whose services were specialized. As a result, the new employees came to see themselves as professional workers. Often familiar names such as "Daddy" George or "Uncle Tom" were avoided, and the formal relationships of social worker to client were substituted.[79] The administrators' request to escape their twenty-four hour responsi-

[79] Clarke Chambers, *Seedtime of Reform: American Social Service and Social Action, 1918–1933* (Minneapolis, 1963), 121–123. According to Chambers, settlement houses encountered this development in the early 1920's.

bilities is understandable to any professional, but George saw it as a basic threat to his anti-institutional scheme. If the superintendent's cottage were "out-of-bounds," his children would belong to a privileged class of juveniles not subject to Junior Republic laws. The distinction between staff children and citizens would become a division between free children and inmates. The whole staff must live at the Republic, George argued, for without them the juvenile community would be quickly dubbed a juvenile institution or reform school. Republic methods failed, George believed, unless every citizen, whoever he might be, was proud of his Republic citizenship.[80]

Surveying the seven Republics established by 1911, George reported to the National Association that not one was operating according to true Republic principles. He listed their deficiencies one after another, especially noting the extreme youth of many citizens, the absence of girls in some Republics, and the unsympathetic trustees in others. But he saved his most severe indictment for the Freeville Republic. The richest, best equipped, and most completely staffed Republic of them all ought to be a showcase for the whole Republic movement, George declared. Instead, the original George Junior Republic was declining from its position as national leader. Comfortable and established, Freeville had replaced experiment and innovation with regularity and routine. The drive and enthusiasm of the Freeville citizens had been dulled into an easy complacency.[81]

George was not without a solution to the Republic prob-

[80] George to the Executive Committee of the George Junior Republic, Nov. 13, 1909.

[81] George, "Annual Report to the NAJR," May 29, 1911, and "Special Report to the Board of Directors, NAJR," Oct. 16, 1911; George to Charles Lee, May 31, 1911, and to Bolton Smith, June 17, 1911.

lems. His new scheme was as simple as it was direct: in addition to the superintendent who was designated to run the business affairs of the institution, George proposed that trustees appoint a "Republic Guardian" whose sole task would be to insure that Republic principles and methods were maintained. The position, of course, was analogous to George's relationship with the Junior Republic when he acted as "Daddy" during the administration of John A. Parker. Most of the trustees must have shuddered at the idea of a Republic Guardian hovering over their work, and they opposed the plan as too expensive and impractical.[82]

Undaunted, George pursued his scheme. Since the appointment of Calvin Derrick as superintendent at Freeville on November 11, 1907, George had become increasingly dismayed over the management of the Junior Republic. Derrick, a former instructor in the Auburn Prison who had successfully organized an association of prison teachers, had been "discovered" by Osborne, and only after considerable persuasion did Derrick consent to leave his position at Auburn. The young prison instructor was clearly oriented toward his profession, and like most institutionalists, he was appalled by the dirt and disorder of the juvenile community; as a strict disciplinarian who demanded efficient organization and routine, he was dismayed at the relative chaos of the Junior Republic. Derrick was a warm, generous man whom George instinctively liked, but immediately the two men clashed. Returning to Freeville from his long lecture trips, George was astonished at the changes proposed by the new superintendent. It was Derrick who suggested abandoning the expensive cottage dining system in favor of central eating facilities. It was Derrick

[82] George, "Annual Report to the NAJR," May 29, 1911; George to Ralph Dennis, Dec. 28, 1910; George to Smith, June 17, 1911; George, Diary, Feb. 18, 1911.

who wanted a separate house for the superintendent and the school principal.[83] Most seriously, it was Derrick who charged that George had been far too lenient with the children. Reportedly, Derrick was unwilling to let Republic justice take its due course. The superintendent also tried to influence the citizen judge, and would arbitrarily jail a boy and "hush up" the nature of his crime.[84] Only three and a half months prior to Theodore Roosevelt's visit, Derrick declared "superintendent's law," and suspended the citizen government because of the inability of the Government to successfully cope with the conditions of lawlessness and rowdyism.[85]

With the former President of the United States due to visit the Junior Republic, one might speculate as to the motives behind Derrick's take-over of the government.[86] There is no question that Derrick, although officially in essential agreement with Junior Republic principles, publicly disagreed with George on the application of self-government methods. George made self-government an end in itself, Derrick thought. To the superintendent, the George Junior Republic was always an institution, and self-government methods were simply useful, limited tools to be used in the reformation of

[83] Minutes of the Executive Committee of the George Junior Republic, July 13, 1912.

[84] George, MS, c. 1910; "Mrs. Albert B. Genung" (Oral History Interview 153, pp. 48–49, Collection of Regional History and University Archives, Cornell University); George to Ralph Dennis, June 26, 1911; John Joseph O'Connor, letter to the editors of the New York *Times*, Sept. 9, 1912.

[85] Derrick to Jack London, president of George Junior Republic, July 15, 1911.

[86] George's diary is not consistent on the issue. Citizen "revolutions," aided and abetted by the administration, were not uncommon in Republic history. Usually administrators tried to work within the fiction of self-government, however. Derrick's suspension of the government, therefore, was a rare outright take-over by the adults.

youth. Problems of work, emotion, and schooling could not be left to self-government, but must be carefully directed by adults, Derrick maintained. To supporters of the Junior Republic the differences between George and Derrick might seem small, but to the founder they loomed large and menacing.[87] As George's criticism of the Freeville administration became more personal and shrill, the Junior Republic moved nearer to its "time of troubles."

iv

The time of troubles, which extended roughly from January 1912 to July 1914, began with an attempt to remove George completely from Freeville, and ended with the resignations of Derrick, Osborne, and most of the Freeville trustees, and the virtual collapse of the George Junior Republic. Its story, which is long, complicated, and sordid, will be told only briefly here.[88] The friction between George, Osborne, and the Board of Trustees resulted from the rapid expansion of the Republic idea. After the founding of the National Association of Junior Republics in 1908, George was supposed to remove himself from the original Republic and devote his full time to developing similar projects in other sections of the country. For this purpose, land had been set aside for a special training colony at which pioneer citizens and prospective workers were to be instructed in the basic Republic

[87] See Derrick's articles "Institutional Management," *The Junior Republic* (journal published by the citizens of the California Junior Republic), IV (March 1915), 3–10; "Self-government," *Survey*, XXXVIII (Sept. 1, 1917), 473, 479; "The Delinquent Adolescent: What the Institution Can Do for Him," National Conference of Social Work, *Proceedings*, 1926 (Cleveland, O., 1926), 195–204.

[88] See Frances Keefe, "The Development of William Reuben (Daddy) George's Educational Ideas and Practices from 1866 to 1914" (Ed.D. dissertation, Cornell University, 1967) 286–333.

principles before being sent off to establish their own self-governing communities. George retained his home in Freeville so that he could keep watch over the training colony. Unfortunately, his home was also "within bounds" of the Freeville Republic. It was too much to expect that George could remain indifferent to affairs involving his own brain child. George's influence was still pervasive, and Derrick complained again and again that his influence with the children was being undermined by the founder. George simply could not let go, and, at last, Osborne determined to take steps to remove him.[89]

The plan was twofold. First, Osborne's associates pushed for a revision of the constitution of the NAJR. In the name of putting the Association "on an aggressive, business basis" and centralizing the activities of the group in a national office, the new constitution authorized the appointment of an executive secretary, who (it was assumed) would maintain an office in New York City. Coupled with this was a new provision appointing the National Director on a yearly basis, rather than for life. George was stung by what appeared to be a vote of no confidence and another broken promise. He was only somewhat mollified with assurances that the change was made with an eye to the future, and would not affect his position in any way.[90]

The major assault on George's prerogatives was frontal. Osborne proposed to purchase all of George's land and to assist him in relocating somewhere else. Ever since the establishment of the Baker State on land given to George by the Millers, George's real estate holdings had been a source of

[89] Chamberlain, *There Is No Truce*, 232–234; New York *Times*, Sept. 4, 1912; George, undated MS.

[90] Minutes of the NAJR, April 20, 1912; George to the Committee on Constitution and By-laws of the NAJR, Sept. 6, 1911; Mrs. William R. George to L. S. Levine, April 22, 1912; Mrs. George to H. L. Platt, April 25, 1912.

irritation. George owned 170 acres, which were strategically located in the middle of the Junior Republic and which were necessary to the Republic Association if they were to expand. But more important than blocking expansion, George's land-holdings gave him great leverage over the Republic admin-istration. As long as he held the property, George wrote to a trustee, he realized he could keep Freeville in line by threat-ening to open a rival Republic under the auspices of the Na-tional Association. George correctly surmised that if he sold his land, he would lose the vestiges of his control over the Junior Republic movement. By his own estimate, the land and buildings in question were worth $13,700, but George de-manded $30,000 so that he could have sufficient cash to begin another Republic if conditions warranted it.[91]

Osborne fumed. George reported: "Mr. Osborne has some-times said to me, 'What would you do if the trustees got out and left you with the Republic on your hands?'" George re-plied that he wished they would so that he could turn the whole Freeville Republic over to his friends in the National Association.[92] Once again Osborne declared he could not con-tinue, but this time he actually submitted his resignation to the Board of Trustees on July 13, 1912.[93] Out of office, Os-borne drove down from Auburn to inform George that he must sell his home and move out of Freeville at once, or the trustees would close the Republic and send all the children away.[94]

Derrick was out, and was soon on his way to California to

[91] George to R. Montgomery Schell, Jan. 2, Feb. 1, Feb. 2, 1912.
[92] George to Schell, Feb. 2, 1912.
[93] Derrick also resigned at the meeting. The two resignations may have been the necessary price paid to get George's land, for at the meeting the trustees authorized its purchase from George. George, Diary, July 13, 1912; New York *Times*, Sept. 4, 1912; Dora Nelson to Mrs. William R. George, July 22, 1912.
[94] C. Spencer Richardson to Lyman Beecher Stowe, Aug. 1, 1912.

introduce self-governing methods in the state reformatories.[95] But when faced with Osborne's ultimatum, even George was unwilling to lose the Auburn reformer from the Republic cause. George had hoped to retire at Freeville "upon the scene where for a score of years a life and death struggle for a principle had been carried on," he wrote Osborne. "Here I have experienced the greatest sorrows and the greatest joys of my life. To this place I brought my bride when we could hardly afford two meals a day composed of the most simple fare, and where during the winter months we almost perished with the cold. Here my children were born and one of them died. . . ." His letter trailed off. Catching himself, George then reaffirmed his resolution: "The removal of my home I feel is necessary for the purpose of demonstrating that the Junior Republic is not what so many commonly term a 'one-man affair.' " [96] The victory was Osborne's. George promised to sell his home and his land, agreed not to undertake a rival Republic, and requested Osborne to reassume his position on the Board of Trustees.

The transition might have gone more or less smoothly had not another unforeseen event upset the carefully negotiated compromises. A "down-and-out" former citizen who aspired to become a newspaper reporter approached the New York *Times* with the story of the Republic's troubles. The youth included in his version a rumor that the cause of the dissension was an ex-citizen's charge that George was the father of her child. The managing editor of the *Times* sent a reporter to Auburn to check the story with Osborne.[97] Believing that candidness was the best policy, Osborne informed the reporter that an investigation by William H. Seward, Jr., had

[95] Mrs. William R. George to Miss Margesson, Aug. 22, 1912.
[96] George to Osborne, Aug. 14, 1912.
[97] John Paul May to whom it may concern, July 10, 1914.

exonerated George from all morals charges. In addition, Osborne explained the entire management problem to the reporter, showing him copies of all pertinent correspondence. To Osborne's chagrin, and George's horror, the whole affair, including the morals charges and the letters, was reported on the front page of the *Times*.[98]

Osborne's blunder was an honest mistake, but coming when it did, George concluded that he had been betrayed. Osborne desperately tried to rectify his poor judgment in the face of spontaneous and genuine outpouring of sympathy for the beleaguered founder,[99] but it was almost impossible not to see Osborne's hand behind the intimate details of the *Times'* story. Two thousands adults and seven hundred children signed a petition in Ithaca assuring George he was welcome there. Already aware that George had decided to settle in Ithaca, Cortlanders nevertheless expressed their support for him. *The Outlook*, although remaining neutral in the controversy, lauded George for his self-sacrificing decision to withdraw from Freeville. From the National Association came genuine support, and even some Freeville trustees were remarkably friendly.[100]

Surprisingly, George maintained his composure throughout the incident while Osborne floundered hopelessly about. In private, however, George fluctuated between anguish over his public exposure and delight with Osborne's embarrassment.[101]

[98] New York *Times*, Sept. 4, 1912.

[99] Telegram from Osborne to George, Sept. 4, 1912; Osborne to New York *Times*, Sept. 5, 1912.

[100] "Ithaca and Mr. George," editorial, Ithaca *Daily News*, Sept. 28, 1912; Ithaca *Journal*, Sept. 28, 1912; Cortland *Standard*, Sept. 21, 1912; "Crisis in the George Junior Republic," *The Outlook*, CII (Sept. 14, 1912), 53–54; Ruford Franklin to George, and R. M. Schell to George, Sept. 4, 1912.

[101] George, Diary, Sept. 4–16, 1912.

The split between the two reformers was now irreparable. A minor incident at the Junior Republic's presidential inauguration during which Osborne left in a huff, followed by a scathing denunciation of the president of the Board of Trustees by an Ithaca paper, practically ended the matter.[102] Osborne's resignation on March 12, 1913, was final. His good friend Charles F. Rattigan had just been appointed warden of Auburn Prison, and Osborne, by going into prison work himself, grasped the chance to demonstrate that Junior Republic principles had an applicability which transcended one man and his institution. Few realized at the time, but the zenith of the George Junior Republic had passed in 1913. The coming war was going to cripple, but not kill, the institution. Thereafter, it never regained its former stature.

v

The extension of the self-government principle into areas unrelated and unconnected to the George Junior Republic marked the final phase of the development of George's ideas. Thomas Mott Osborne had been one of the first to recognize the importance of the Republic's anti-institutional principle. He understood immediately how George's methods could be adopted by schools, and later, advocated their application within the prison. He wrote, "Mr. George opened my mind to the possibility of the same principle being used as a basis for an intelligent and *reforming* Prison System . . . at first I laughed; then I saw the Truth." [103]

George magnanimously endorsed Osborne's new project at Auburn Prison. Believing that he had found a solution to the

[102] Chamberlain, *There Is No Truce*, 234; Ithaca *Journal*, Jan. 16, 1913.
[103] Osborne, "Introduction," in William R. George, *The Junior Republic* (New York, 1910), x.

internal problems of his several Republics, George hoped that by encouraging formal institutions such as Auburn to adopt partial self-government he could find an outlet for helpers and trustees who did not support absolute self-government. Those who did not fully accept Junior Republic principles as defined by George could transfer their support to an institution whose work was more to their liking. In this way, he intended to rid himself of those who wished to modify the Junior Republic, and, at the same time, retain their good friendship and cooperation. Such an alternative, he hoped, would not leave him completely alienated from many old friends.[104]

Events had come full circle, only this time it was George who pragmatically advocated the extension of the self-government movement as a safety valve for the excessive zeal of Republic advocates, and Osborne who idealistically dreamed of self-government conquests. But to the end, Osborne's will vacillated. Although he had sought an easy escape from the George Junior Republic Association, Osborne was temperamentally incapable of gracefully abandoning his untenable position. Since both men interpreted their struggle in personal, as well as practical and ideological, terms, it was almost impossible for their relationship to end in anything but bitterness. Consequently, when the accumulating pressures finally erupted in the explosion of 1913, the Republic movement was shattered, leaving isolated fragments here and there around the world.

The conclusion of the Junior Republic story cannot be told independently from the history of the Progressive Era, which, in 1913, was approaching a climax of its own. The disintegration of the Junior Republic movement owed as

[104] George, "Report to the NAJR," Minutes of the NAJR, Nov. 18, 1912.

much to external forces as to internal pressures. The mercurial rise and fall of the George Junior Republic outlines a significant chapter in the history of Progressive education and penology, recording subtle yet vital shifts in the intellectual and social history of the age. Finally, Junior Republic actors rarely distinguished carefully between their public and private lives (in the case of Osborne and his masquerades they were hopelessly confused). For these reasons, we must now shift the scene from the private to the public level of the Republic drama.

V

FROM FREEVILLE
TO SUMMERHILL

——————— The George Junior Republic, although variously described as an orphanage, a children's home, and a reformatory, was essentially a school whose educational functions transcended the limitations of the ordinary classroom. It was one of the first institutions that self-consciously attempted to fill the educational vacuum created by the decline of America's agrarian communities. John Dewey was not alone in recognizing the need for schools to assume the educational functions once performed by the family, farm, neighborhood, and shop. In a scheme remarkably similar to Dewey's Laboratory School and to the Gary Plan, George attempted to create an "embryonic community" which reflected the realities of life in the larger society. The Junior Republic was not a refuge from life, but rather brought the child face to face with the struggle for existence. "Daddy" George, "Uncle Tom," "Mama" Griswold, the Republic farmer, plumber, printer, and teacher assumed the roles of the extended family, the friendly neighbors, and the village artisans. Even the young citizens became surrogate siblings and cousins for one another.

Originally, the task of the Junior Republic was to Americanize the immigrant youth and "fit the child" for a vanishing agrarian society, but in doing so George was swept into the ranks of the Progressive educators. Few of George's contemporaries were distressed by his ardent patriotism or his conservative political and economic beliefs. Lawrence Cremin has noted that Progressives were essentially moderates, and for all their sense of moral outrage, moderates proceed slowly.[1] Reluctant to lay their hands on the nation's political and economic institutions, supporters of the Junior Republic clung tightly to the American myth that education could cure all social ills. Those who gathered around George were not as sophisticated as Dewey. They tended to believe that the best education exercised latent faculties for the purpose of moral and civic training, and preparation for a specific vocation. But they shared with Dewey the belief that democracy was more than a form of government, and moved close to Dewey's dictum that democracy "is primarily a mode of associated living, of conjoint communicated experience." [2] The Junior Republic educated the "whole" child in a "total environment." "Learning by doing" was literally practiced in the child-centered, antiformalistic juvenile society, and throughout its early history the Republic took pride in the fact that the functions of education, nurture, and correction could not be clearly differentiated. Ultimately, the George Junior Republic has been remembered as a juvenile reformatory rather than a Progressive school. Probably this conception has not greatly impaired our understanding of Progressive education, but it has led to a more subtle impairment of our appreciation of the interrelatedness of Progressive pedagogy and penology.

[1] Lawrence Cremin, *The Transformation of the School: Progressivism in American Education, 1876–1957* (New York, 1961), 89.

[2] John Dewey, *Democracy and Education* (New York, 1916), 101.

i

William R. George never tired of his errands to the Freeville railroad station. The railroad had been his symbolic link
to the outside world when he was a child, and through his
adult years the traffic that passed through the station served
as a rough gauge of the popularity of the Junior Republic.
But on a fall afternoon in 1896, George paced nervously on
the platform, awaiting the arrival of the train from Ithaca
bearing a young assistant recommended to him by Jeremiah
Jenks of Cornell University. Noting that Willard Hotchkiss
had prudently sent his trunks ahead, George wondered
whether he would prove as efficient in managing the new
Republic school. As an unemployed member of Cornell's
class of '96, Hotchkiss had accepted the position in Freeville
with the undisguised hope that something else would soon
turn up. When the high school drop-out and the college graduate met on the station platform that afternoon, neither had
a premonition that together they would become educational
pioneers.[3]

When George founded the Junior Republic in July 1895,
none of his original recruits regularly attended New York
City schools. The first winter, three boys often walked to
Dryden High School, and seven others took intermittent advantage of the local grammar school. Since neither George
nor the boys cared much for formal schooling, educational
provisions were virtually neglected. By the fall of 1896 the
permanent Junior Republic population had mushroomed to
forty school-age citizens, ten of them girls. George continued
his lax school policy, however, until after the State Board of
Charities included neglected education among its most serious
indictments of the youth community. George was persuaded

[3] Willard E. Hotchkiss to Mrs. William R. George, Feb. 17, 1950.

that his failure to provide educational opportunities for the children would prove fatal to the Junior Republic, and accordingly he hastily arranged for all high-school-age citizens to attend the Dryden High School. But the local school district was unprepared and unwilling to accept the remaining primary children in its classrooms. The situation became even more serious when the reorganized Junior Republic Association discovered it lacked the ready cash to hire a full-time school teacher.

In order to ease the educational crisis and to forestall further unfavorable reports, Susan Dixwell Miller, wife of Gerrit Smith Miller, presented the Junior Republic with an excellent library of over 1,000 volumes.[4] The library soon doubled as friends from Cornell and mission societies contributed old books, popular magazines, and periodicals. From Frank Boynton, superintendent of Ithaca schools, came a wagonload of discarded mathematics, English, geography, and history textbooks. In time the George Junior Republic library, far superior to that of most rural high schools, justifiably became one of the major attractions of the institution.[5]

But a new library, for all its excellence, could not substitute for a school, and although the Millers' donation temporarily silenced Republic critics, it provided no remedy for the Republic's instructional shortcomings. George recognized that the future of the Republic demanded the establishment of a regular school, but he also feared that the presence of a school might wreck his self-government scheme as surely as no school at all. The principle of "Nothing without Labor" assumed that each citizen worked to earn his own room and board. How could the Republic standards of self-government

[4] William O. Dapping, *Susan Dixwell Miller* (Peterboro, N.Y., 1926), 24–26.

[5] George, *The Adult Minor* (New York, 1937), 106–107.

and self-support be maintained, George wondered, if the majority of his citizens idled away their day in the school room?

Frank Boynton's wagon carried within it the solution to the dilemma. George cheered its arrival not only because it brought a welcome addition to the Republic library, but because it brought a few hours of much needed work to the lagging Republic economy. As a gang of boys eagerly set to work unloading the cargo, George could only wish that each book were itself a wagon of books. A thousand wagons were needed to provide enough year-round employment to keep everyone busy. Suddenly George recognized that each book in fact held the solution to his unemployment and educational problems. Though he did not fully work out his scheme on that day, George had begun to formulate his plan for employing citizens in a school which he called "the Publishing House." [6]

"The Publishing House" allowed George to fit an educational system under the rubric of "Nothing without Labor." The curriculum of the Republic school was traditional and paralleled that of the public schools throughout the state. But the pedagogical methods, being wholly consistent with Republic principles, were radically different from those of the public schools. Not surprisingly, one of George's major aims was to avoid the appearance of an institutional school as far as possible. He accomplished this by pretending that the school was not a school at all. Instead the teacher was to be one of the regular Republic employers, or more accurately, the foreman of the Publishing House. The school was run as if it were one of the Republic's businesses. Each student contracted with the foreman-teacher to prepare a specified lesson and was remunerated at an hourly rate comparable to that for manual labor in other sections of the Republic. In addi-

[6] *The Adult Minor*, 107; "The Publishing House," MS, 1919.

tion there was incentive pay: the more difficult and exacting the work, the higher the wage. For example, a student might contract to prepare a "book" in the fields of geography, English, history, and civics. If his report was accepted by the teacher, he was paid according to the accuracy of his facts and grammar and the legibility of his writing. Upon completion, the student's "book" was bound in plain brown paper and added to the Republic library. In mathematics a note of realism was occasionally added when the Republic bank let its bookkeeping contract through the school.[7] George served as the first—and last—Publishing House foreman during a school year which must have bewildered and shocked most traditional educators.

The Board of Trustees indulged the Publishing House scheme as a stopgap measure until it could afford to hire a full-time instructor and establish a regular school system. Thus when Hotchkiss came to the Republic, he not only replaced "Daddy" George as teacher, but was expected to introduce more conventional teaching methods in the classroom. Fortunately, Hotchkiss was a sensitive and intelligent young man who recognized the merits of George's unorthodox educational experiment. Impressed by the high spirit of George's students, Hotchkiss determined to incorporate as much of the Publishing House as possible into the new Republic school.

Two features of the Publishing House system were especially attractive to Hotchkiss. First, the scheme had demonstrated the unquestionable value of an ungraded educational system for children from deprived backgrounds. Faced with the task of educating immigrant children with vastly differing

[7] John R. Commons, "The Junior Republic, II," *American Journal of Sociology*, III (Jan. 1898), 433–434; Willard Hotchkiss, "The Publishing House," MS, 1897; George, "The Publishing House Scheme," MS, 1913; "The George Junior Republic," *Municipal Affairs*, I (Sept. 1897), 562–564.

educational, cultural, and emotional skills, and unable to implement a rational grading system, the Publishing House was forced to develop an individual program for each child. If Hotchkiss' first task was to create order out of the curricular chaos, he was careful not to crush the spirit of the Publishing House reform. Despite all its shortcomings, it could not be denied that the freewheeling Publishing House had inspired children who had hated school before. George had accomplished this miracle by eliminating recitation and allowing childen to work at their own pace on projects of their own interest. Although Hotchkiss soon introduced traditional classes, the permissive and experimental flavor of the Publishing House was never entirely lost.[8]

The second feature Hotchkiss retained was the "learning by earning" principle, which paralleled George's old "law and order" idea. George believed that disorderly, antagonistic, and inattentive children would perform satisfactorily in school if they were given a "stake" in their education through payment of wages for school work. George conceded that initially the incentive, like the law and order principle, was frankly mercenary. But he argued that it was impossible to bring poverty-hardened youth to an immediate respect for learning for its own sake. The old appeal to self-interest provided a ready handle by which to catch the child. For whatever reason the disadvantaged child *begins to study*, George emphasized, the cause of general education is advanced. Disinterested motives, though rarely pure, almost invariably followed. "Until any who are disposed to question the quality of our incentive furnish more effective means of aiding the cause of 'education for education's sake,'" George wrote, "learning by earning may stand as the most practical under general conditions." [9]

[8] Hotchkiss, "The Publishing House."
[9] *The Adult Minor*, 130–131.

To a generation of educators disgusted by the practice of indulgent parents paying their children for good school marks, the learning by earning idea may appear crass and unattractive. But to many Progressives, George's emphasis was anything but distasteful. If George accomplished nothing else, he succeeded in elevating intellectual work to a par with manual labor. Not only did the Publishing House demonstrate that mental work was as valuable as physical labor, but in a few instances it was shown that study in school could produce greater rewards than work in the shops. Far from being anti-intellectual, in the context of the Junior Republic the learning by earning principle increased the prestige of education among students who ordinarily cared little for formal learning.[10]

By most standards, the George Junior Republic developed a respectable, if not outstanding, curriculum and record. The institution was transformed from a recreational refuge for New York City's underprivileged into an "educational gymnasium." Boys from poor families were solicited with the promise that the training they received would prepare them for a college education financed by the generosity of philanthropic backers.[11] William O. Dapping, bright but poverty-stricken, became one of the Junior Republic's most notable protégés.[12] Dapping's career was atypical of Republic graduates, but it demonstrated the fullness of opportunity that the Republic offered. Recruited by George, Dapping soon won the heart of Osborne, who admired the boy's crusading liberalism. Building on the foundation obtained at the Re-

[10] George, *The Adult Minor*, 131–136; George, "The Publishing House," MS, 1919.

[11] Rudolph W. Chamberlain, *There Is No Truce: A Life of Thomas Mott Osborne* (New York, 1935), 224.

[12] John Balderston, the noted playwright and author, was another.

public, Osborne sent Dapping successively to Auburn High School, Fort Plain Military Academy, the Hackley School, and finally to Harvard where he earned an A.B. in 1905. After graduation Dapping joined the staff of the Auburn *Citizen*, Osborne's newspaper, and steadily rose to the position of editor. In 1930, he was awarded the Pulitzer Prize for local journalism.[13] By 1906 the George Junior Republic counted among its alumni two A.B.'s and a civil engineer from Cornell, an A.B. and an LL.B. from Harvard, and an A.B. from Ohio University. In addition, three more students were enrolled at Cornell and Harvard.[14]

As a prep school for poor but deserving students and wealthy but troublesome boys, the George Junior Republic won considerable acclaim. Europeans were especially impressed with the intermingling of social classes on a basis of absolute equality. The rich student had no advantages in Freeville, and was often initially at a disadvantage when compared to the child from the slum who had learned to live by his wits. It appeared literally true that, regardless of social class or wealth, all Republic citizens of sufficient ability and interest could aspire to a college education and middle-class gentility.[15]

Actually, Junior Republic leaders did not seek to abolish social classes but joined with Francis W. Parker and John

[13] Chamberlain, *There Is No Truce*, 227.

[14] "Outline of the Work of the George Junior Republic," George Junior Republic Association pamphlet (Freeville, N.Y., 1906). Although two of the degrees may have been held by the same person, this record is still impressive.

[15] A. Ferrière, "Ecoles nouvelles en Amérique: Une République d'adolescents aux Etats-Unis," *Education Nouvelle et Populaire* (Geneva), April 7, 1921, 125, 133–139; Frederic J. Haskin, "Conservation of Child Life—Junior Republics," New York *Globe* (Feb. 24, 1909); Jeanne Robert, "A Republic for Boys and Girls—After Twenty Years," *American Review of Reviews*, IV (Dec. 1910), 705–712.

Dewey in advocating an educational curriculum which served the needs of all social classes. Accusing both private and public schools systems of being too aristocratic and paternalistic, Osborne demanded that American schools practice democracy as well as give lip service to democratic values. Like Dewey, Osborne believed democracy to be the basis of associated living as well as a system of politics.[16] Republic graduates who satisfactorily adjusted to life in the Great Republic were deemed as successful as college graduates. The Junior Republic anticipated most public high schools in the variety of its educational offering and by 1912 was graduating more students with vocational than with academic degrees.[17] With its simple application of the "learn by doing" principle in all departments, the George Junior Republic became an important testing ground for the theories of Progressive educators.[18]

George and Osborne made no claims that their educational methods were original. When constantly reminded of the precedents to his work, George admitted: "I feel guilty when I consider the share that has been put upon me in world wide attention paid to the Junior Republic. . . . I have done nothing. It is no invention. I didn't sit down and evolve it. It is

[16] Utica *Daily Press*, Feb. 2, 1909; Cremin, *Transformation of the School*, 122.

[17] The George Junior Republic Papers contain several dated and undated lists of former citizens. Among them are the "Republic Roster," Jan. 1898; "List of Graduates and Citizens of the George Junior Republic," 1903; Thomas Mott Osborne, address before the National Conference of Charities and Corrections, Washington, D.C., May 13, 1901; and a detailed "List of 900 Graduates," July 1912.

[18] A decade ago Timothy L. Smith discovered, to his surprise, "that progressive educators regarded private, as distinct from sectarian, institutions as staunch allies." Institutions like the George Junior Republic were "indispensable for experiments which political or other pressures made impossible in tax supported schools" ("Progressivism in American Education, 1880–1900," *Harvard Educational Review*, XXI [Spring, 1961], 191).

no product of my ingenuity. It is as old as Plato, as old as man, as old as the earth." [19]

If the Junior Republic was not an absolutely original scheme, the New York *Herald* noted, George himself was no less an educational pioneer. The founder of the Junior Republic focused attention on a long-neglected principle of education, and years in advance of most educators he perceived the need for an adolescent education especially designed to meet the needs of an urban-industrial society. George did not consciously attack the theories of William Torrey Harris, the *bête noire* of Progressive educators, but in practice the George Junior Republic rejected the formalism characteristic of classical education. George's emphasis on industry confirmed the first principles of Harris' social philosophy, but his conservatism did not prevent George from vigorously contributing to the Progressive attack on educational formalism. Rote memorization was banned from the Junior Republic. George stressed interest, exploration, and spontaneity in his school at the expense of order, regularity, and silence. The best teacher, he asserted, was practical experience which tested a student's ideas and theories. "Learn by doing," the slogan of Progressive educators, was simply and literally understood by George, yet even his lack of sophistication en-

[19] Interview of George in the New York *Herald*, March 19, 1911. See also George to Frank Fetter, Feb. 13, 1912. George's close friend Richard Welling, writing for the National Education Association, traced the origins of student self-government to the Italian humanist Vittorino da Feltre (1378–1446), founder of the famous boys' school at Mantua. In the United States, Catherine Beecher's Hartford School and Bronson Alcott's Temple School anticipated the main features of George's anti-institutionalism (Welling, "Pupil Self-government as a Training for Citizenship," National Education Association pamphlet [San Francisco, 1921]). For a brief description of Vittorino's work, see Paul Munroe, ed., *A Cyclopedia of Education*, V (New York, 1913), 737–738.

deared him to many reformers. By 1925, his friend and supporter Alexander Forbes was able to say that "the George Junior Republic is the embodiment of the best that Progressive educators have achieved." [20]

ii

The George Junior Republic was founded at a critical moment in the history of American education. The explosion of the urban slums had seriously weakened traditional centers of education—the family, the church, and the apprentice system. Rural schools, bright symbols of American agrarian democracy in the 1840's and 1850's, had fallen into disrepair and disrepute, victims of exodus from farm to city. City schools, on the other hand, all but collapsed under the weight of increased enrollments. With an average of sixty students in a class, the public schools had neither facilities nor curriculum adequate to the educational needs of an urban society.[21]

John Commons, one of "Daddy" George's closest friends, warned that public education would not be redeemed in the United States until American educators remembered that it was the community more than the school that gave the child

[20] Forbes, "The George Junior Republic: A Community Vital to the United States," pamphlet (Freeville, N.Y., 1925). See also Jeanne Robert, "A Republic for Boys and Girls"; J. F. B. Tinling, "Juvenile Self-governing Communities," *Progress, Civic-Social-Industrial*, IV (Jan. 1909), 1–12; Jacob Smith to Richard Welling, Feb. 14, 1939; Cremin, *Transformation of the School*, 19–20. Timothy L. Smith has noted that as early as 1882 Joseph R. Buchanan's *The New Education* rejected rote memorization in favor of "training the whole child for the practical requirements of real life" ("Progressivism in American Education," 185).

[21] Cremin, *Transformation of the School*, 20–21; Smith, "Progressivism in American Education," 168–170; Sol Cohen, *Progressives and Urban School Reform: The Public Education Association of New York City, 1895–1954* (New York, 1963), 5–8.

his actual working ideals, habits, and attitudes toward life. In the great city, he believed, the dominant educating community was the slum. Commons observed that the schoolbooks given to slum children described no American institution or value with which they were familiar. Few Americans lived within the immigrant's community—the American churches and American employers were in other parts of the city. The Americanization of the slum child was thus left to harassed and indifferent teachers, policemen, and ward politicians. But on the farm, Commons continued, the immigrant child "sees and knows all classes, the best and the worst, and even where his parents strive to isolate their community and to preserve the language and the methods of the old country, only a generation or two are required for the surrounding Americanism to permeate." [22] The lesson was clear to the young socialist. Life in a farm community still provided the most healthful employment and inspired industrious and thrifty habits which allowed the immigrant to realize his greatest potentiality. Commons' analysis was almost identical to that of Jacob Riis,[23] and it is not surprising that both reformers discovered in the George Junior Republic a virtual educational panacea.[24] Yet Commons and Riis were not merely nostalgic and sentimental in their support of the Junior Republic, for the Freeville institution was not simply a reconstructed nineteenth-century rural village. The major currents of Progressive education were evident in the work at Freeville, and three themes were decidedly the most significant: vocational

[22] *Races and Immigrants in America* (New York, 1907), 216–217.

[23] For example, see Riis, "One Way Out," *The Century*, LI (Dec. 1895), 303–308.

[24] See Commons' articles in the *Journal of Sociology* for Nov. 1897 and Jan. 1898. Riis's endorsement of the Junior Republic can be found in a manuscript entitled "Introduction" in the George Junior Republic Papers.

education, the child-centered school, and education as social reform.[25]

The George Junior Republic had a justified reputation as a model vocational school. The principle "Nothing without Labor," which demanded that all citizens be employed in a "gainful" occupation, meant, after the establishment of the educational system, that most students were enrolled in vocational training courses. Plumbing, steamfitting, and metalworking were taught in the plumbing shop. The printing office did job work, published the Republic paper *The Junior Citizen*, and printed reports, pamphlets, and forms for the George Junior Republic Association. Some citizens learned the bakery trade while producing the locally famous George Junior Republic wafers. Others were employed in the carpentry shop building mission furniture. A large number of citizens worked on the farm or in landscape gardening. Both boys and girls received training in hotel management at the Republic Inn, and girls were taught housekeeping, millinery, laundry work, and cooking.[26]

The vocational program served a number of special interests. Most advocates of industrial training for indigents, im-

[25] Two other themes were strong, but not dominant: conservation of children and efficiency of education. Cf. J. W. Callnon, "Conservation and Progress," *The Junior Republic* (journal published by the citizens of the California Junior Republic), IV (Oct. 1914), 6; Haskin, "Conservation of Child Life"; J. George Frederick, "Applying Efficiency Principles to Educating Children," New Orleans *Item*, June 7, 1914; A. E. Winship, "Projected Efficiency of the Junior Republics," *Journal of Education*, LXXVI (Sept. 18, 1913).

[26] George, "Industries of the Republic," *The Junior Republic* (New York, 1910), 208–235; Orestes M. Brands, "The George Junior Republic," *Journal of Education*, LXXII (Nov. 17, 1910), 483–484; "The George Junior Republic," *Municipal Affairs*, I (Sept. 1897), 562–564; William I. Hull, "The George Junior Republic," *Annals of the American Academy of Political and Social Science*, X (Aug. 10, 1897), 73–83.

migrants, and Negroes argued that vocational training was the key to social control and thus to economic and civic progress. "The industrial school plants itself squarely in the gap between the tenement and the public school," Jacob Riis wrote. "Wherever the greatest and poorest crowds are, there also is the industrial school." [27] Progressive social workers seeking to save the disadvantaged classes knew that economic self-sufficiency usually preceded civic responsibility and social equality. It was not enough for the schools to teach reading and moral philosophy. In addition to civics and geography, hygiene and physical culture, classes in mechanical, agricultural, and household arts were necessary.[28] The George Junior Republic was certainly one of the outstanding institutions promoting civic and social stability through vocational training. Riis praised the Republic for teaching young toughs that it "costs more to be bad than good. I believe thoroughly in the plan of the Junior Republic as applied to the slum," he continued. "[Slum] gangs are only 'Industrial Classes' waiting to be enrolled in the Republic." [29]

If the Junior Republic was known as a poor-man's prep school, it was also compared favorably to Tuskegee and Hampton Institutes. The Carlisle Indian Industrial School borrowed directly from Junior Republic methods and principles, and the Atlanta *Journal* suggested that a series of Republics might provide a convenient solution to the Negro problem in the South.[30] The Freeville Republic had admitted its first Negro in 1897, and thereafter admitted Negroes on a regular basis, including a few transfer students from Tuskegee

[27] *The Children of the Poor* (New York, 1902), 187.

[28] Daniel Levine, *Varieties of Reform Thought* (Madison, Wis., 1964), 27; Smith, "Progressivism in American Education," 171.

[29] "Introduction," MS, George Junior Republic Papers.

[30] Atlanta *Journal*, March 8, 1914; George, "About the Negro," MS, 1920.

Institute. But George's continued policy of toleration and integration of both races and sexes foreclosed any possibility that his scheme would be widely adopted in the South.[31]

Finger Lakes businessmen and manufacturers also enthusiastically endorsed the vocational efforts of the Junior Republic. Local businessmen who hired Republic graduates were spared the expense and uncertainty of training unskilled laborers. George enjoyed invaluable contacts with area entrepreneurs and seldom had difficulty finding satisfactory skilled or semiskilled employment for his boys. D. M. Osborne and Company and Smith-Corona were two of the most prominent manufacturers regularly employing former citizens, and several other businesses hired Junior Republic boys whenever there was a vacancy on their small staffs. Proud, self-controlled, and self-reliant, disdainful of those who could not "make it on their own," Republic graduates were relatively immune to the enticements of organized labor. They often transferred their intense loyalty for "Daddy" George to their employer, a fact which may explain why so few Republic graduates lost their jobs during the Great Depression.[32]

[31] Caroline W. B. Chapin to Mrs. William R. George, Sept. 29, 1897; Elizabeth B. Grannis to George, June 20, 1910. For a Progressive, George's record with the Negro is good. He refused to segregate or discriminate against Negroes in the Freeville Republic, and as National Director of the National Association of Junior Republics, he severely criticized those Junior Republics that did. Much to his consternation, Negroes were occasionally excluded from other Republics; where admitted, they were usually segregated (E. D. Bruner to Lucy More, March 22, 1929, Papers of the Western Pennsylvania George Junior Republic, Cornell University).

[32] A. E. Winship, "The George Junior Republic, I," *Journal of Education*, LI (Jan. 4, 1900), 3; Brands, "George Junior Republic," 483–484; George, *The Adult Minor*, 28–29. For a discussion of the support given to manual training and industrial education by the National Association of Manufacturers, see Cremin, *Transformation of the School*, 34–38.

The vocational efforts of the George Junior Republic were not limited to training the urban masses and disadvantaged minorities for positions in upstate New York businesses and factories. Begun as a Fresh Air camp, the Junior Republic needed little modification in either ideology or method to make it one of the important farm schools of New York State. With the aid of Osborne's implements company and the assistance of students from the College of Agriculture at Cornell University, the Junior Republic became one of the nation's foremost high schools in the teaching of agricultural science. Junior Republic boys were taught the latest methods of planting, cultivating, draining, and harvesting. They built modern barns and other farm buildings and kept a large herd of registered Holsteins (donated by Miller), and several pigs and chickens.[33]

Cornell professors and students were especially eager to assist the Junior Republic in its agricultural program. Liberty Hyde Bailey, Cornell's first professor of horticulture and dean of the agricultural school, was the nation's foremost advocate of country life. If country schools were to be effective, Bailey wrote, they must represent the civilization of their time and place. Supporting the manual training advocates, Bailey argued that schools must be broad rather than narrow, active rather than passive. If manual training provided urban workers with moral and economic training, then agricultural studies were the key to rural regeneration. Let the students enter the shops, fields, and gardens, confronting firsthand the virtue of country living and the depth of rural problems. Country schools had failed, Bailey argued, because they had

[33] Preston Search, *An Ideal School* (New York, 1901), 78–79; Henry Bush-Brown, "Farm Schools," Detroit *Tribune,* Jan. 31, 1901; Winship, "The George Junior Republic, I," 3; Brands, "George Junior Republic," 484.

isolated themselves from the rural community and taught little that was relevant to country living. Urging rural communities to revitalize their schools, Bailey reminded American farmers that "agriculture is not a technical profession or merely an industry, but a civilization." [34]

The George Junior Republic, with its country store, its rural, nondenominational church, its village government, and its agricultural employment, represented the best of Bailey's agrarian civilization. This alone would have warmed the heart of any country-life exponent.[35] But the Junior Republic was also a rural version of the famous settlement house. Many young agricultural extension agents first practiced their craft in Freeville. The Junior Republic became both a model farm and a modest training center for Cornell University.

The purpose of vocational and agricultural studies at the Junior Republic was not simply to prepare mechanics and farmers for their jobs, however. Although George did not go as far as Calvin Woodward of Washington University in St. Louis who believed that manual training was as essential to the growth and development of the child as physical education, George regarded vocational studies as a valuable coordinate to a liberal education. He was proud of the fact that Republic experience often enriched a student's formal studies, and, like Dewey, he was only incidentally interested in pre-

[34] *The Country-Life Movement* (New York, 1911), 63; Cremin, *Transformation of the School*, 75–78. See also, *The Report of the Country Life Commission* with introduction by Theodore Roosevelt (New York, 1911); Clayton S. Ellsworth, "Theodore Roosevelt's Country Life Commission," *Agricultural History*, XXXIV (Oct. 1960), 155–172; Philip Dorf, *Liberty Hyde Bailey* (Ithaca, N.Y., 1956).

[35] See Bailey as quoted in George and Lyman Beecher Stowe, *Citizens Made and Remade* (New York, 1912), 92.

paring children for particular professions and jobs. More important than teaching children a specific task, manual and agricultural training taught habits of self-discipline, order, and industry, and inculcated in the child a sense of high character and social responsibility.[36] Thus what saved the Junior Republic from being a mere training school for local farmers, businessmen, and manufacturers was the institution's close association, in both theory and practice, with the newly established child-centered schools.

iii

Throughout his career, George was identified with such great educational pioneers as Maria Montessori, Johann Pestalozzi, and Friedrich Froebel.[37] George, of course, knew nothing of these educational theorists when he founded the Junior Republic in 1895. Two years later, when he established the Publishing House, he was still unaware that his educational scheme was almost an exact copy of the famous demonstration school established at the Cook County Normal

[36] George, *The Junior Republic*, 308 and *passim.;* John Dewey, *The School and Society* (1900; reprint ed., Chicago: Phoenix Books, 1956); Cremin, *Transformation of the School*, 29–33; Smith, "Progressivism in American Education," 178.

[37] The Little Commonwealth, the English version of the George Junior Republic, was founded with the assistance of the Montessori Association of England. Frank Fetter, professor of economics at Princeton, reported that Dr. J. Guillaume, author of *Pestalozzi: Etude biographique* (Paris, 1890), had characterized George as the "American Pestalozzi" (Fetter to George, Feb. 1, 1912). Perhaps the most typical comparisons of George, Ben Lindsey, Jane Addams, Maria Montessori, and Friedrich Froebel can be found in Mary Heaton Vose, "The New Freedom for Little Children," *Woman's Home Companion*, Nov. 1913, 18; and Thomas R. Croswell, "Amusements of Worcester School Children," *Pedagogical Seminary*, VI (Sept. 1899), 45–46.

School by Francis W. Parker, America's foremost disciple of Froebel and Pestalozzi.[38]

Charles W. Eliot, President of Harvard University, was one of the first observers to link the educational theories of Froebel to the educational practices of the George Junior Republic. Eliot noted that the Junior Republic had successfully tested three of Froebel's most basic principles. First, the Junior Republic had demonstrated that self-reliant and autonomous children could be taught the social necessity of civic responsibility. The Republic taught, "not a habit of submission to an overwhelming, arbitrary, external power, but a habit of obeying the dictates of honor and duty, as enforced by active will power within the child." [39] Second, the Junior Republic illustrated that the child was best educated by appealing to his natural instincts, impulses, and activities. George had intuitively discovered Froebel's principle while organizing his Law and Order Gang. Later, "Nothing without Labor" and "Learning by Earning" were self-conscious devices used to turn the child's base instincts toward socially constructive activity. Even the child's love of playing "grown-up" was systematically exploited by Junior Republic leaders.[40] Third, the Junior Republic implemented Froebel's theory that education was most effective when it involved productive, visible achievement in doing, making, or producing something.[41]

---

[38] Colonel Parker described his school as a "model home, a complete community and embryonic democracy" (Francis W. Parker, *Talks on Pedagogics* [New York, 1894], 450, as quoted in Cremin, *Transformation of the School*, 132).

[39] Charles W. Eliot, New York *Tribune*, Nov. 2, 1900, as quoted by George in *The Adult Minor*, 57–58.

[40] *The Adult Minor*, 18–58; *Citizens Made and Remade*, 139–161.

[41] Eliot as quoted in *The Adult Minor*, 58; Lyman Beecher Stowe, "Democracy in the Schools," *The Junior Republic*, I (March 1912).

Yet the system of using the child's natural instincts to produce a self-consciously social individual through productive activity was not without its pitfalls. If George had difficulty in finding sympathetic and cooperative trustees and administrators, he had an even more difficult time finding and keeping qualified teachers and housemothers. George's problem was not unique among child-centered educators. Well-meaning helpers, more accustomed to the silent discipline of the traditional school than the noisy confusion of a functioning Junior Republic, often could not resist the temptation to bring systematic order into the Republic's educational affairs. The Republic citizens were quick to detect a sham, however, and when it became evident that a teacher was using her position to influence the administration of justice or the selection of Republic officers, the citizens (even those who had been the victims of injustice) did not hesitate to express their resentment. Artificial government was worse than no government at all, George warned, because its hypocrisy destroyed all respect for duty and authority. Proper education, he continued, was neither authoritarian in its methods nor dilettantish in its results. The skillful teacher realized that difficult and productive work was usually accompanied by the noisy expenditure of energy.[42]

iv

George Junior Republic methods and principles gradually worked their way into the mainstream of American educa-

---

Eliot's analysis of the George Junior Republic was undoubtedly based on his reading of John Dewey's chapter on "Froebel's Educational Principles," in *School and Society*, 116–118.

[42] Croswell, "Amusements of Worcester School Children," 45–46; George, *Junior Republic Principles and Bulletins* (Freeville, N.Y., 1941), *passim*.

tional reform. George accepted numerous invitations to address school committees, educational associations, and teachers' colleges. Without fee, he advised several school officials on the best means to implement self-government in their institutions.[43] Osborne also aided the Junior Republic cause by advocating Republic methods for Hackley Hall and Milton Academy. Anticipating the modern honor system, Osborne advised that cheating could be reduced by abolishing the monitor system in favor of student self-government. Self-government taught responsibility and self-respect, Osborne suggested, "and will introduce a manly tone into the school, taking a large burden of discipline off the shoulders of the teachers." [44] When Arthur E. Morgan, the controversial president of Antioch College, first proposed his scheme of alternating five weeks of study with five weeks of industrial work, he turned to William R. George for advice and criticism. And when the School of Pedagogy of New York University decided to offer a course in student self-government, it naturally called upon George to help plan the syllabus.[45] During his visit to the Junior Republic in 1908, Theodore Roosevelt had wondered how the headmaster at Groton, the Reverend Endi-

[43] George aided such schools as the Texas Industrial School for Boys (R. E. Grabel to George, Sept. 26, 1908), the Wisconsin Home and Farm School (Frank G. Swoboda to George, Feb. 20, 1909), the public schools of Oklahoma City (J. B. Taylor to George, March 8, 1909), Union City, Indiana, Public Schools (Carl H. Mote to George, April 5, 1909), Ruskin College, Florida (Harry C. Moffett to George, Feb. 10, 1912), and Central High School, Syracuse, New York ("John J. Kinane," Oral History Interview 154, p. 17, Collection of Regional History and University Archives, Cornell University).

[44] Thomas Mott Osborne to T. C. Williams, Feb. 14, 1900; Osborne Papers, Syracuse University.

[45] Arthur E. Morgan to George, June 11, 1921; Thomas M. Balliet to George, July 18, 1909.

cott Peabody, would like the Republic. Four years later, in a letter to George, Peabody answered the question:

I have not talked much about anything but the George Junior Republic since I left you last Friday night. I trust I shall prove a good missionary in your service. . . . The spirit of the place and the love and devotion which flow out from you I am determined, with God's help, to bring in as they have not been brought before. My only regret is that I did not see the Republic and did not come into close touch with you years ago. However, there is all eternity before us—and I hope that you will give me the privilege of knowing you better still as the years go on.[46]

This glimpse of George's contribution to American public and private education is tantalizing, but its importance is inconclusive. Because George was reluctant to encourage publicly or assist partial or pseudo self-government schemes in schools and institutions, we may never know the full extent of his influence on Progressive educators. In the absence of his cooperation, many reformers developed his ideas on their own, quite correctly taking full credit for the innovations they worked out.

The School City founded by Dr. Wilson Gill in 1897 is an excellent example of an important reform inspired, but not encouraged, by the founder of the George Junior Republic. Gill, another disciple of Pestalozzi and Froebel, spent much of the summer of 1895 or 1896 at the Junior Republic in Freeville.[47] President of the Patriotic League before coming to the Junior Republic, Gill returned to New York City convinced that self-government introduced into the public schools would be the best means of Americanizing immigrant children. With

[46] Peabody to George, Jan. 3, 1912.
[47] George, "History of Self-government," MS, c. 1930; Mrs. Willian R. George to Jacob Smith, Feb. 15, 1937; "The Gill School City," *Municipal Affairs*, I (Sept. 1897), 564–565.

the encouragement of Mayor William Strong, Theodore Roosevelt, Charles W. Eliot, and the Federated Women's Clubs—but without that of George or Osborne—Gill established his self-government school for 1,200 youths in the midst of the New York City slums.[48] The School City, as Gill called his experiment at Public School No. 69, was organized into a miniature municipality governed by a junior mayor and alderman, and with police, sanitation, and health departments. The School City idea soon caught the imagination of American educators. From Public School No. 69, student self-government, in one form or another, gradually worked its way into the New York City school system and then into the vast majority of public and private schools in the country. Perhaps the most important boost to the School City idea came from the State Normal School at New Paltz, New York, which organized a model School City on its campus. Scores of teachers, indoctrinated with Gill's philosophy and methods of student government, formed School City committees, sponsored symposiums, and published literature on Gill's theories.[49]

[48] George apparently wished Gill well but predicted early failure for the scheme (see George's "History of Self-government"). Osborne was not so kind: "I have not much faith in the man himself and think that the 'School City' is apt to prove seed sowed in very shallow places" (Osborne to Mrs. B. Vaughan, July 27, 1903, Osborne Papers).

[49] "The Gill System of Moral and Civic Training," *Normal Review*, May 1900; Wilson Gill, *School City Helps* (New Paltz, N.Y., n.d.); Gill, "Child-Citizenship and the School City," *Addresses and Proceedings of the National Education Association* (Cleveland, O., 1908), 285–289; William R. Ward, *Student Participation in School Government* (Poughkeepsie, N.Y., 1906); Bernard Cronson, *Pupil Self-Government* (New York, 1907); Albert Shaw, "School City— A Method of Pupil Self-government," *Review of Reviews*, XX (Dec. 1899), 673–686; Anna McCormick, "The School City," MS, George Junior Republic Papers; "The Development of the Student Participation Movement," *The Student Council in the Secondary Schools*,

Reviewing a quarter of a century of reform, B. O. Flower
wrote:

Mr. Gill held, and rightly held, that so long as children passed
from the primary grades through the universities without being
taught self-government in a practical way, they would be the
easy victim of the boss and the machine. Moreover, he believed
that no part of education was more essential to the young than
the teaching at an early age of the principles of free government
and developing the ideals of good citizenship in the child.[50]

Perhaps even more influential than Wilson Gill in promoting student government was the National Self-Government
Committee (NSGC). Founded in 1904 by Richard Welling
(and originally named the School Citizens Committee), the
NSGC was an offspring of the Good Government movement.
Richard Welling, Harvard classmate of Theodore Roosevelt,
had been one of the organizers (and later president) of the
anti-Tammany City Reform Club in 1882, and secretary of
the Commonwealth Club founded by Carl Schurz and E. L.
Godkin; he campaigned for the Australian ballot, civil-service
reform, separate municipal elections, and New York City
home rule. Out of the City Club grew the famous Good
Government Clubs organized by Welling and Edmund Kelly.
Twenty-three Good Government Clubs were founded, one
for each Assembly district, and Welling became the leader of
Good Government Club D. The Good Government Clubs
employed poll watchers such as George's Law and Order
Gang during the mayoralty campaign of 1894, and it is pos-

Proceedings of the National Association of Secondary School Principals (Washington, D.C., 1950); Lillian K. Wyman, *Character and
Citizenship through Pupil Self-government* (Philadelphia, 1935).

[50] B. O. Flower, *Progressive Men, Women, and Movements of the
Past Twenty-five Years* (Boston, 1914), 210–211.

sible that it was in this connection that George and Welling first met.[51]

Welling's interest in Good Government was not extinguished by the disillusionment that followed the election of Mayor Strong in 1894. He battled hopefully for Seth Low in 1897, and was encouraged when the fusion candidate won in 1901. But when the Tammany politicians redistricted the city at the end of Low's term of office in 1903, Welling joined the ranks of disappointed reformers. Yearning to get out of town for a while, he remembered a magazine article which had picturesquely described the George Junior Republic and shortly thereafter arranged an appointment with George in Freeville.

Like so many other visitors to the Junior Republic, Welling was overwhelmed by George's personality, enthusiasm, and zeal, and fascinated by the spectacle of adolescents governing themselves better than the people of New York City. "Why are not our New York schools doing the same?" Welling asked himself. After bringing his question to the attention of Charles W. Eliot, then President of the National Education Association, Welling was invited to address the Association's annual meeting in Boston. Warning the assembled teachers and principals that they were teaching only the *form* of democracy and not its practice, he urged his listeners to adopt student government in their own schools.[52]

As letters came from all parts of the country congratulating him on his speech, or inquiring how best to implement self-

[51] Richard Welling, *As the Twig Is Bent* (New York, 1942), 23–64; Welling, "Are We Educating for Democracy?" *International Observer*, May 1936, 40, 51.

[52] Welling, untitled MS, Jan. 8, 1941, George Junior Republic Papers; *As the Twig Is Bent*, 91–92; "Are We Educating for Democracy?" 40.

government methods, Welling realized that he had found a new and promising cause.[53] Encouraged by his friends to form a new committee, Welling organized the NSGC with such influential friends as Charles S. Fairchild, Samuel McCune Lindsay, George Haven Putnam, and Lyman Beecher Stowe.[54]

Initially, the Committee promoted self-government in factories, businesses, labor unions, and prisons, but it soon became so busy with its work in schools and colleges that it was forced to neglect all other aspects of the work. Welling's National Education Association address was published by the Committee and sent to schools throughout the country. Later, Lyman Beecher Stowe persuaded Eliot to write his views on the self-government movement, which were also published and distributed by the Committee. In addition the NSGC helped New York University's School of Education organize a course on self-government with such men as G. Stanley Hall, William R. George, and Lyman Beecher Stowe as lecturers.

Welling's Committee promoted self-government wherever it was practical. It cooperated with William R. George and Wilson Gill, but believed that both men held too rigidly to a mechanical system. The Committee actively advertised the

[53] It is also possible that the success of the neighboring Good Government Club E in sponsoring educational reform encouraged Welling to turn from political reform. See Cohen, *Progressives and Urban School Reform*, 30–38.

[54] Welling, *As the Twig Is Bent*, 120–125; Robert Muccigrosso, "The City Reform Club: A Study in Late Nineteenth Century Reform," *New-York Historical Society Quarterly*, LII (July 1968). Eventually John Dewey, Julia Richman, Alfred E. Smith, Lillian Wald, Hermann Hagedorn, William McAndrew, Mary K. Simpkovitch, Nicholas Murray Butler, Harry Emerson Fosdick, and Stephen Wise became associated with the committee in one capacity or another.

work of the Junior Republics and the School Cities, however, praising them without reservation.[55] The main effort of the NSGC was directed toward self-government in public and private schools. Welling and Stowe missed no opportunity to address teachers, administrators, and businessmen on the topic.

Welling personally claimed to have converted Julia Richman, Nicholas Murray Butler, Charles W. Eliot, Frank Kiernan, Dean Balliet, Endicott Peabody, and Walter Damrosch to the cause. Each of his supporters had raised a different objection: Did children possess sufficient maturity to be self-governing? Would children, when vested with power, become arrogant and tyrannical? Did adult supervision of self-government programs make the students merely puppets? Would self-government undermine the authority of the teacher? The objections, Welling discovered, were almost endless. Julia Richman, for example, argued that self-governing students would be forever talking about their rights, while in vain teachers would try to convince students of their obligations. Nicholas Murray Butler, concurring with Julia Richman's conception of youth, believed that classroom anarchy would result without the most strict discipline. In his reply to skeptical educators, Welling relied on theory and fact. Referring first to the publications of the NSGC and the precedents for student self-government set by Catherine Beecher and Bronson Alcott, Welling finally answered each objection by carefully describing how the question had actually been satisfied through the successful application of the self-government principle in the George Junior Republic.[56]

[55] Welling, "The Teaching of Civics and Good Citizenship in the Public Schools," in his *Self-Government Miscellanie, 1903–1915* (New York, 1917), 2–3. Much of this book was later incorporated into *As the Twig Is Bent*.

[56] *As the Twig Is Bent,* 94–100.

By 1913, the Committee had supervised the establishment of self-government in 25 New York City schools, and had advised 163 schools throughout the county on student government methods. Moreover, the Committee worked strenuously for the improved teaching of civics in the schools. The most popular pamphlet published by the Committee was "The Truth about Politics—Civics as It Should Be Taught." In just fifteen pages it outlined topics usually omitted from civics classes: practical politics, newspaper-reading, current events, the district attorney, the grand jury, proportional representation, the merit system, and so on. The pamphlet also suggested for supplementary reading such books as *New York and the Seabury Investigation* edited by John Dewey, *What's the Matter with New York?* by Norman Thomas and Paul Blanshard, *Tammany Hall* by Gustavus Myers and M. R. Werner, *The Shame of the Cities* by Lincoln Steffens, and also Steffens' *Autobiography*. In 1932 and again in 1935, Dewey, Welling, Stowe, and Wise joined together in requesting the New York Board of Regents to stress a citizenship program that would follow the outline of "The Truth about Politics."[57] In 1941, the NSGC counted over 6,000 members and proudly announced that student government, in one form or another, was practically universal in the United States. From its offices in New York City, the Committee also advised and encouraged the founding of the Boys' Brotherhood Republic, the American Legion Boys' State, Junior Cities, mayor- and governor-for-a-day programs and numerous other bona fide and quasi self-government schemes.[58]

At the close of World War II, Welling recognized that the greatest threat to the self-government movement was its

[57] *Ibid.*, 120–141.
[58] Welling, untitled MS, Jan. 8, 1941, George Junior Republic Papers.

overpopularity. Student government was caught up in the great postwar boom in extracurricular activities. Welling soon was confronted by William R. George's most difficult problem. To be successful, child-centered educational programs needed child-centered teachers. The major threat to student self-government, Welling concluded, came not from disruptive and uncontrollable children, as Julia Richman and Nicholas Murray Butler had warned, but from overprotective and authoritarian adults. No student government plan that he knew of had failed because of student mismanagement, he reflected. But several had collapsed after being sabotaged by their adult leaders. The teachers preached democracy, but usually practiced something else. Colleges of education made no attempt to weed out young martinets, Welling noted, and when they taught the theory and method of student self-government, teacher training institutions usually included a course on extracurricular activity. But self-government regarded as simply another activity like football or cheerleading became, in George's terms, only partial self-government, and thus not real self-government at all. Gradually elections for student councils and class officers became just another arena in which Homecoming Queens and Handsome Harrys vied for popularity. Toward the end of his career, Welling melancholically accepted the panegyric offered him some years years before by William McAndrew, superintendent of the New York City schools:

> He grasped the intent of the founders of public schools
> He marvelled at its neglect
> He organized good citizens to realize it
> He gave of his time and labor and earnings to foster it . . .

With what success? God knows.[59]

[59] Welling, *As the Twig Is Bent*, 276.

V

The Progressive movement, George Mowry noted in his study of the California Progressives, "was a western European phenomenon, its impulse being felt all over the Western world at the end of the nineteenth and the beginning of the twentieth century. Wherever one found that characteristic ferment arising out of Western society's attempt to adjust its archaic agrarian social system to the new industrial and urban world, there one found the moral, humanitarian, and democratic strains of progressivism." [60] Other historians, especially social and intellectual historians, have noted the European impact on American Progressive reform and thought. [61] But comparatively few studies have been made of the influence of American Progressivism on the industrial and urban world outside the continental limits of the United States. This is not surprising. American historians have been more interested in tracing the roots of American reform thought than they have been in measuring the impact of American Progressive reform abroad. Furthermore, although foreigners borrowed selectively from Progressive principles, the application of American reforms abroad transcends the usual limits of American history. The result has been an unconscious emphasis on the derivative aspects of American Progressive thought with-

[60] George Mowry, *The California Progressives* (Berkeley, 1951), 88.

[61] See for example, Richard Hofstadter, *Social Darwinism in American Thought,* (Philadelphia, 1944); Arthur Mann, "British Social Thought and American Reformers of the Progressive Era," *Mississippi Valley Historical Review,* XLII (March 1956), 672–692; Henry F. May, *The End of American Innocence* (New York, 1959); David Noble, *The Paradox of Progressive Thought* (Minneapolis, 1958); Morton White, *Social Thought in America* (New York, 1949).

out an appropriate appreciation of American contributions
to international reform in the period 1890–1914.

A study of the contributions of the George Junior Republic
to international educational and penal reform gives an especially interesting insight into "international Progressivism,"
because the Freeville Republic was somewhat more influential
abroad than might be expected. In addition, a study of the
exported versions of the Junior Republic provides insights into
the basic structure of the original institution. Under the stress
of foreign cultures, the Junior Republic plan exhibited surprising strengths and telling weaknesses.

The George Junior Republic files are filled with inquiries
from foreign countries. Teachers, penologists, social reformers, and diplomats were the most frequent correspondents.
The visitor's book also indicates that the Junior Republic was
as popular among foreign tourists as it was among Americans.[62] In addition, George was requested to address several
organizations outside the United States. He found it convenient to speak to the Canadian Club of Ottawa, but regretfully declined an invitation to address the Second International Congress of Moral Education held at The Hague in
August 1912. At the urging of H. A. Overstreet, however,
George prepared a paper on "Self-government as a Means of
Moral Education" which was sent to the conference. Lack
of finances also forced George to decline an invitation to assist
in the establishment of a Junior Republic in England (an
invitation which Osborne, however, accepted).[63]

[62] Inquiries and visits came from persons representing more than
twenty-four nations.
[63] George to Herbert I. Thomas, Secretary of the Canadian Club,
Ottawa, Sept. 5, 1911; George to H. A. Overstreet, professor of
philosophy, The College of the City of New York, April 23, 1912;
George to Rose C. Barran, June 1910; George to George Montagu,
Jan. 9, 1911. George was one of about forty members of the Inter-

The first exportation of the Junior Republic idea rode the outgoing wave of American imperialism. It was logical that reformers who had sought to Americanize immigrants with Junior Republic methods concluded that juvenile self-government introduced into foreign lands would facilitate the Westernization and civilization of backward peoples. Osborne professed admiration for the civilizing influence of the English colonial system until he became acquainted with the Junior Republic. "It seems to me a startling fact," Osborne wrote to Samuel Langhorne Clemens, "that Mr. George, starting with a pure autocracy . . . should have landed his charges in a free republic. He has, after all, not only repeated the experiences of the world, but he has proved the value of free existence in a new field." In Osborne's scale of values there was one thing more valuable than good government and that was self-government. He counciled V. Everit Macy: "We who are trying to free the children from the application of the idea of a beneficial tyranny ought to be the first to recognize that Imperialism is only the reform school principle on a larger scale." To William Lloyd Garrison, Jr., Osborne confided that the more he saw of the work in Freeville the more he was convinced that the true answer to educating America's Cuban and Philippine wards was the Junior Republic.[64]

Osborne's plan for Americanization began with the modest proposal that Cuban and Philippine students bound for American preparatory schools spend a short time in the Junior Republic learning the basic principles of American culture

national Committee on The New Educational Movement, whose membership included Felix Adler, John Dewey, Booker T. Washington, and L. D. Harvey, President of the National Education Association.

[64] Osborne to Clemens, Oct. 16, 1901; Osborne to Macy, Aug. 1, 1900, Osborne to Garrison, June 19, 1900; Osborne Papers, Syracuse University.

and education. The program began with two Cubans whom Osborne hoped to send on to the Hackley School. Shortly thereafter, he proposed bringing two boys from the Philippines for the same purpose.[65]

Just as he was opposed to the proliferation of Junior Republics in the United States, Osborne discouraged founding self-governing schools in Cuba and the Philippines. But he did so for different reasons. The major task of Junior Republics was to fit children for the actual conditions of the country in which they lived. Obviously, juvenile self-government was not practical in a country which was not itself self-governing. Thus, as Osborne puzzled over exactly what kind of junior government could be produced in America's insular possessions, he was forced to concede one of the major theoretical limitations of the Junior Republic method.[66] If George's theories were literally followed, Junior Republics could be founded only in those countries where the principles of democracy and capitalism were already firmly established.

As usual, Republic officials were not left to decide how best their Junior Republic model could be adapted to foreign conditions. The Cuban census of 1899 revealed that 66 per cent of the people were illiterate, and only 21,000 children were actually enrolled in school. General Leonard Wood, governor-general of Cuba, saw that his first task in reform was to establish an adequate school system for Cuba. Wood first attempted to model his Cuban school system after that in the State of Ohio. But the irrelevancy of the Ohio curriculum to Cuban life, and the apparent incapacity of Cuban children to learn after years of harsh Spanish rule, discouraged Cuban school reformers. President Roosevelt, believing the problem

[65] Osborne to Miss Sarah Hunt, Oct. 31, 1901, Osborne Papers.
[66] Osborne to Grace W. Minns, Dept. of Charities, Havana, Cuba, April 4, 1902, Osborne Papers.

of educating Cuban children was similar to Americanizing young immigrants, reviewed Wilson Gill's successful work with the slum children of New York and recommended to General Wood that Gill be asked to organize Cuban schools into self-governing communities. At the outset Gill established six schools on a self-governing basis and then invited the Commissioner of Public Education to inspect his work. The surprised Commissioner reported that discipline in Gill's schools was superior to that of all other schools in his jurisdiction. Following the Commissioner's recommendation, the School City plan for moral and civic training was added to the curriculum of all Cuban schools, making Cuba the first country in the world to have universal student government in its schools.[67] When Wood was later transferred to the Pacific he took Gill along with him to institute a similar educational system for the Philippine Islands.[68]

Gill's dramatic success and the publicity given the George Junior Republic inspired numerous missionaries and colonial officers to attempt Junior Republics of their own. From a missionary in Shanghai, a representative of the International Reform Bureau combating opium addiction, and the president of Fukien Union College, in Foochow, George received proposals for establishing a Chinese Junior Republic.[69] The North China Presbyterian Mission also requested aid from the Junior

[67] "The School City," Circular No. 11, Office of the Commissioner of Public Schools, Havana (Feb. 8, 1902), in *Civil Report of General Leonard Wood, Military Governor of Cuba*, I (1902); Aurelio Hevia, "General Leonard Wood and Public Instruction in Cuba," *Inter-America*, IV (1920–1921); David F. Healy, *The United States in Cuba, 1898–1902* (Madison, Wis., 1963), 179–182; Hermann Hagedorn, *Leonard Wood*, I (New York, 1913), 303.

[68] Tinling, "Juvenile Self-governing Communities," 6.

[69] Mrs. Charles Edge to George, Sept. 29, 1909; Edwin C. Jones to George, July 5, 1917; Mrs. E. W. Thwing to George, June 17, 1912.

Republic in the winter of 1917. Against the background of the chaotic and tottering government of the new Chinese Republic, American, European, and Chinese residents of Peking drafted a constitution for the North China Junior Republic Association. Because the future of republican government in China was precarious, the Association planned to establish a self-governing industrial school where the principles of the George Junior Republic would be followed as literally as conditions permitted. The aims and problems of the China project were familiar enough. Founded to assist youthful citizens of the Chinese Republic in acquiring skills in self-government and to help relieve the terrible and hopeless poverty of Peking, the organizers of the North China Junior Republic found themselves without land, money, or men to run the school.[70] Except for sending his encouragement and a suggested reading list, George was unable to give any assistance to these endeavors.

Efforts to establish Junior Republic schools in India, South Africa, and northwest Rhodesia also failed. Colin A Mac-Pherson of the Imperial Indian Police and the Reverend L. S. Gates of Sholapur proposed Junior Republic methods for controlling India's "criminal tribes" and orphan children.[71] In Africa, proposed Junior Republics were to perform three separate functions: they were to bring the rudiments of civilization among the rawest specimens of humanity whose superstition, slavery, and heathenism hampered self-government; they would be used to instill a sense of self-reliance and independence among white children grown soft and lazy

[70] Ada Haven Mateer to George, Oct. 19, 1916, and Feb. 9, 1917; S. Moore Gordon to George, Feb. 19, 1917.

[71] Colin A. MacPherson to George, Sept. 19, 1917 (MacPherson was referred to George by Ben Lindsey and Winthrop D. Lane). L. S. Gates, "Self-governing Orphanage in India," undated MS.

from dependence upon black servants;[72] and they were suggested as the best means to control the most troublesome class of South Africans, the "Coloureds."[73]

From Capetown to Peking, from Manila to Havana, adherents of Junior Republic methods sought to bring order and cohesion to disrupted societies. With motives similar to George's, they attempted to establish a new sense of community among peoples whose identity had been seriously eroded by the acid of imperialism. George soon discovered that if ever he was willing to admit that partial self-government was better than no self-government at all, he could sanction the use of Junior Republic methods by almost any imperialist or authoritarian regime.[74]

European interest in the George Junior Republic was high, but communications between New York and the continental experiments in self-government were faulty, and in no important way did George influence continental developments. Once again, he was forced to decline invitations to address the International Congress for Common Education held in Leipzig in 1914, and the Third International Congress of Moral Education at Geneva in 1922, thus missing important opportunities to personally represent his views before an European audience.[75] *The Junior Republic* was reviewed in, and translated into, French, German, and Swedish,[76] however,

[72] Rev. John M. Springer to George, Sept. 25, 1911.

[73] W. Cumming George to William R. George, June 16, 1924.

[74] William R. George to Acting House Father, Government Industrial School, Standerton, Transvaal, South Africa, Dec. 22, 1909.

[75] Lyman Beecher Stowe to V. Hattingberg, July 26, 1914; Adolphe Ferrière to George, Jan. 27, 1922.

[76] The Swedish edition was translated by G. H. vonKoch, *Ungdomsrepubliken I Amerika* (Stockholm, 1912). The French edition apparently was published by the J. J. Rousseau Institute in Geneva in the *Collection d'Actualités Pedagogiques*. William Stern planned a full translation to follow his article, "Die Jugendrepublic,"

and comparisons were immediately and favorably drawn between the Freeville institution and the Munster School at Frankfurt am Main, the Eichwald School at Abo Akademi, Finland, and the Semestarungdomen in Västerås, Sweden, each of which had independently developed its own self-government plan.[77] But the link between the American and the continental versions of student self-government was so tenuous that the National Association of Junior Republics, announcing the foundation of the Little Commonwealth, merely noted the existence of the other schools.[78]

vi

On the other hand the Little Commonwealth, established in England in 1913, was perhaps the most successful foreign imitation of the George Junior Republic. At the purported urging of the Duchess of Marlborough, the former Consuelo Vanderbilt, the British Embassy sent Harold Beresford Hope, cousin of Lord Beresford, to study the Junior Republic in the fall of 1908.[79] Earlier, the Freeville institution was visited by George Montagu, the nephew and heir to the Earl of Sandwich, who returned to England determined to open an En-

---

Zeitschrift für angewandte psychologie und psychologische sammelsorschung (Leipzig), III (1910), 334–335. Other reviews appeared in: "Ecoles nouvelles en Amérique," *Education Nouvelle et Populaire*, April 7, 14, 21, 1921; Julia Gyllich, "Selvstyrende Børnerepublikker," *Maaneds-Magasinet*, IV (March 3, 1912), 185–191; Einer Gauffin, "George Junior Republic," in *Karaktarsdaning, Genom Social Fostran* (Stockholm, 1928); G. H. vonKoch, "George Junior Republic," *Social Tidskrift*, VIII (Aug. 1908), 341–355.

[77] Stowe to Herman Rost, Leipzig, Aug. 12, 1912; George to Alexis Eichwald, July 2, 1924; Alletta Korff, Helsinki, to Stowe, Nov. 18, 1912; Edgar Swenson to George, July 31, 1921.

[78] "The Growth of the Junior Republic Idea," *The Outlook*, CIV (July 5, 1913), 500.

[79] Ithaca *Daily News*, Sept. 29, 1908.

glish version of the self-governing community. With the endorsement of James Bryce, Ambassador to the United States and author of *The American Commonwealth*, Earl Grey, governor-general of Canada, and General Baden-Powell,[80] and the assistance of Lander McCormick Goodhart, the grandson of Cyrus McCormick, Montagu was finally able to enlist an impressive galaxy of British notables and peers in the venture. Backed by the Duchess of Marlborough, Earl Grey, Lady Evelyn Jones (Grey's daughter), Lady Elcho, and Lady Somerset (president of the British and World's Women's Christian Temperance Union), Montagu persuaded his uncle to donate, rent-free, a 190-head dairy farm in Dorsetshire to be used as the site of the Little Commonwealth.[81] Interest in Montagu's project was in no way confined to British nobility. Conservative Arthur Balfour, Liberal Arthur Biggs, and Laborite John Burns were attracted by Montagu's proposal, and Secretary Reginald M'Kenna of the Home Office promised to follow developments closely with the view of applying self-government principles to schools, reformatories, and prisons throughout the country.[82] Other prominent Englishmen served on the general committee of the Little Commonwealth.[83] The list of supporters was so long, Lyman Beecher Stowe reported to George, that it was sufficient to note that an organizational meeting held at the residence of

[80] James Bryce to George P. Day, March 25, 1911; Earl Grey to George, Feb. 24, 1910; Baden-Powell, "The Little Commonwealth," *Headquarters Gazette*, April 1914.

[81] George Montagu, "The Little Commonwealth," pamphlet (n.p., 1914); London *Observer*, July 7, 1913.

[82] Auburn *Citizen*, Oct. 23, 1911.

[83] London *Observer*, July 13, 1913. Important individuals were: Beresford Melville, chairman of the Montessori Society, Percy Machell, alderman of the London County Council, and Cecil Chapman, metropolitan police magistrate.

the Duchess of Marlborough and presided over by Earl Grey attracted over 700 of England's civic, philanthropic, and social leaders.[84]

It is not quite clear why the Junior Republic gained such popularity in England. To some extent, no doubt, it was a fad touched off by the Americans Consuelo Vanderbilt and Alberta Sturgis, the wife of George Montagu. Lander McCormick Goodhart's American connections also helped advertise the Junior Republic among English society. In addition, the high praise given the movement by Bryce and Baden-Powell, both of whom described the Junior Republic as one of America's most significant contributions to social reform, was re-enforced when Baden-Powell opened a self-governing scout camp in Sussex on his return from America.[85] The Junior Republic's emphasis on self-help and self-government allowed England's society matrons to embrace the scheme as "a broad-minded and liberal" solution to the problem of London's poor.[86] Rarely more frank or candid, George reminded Montagu that the mission of the Junior Republic was "to take the forms of government and customs as they exist and to adjust future citizens to meet those conditions." [87] English society, like American, did not have to fear radical or socialistic threats from the self-government movement.

Like its American counterpart, however, the Little Commonwealth also offered reform-minded Englishmen an excellent opportunity to test their social theories. Led by Beresford Melville, the English Montessori Society used the Little Commonwealth to determine whether Maria Montessori's

[84] Stowe to George, July 2, 1912.

[85] London *Observer*, Nov. 5, 1911.

[86] Baden-Powell, "The Little Commonwealth"; Bryce to George P. Day, March 25, 1911.

[87] George to Montagu, Jan. 9, 1911.

educational methods could be adapted for the instruction of older children. On the surface, it appeared to most observers that the basic principles of the Junior Republic and the Montessori Method were related. Neither rigidly separated children by age or sex, and both stressed freedom of choice, individual work, and personal responsibility. George and Montessori stressed "practical life exercises" which led to specific educational objectives. Ideally, they believed that the teacher "creatively" assisted the student to educate himself. Both the American and the Italian insisted that the best teacher taught the least. They were, of course, uncompromising critics of the rigid classical curriculum that typified the traditional English public school.[88] Thus, when, for whatever reason, English gentlemen contributed more than £15,000 to found the school and another £4,000 annually to run it, apparently no one was disturbed when a Montessori school was established at the Little Commonwealth with a teacher trained by Maria Montessori and supported by the Montessori Society of England.[89]

Perhaps the educational innovations introduced into the Little Commonwealth failed to cause alarm among aristocratic sponsors because from the outset the school was viewed primarily as an experiment in juvenile penology. The British press rarely described the Dorsetshire school as anything but a model correctional institution. Unlike their American counterparts, the English advocates of juvenile self-government publicly confessed that their general object was to provide a self-governing community for delinquent boys and girls who

[88] London *Times*, Jan. 6, 1914; Mrs. Reno Marguiles, "How to Teach Mothers the Montessori Method of Child Control," New York *Times*, Nov. 24, 1912; R. C. Orem, *Montessori for the Disadvantaged* (New York, 1967), 146.

[89] Montagu, "The Little Commonwealth"; "Junior Republics in England," *Journal of Criminal Law*, III (Sept. 1912), 470–472.

would otherwise be sent to a reformatory or to an industrial school. In further contrast to the Americans, the Englishmen showed no reluctance to refer to their school as an "institution," or to their students as "inmates." George Montagu, the prime mover of the Little Commonwealth, did not come to the Republic movement from a background of general social reform, as had George, Osborne, and Stowe. As a member of the Borstal Committee of the Prison Board of Aylesbury, Montagu was primarily interested in the penological applications of self-government, and it was only natural that his first choice for superintendent of the Little Commonwealth was Arthur St. John, the chief lobbyist of the Prison Reform Society.[90]

The emphasis on correction rather than education not only made the Little Commonwealth an interesting variant of the George Junior Republic, but it revealed basic weaknesses in the Junior Republic method which were ultimately to prove embarrassing to the parent Republic. In the tension between George and his English followers, there can be detected a harbinger of the traumatic "time of troubles" which almost destroyed the experiment at Freeville. George's guarantee that Junior Republic methods could be adapted to almost any society or culture gave Montagu confidence that his junior England need adopt "only those methods which harmonize with English life and English traditions." [91] Superficially, the Little Commonwealth borrowed intact the governmental and economic provisions of the Junior Republic. Learning by experience was the keynote of the English institution, and to

[90] London *Times*, Jan. 6, 1914; London *Observer*, Nov. 5, 1911; "Junior Republics in England," *Journal of Criminal Law*; Montagu to George, Sept. 1910; London *Observer*, July 7, 1913.

[91] "Junior Republics in England," *Journal of Criminal Law*; Montagu, "The Little Commonwealth."

the casual observer slight differences between the American and English institutions only reflected the differences in national culture and history.[92]

In fact, however, the deviation was fundamental and profound. The appointment of an American, Homer Lane, as superintendent in 1913 signaled a break with traditional Republic methods. While Lane was head of the Ford Republic near Detroit, he was invited to join the National Association of Junior Republics, but attempts to work out differences between the Ford Republic and the George Junior Republic failed. Heartily thanking Lyman Beecher Stowe for his invitation, Lane declared he could not affiliate with the NAJR as long as the prison and the court system were essential features of the Republic method. Like George, Lane believed that children could be saved by appealing to their natural impulses. But sitting in legal judgment of their peers and throwing each other in prison was unnatural, Lane believed, and only succeeded in corrupting and hardening the children's finer instincts of compassion and fair play. Shocked by the brutality of prison discipline, Lane contended that the Republic should offer an alternative to, not a duplication of, standard penal methods.[93] Once again, George described such impressions as "Utopian fallacy." If the world became a Utopia, George admitted, prisons and courts could be abolished, but until that time such reforms were dangerously sentimental and absolutely unsound.[94]

Homer Lane suspected that George and his helpers formed a hidden aristocracy which surreptitiously manipulated the inner workings of the Republic government.[95] Turning

[92] Howard Jones, *Reluctant Rebels* (New York, 1960), 18–19.
[93] Lane to Stowe, June 11, 1912.
[94] Stowe to Lane, June 14, 1912.
[95] Lane to Stowe, June 11, 1912.

George's own arguments against him, Lane reminded the NAJR that sham self-government was worse than no self-government at all. Realistically, Lane maintained, no adult leader could (or should) neutralize his influence over the young citizens. Probing to the heart of the Republic system, Lane charged that George was wrong in hiding from the community and himself the extent to which Republic superintendents played an active part in the success of their communities. The superintendent was not simply a negative factor acting as the bulwark against outside interference into Republic affairs by adult helpers and trustees. Lane explicitly recognized the active role that the adult must assume, and so emphasized what he called "shared responsibility" rather than self-government.[96]

For his model of the junior community Lane chose the family rather than the village. As a result, all of the adults, including the superintendent and administrators as well as the shop foremen and helpers, were integrated into the Little Commonwealth's society. Lane believed in systems even less than George, including "freedom systems."

"Give the child freedom" is the insistent cry of the New Education, but then its exponents usually devise a "system" which, although based upon the soundest of principles, limits that freedom and contradicts the principle. . . . The point is, freedom cannot be given. It is taken by the child. Freedom involves discovery and invention, neither of which by their very nature can be embodied in any system. Freedom demands the privilege of conscious wrongdoing, and above all things freedom cannot exist in the presence of authoritative punishments.[97]

[96] Jones, *Reluctant Rebels*, 21; E. T. Bazeley, *Homer Lane and the Little Commonwealth* (London, 1928), 13–18.

[97] *Talks to Parents and Teachers* (New York, 1949), 124–125.

Unlike the Junior Republic, therefore, the Little Commonwealth did not impose upon its citizens a system of government copied from the institutions of the adult world. The family model of the Little Commonwealth allowed the children to fashion, often painfully and slowly, social structures that satisfied their own needs. Led and advised by its adult members, each "family" was free to devise its own standards of behavior and discipline. As a result, only conflicts between members of different families were left to the jurisdiction of the entire community.

The family model not only allowed Lane to incorporate adult leaders into the community life and to achieve a greater flexibility in experimenting with various social structures, but it also enabled him easily to dispense with Junior Republic features he thought unhealthy. Since no family sent its own members to jail, Lane was able to abolish that institution, and at the same time reduce to a minimum the role of the court. Elimination of the jails removed from the Little Commonwealth the last vestiges of the authoritative reformatory system and helped Lane solve two additional problems: the socializing of the principle of self-support and the accommodation of girls with a correctional system.

The economic aim of the Little Commonwealth, like that of the Junior Republic, was self-support, but the family orientation of Lane's institution significantly altered the meaning of the principle. Under the village model of the Junior Republic, the cottages were boarding houses occupied by guests who paid room and board; a citizen's tenancy was terminated if he could no longer pay his rent, and if he could not even afford a bed in the "Garroot" he was sentenced to jail as a vagrant. In the Little Commonwealth, the cottages were occupied by "families," gathered from among those who cared for one another. No member of a family was tossed out merely because he lost his job or had fallen on hard times. No unfortunate citizen suffered an immediate loss in his standard of living due to personal misfortune. The principle "Nothing without Labor" was not lost, but it was the family, not the individual, which suffered the loss of earning power. "In this way," Howard Jones explains, "the economic sanction was preserved, but it was much less impersonal and hard—it was infused through and through with warm personal relationships and incentives." [98] By softening the consequences of dependency, Lane appealed to the sentiments of the tenderhearted. Love, not self-interest, was to be the motive power of the Little Commonwealth.

If friends of the Little Commonwealth were apprehensive of George's "work or starve" principle, they also recognized the danger of admitting girls into a correctional school. Although the Montessori educational system suggested that the Little Commonwealth was an academic as well as a reform school, fears of allowing boys and girls to live together in the same community persisted.[99] By abolishing the jail and adopting the family model, Lane hoped to minimize the problems involved in handling girl vagrants and prisoners. Lane agreed with George that a juvenile community without both sexes was unnatural, but he also believed that adolescents, and especially girls, living without families were even more unnatural and dangerous. Lane rationalized that young girls would be far less subject to corruption and sexual molestation in the families of the Little Commonwealth than in the slums of London. Quite often, of course, public concern was just the opposite—that bad girls would contaminate innocents of both sexes. Accordingly, Lane secured four girls convicted of shop-

[98] *Reluctant Rebels,* 20.
[99] Harold Large to George, June 21, 1912.

lifting for the nucleus of his first family at the Little Common-wealth. He reasoned that he could more easily bring boys into an established girls' community or family than the opposite. Determined that his girls would not sexually corrupt prospective citizens, Lane began the slow and careful process of building the Little Commonwealth.[100]

Homer Lane's Little Commonwealth was barely begun when it was mortally struck by two catastrophes. First, World War I robbed the struggling community of much of its vital force. As England's energies were mobilized, the dedicated philanthropists and strong, young boys upon whom the success of the venture rested were engulfed by the war. Unlike the George Junior Republic which had grown to over 200 citizens shortly after it was founded, by 1917 the Little Commonwealth counted but two families of eighteen members each, mostly girls.[101] In his original vision of the Commonwealth, Lane had planned for the gradual evolution of a village. As older boys and girls grew to maturity, Lane hoped that they would marry, build cottages within the community, and form the nuclei of fresh, young families. He apparently expected that the best of the citizens, once married and raising families of their own, would undergo a conversion similar to his. The "true graduation" of the citizens would come when they discovered that the highest purpose in life was to make the world a better place for all children, not just their own.[102]

The war ground away at Lane's hopes. The Common-wealth gradually became a community of very young boys

[100] Bazeley, *Homer Lane and the Little Commonwealth,* 29–36.
[101] At its height it contained five adults, forty-two citizens fourteen to nineteen years old, and nine younger children, living in three families (Lane, *Talks to Parents and Teachers,* 207).
[102] Bazeley, *Homer Lane and the Little Commonwealth,* 148–149.

and girls led by a handful of older adolescents who in many ways were childish young women. Stunted and distorted by the war, the Little Commonwealth became increasingly vulnerable to the second disaster—scandal. With all of the young men swept away by war, the older girls became increasingly restive. Only Lane remained as an object of their fantasies. Harassed and overburdened by the duties thrust upon them by the emergency, stifled and frustrated in finding normal outlets for their adolescent vigor, some of the more unscrupulous girls used accusations against Lane as a means of liberating themselves from the discipline of the Little Commonwealth. Not wanting to permanently damage the reputations of the offending girls, Lane did not move quickly enough to quash the incipient scandal. His caution seemed to lend credence to the girl's charges, forcing the Home Office to instigate an investigation of the matter. The inquiry, Lane's friends have claimed, was handled by J. F. Rawlinson, K.C., then Recorder of Cambridge, whose training did not enable him to understand or sympathize with the unconventional methods of the Little Commonwealth.[103] Although Rawlinson neither proved the charges nor exonerated Lane in his report, the Home Office threatened to withdraw their certification of the school if Lane remained as superintendent. Rather than lose Lane, the directors chose to close the Commonwealth without publishing an explanation for their action. Consequently, haunted by suspicion in official quarters, Homer Lane was forced from youth work. He died tragically in September 1925, shortly after a recurrence of the scandal led to his conviction and sentence of one month in jail on the technicality of being an unregistered alien. Though his sentence was quashed on appeal, Lane was deported. Broken

[103] Cf. Albert Liverpool, "Introduction" to Lane, *Talks to Parents and Teachers*, 18–19.

in body and spirit, he contracted typhoid and pneumonia in Nice, and later died in the American hospital in Paris.[104]

Despite its small size, its short life, and its calamitous end, the Little Commonwealth was not without influence on English educational and penal reform. George Montagu, the Earl of Sandwich by 1926, reflected with some pride that Lane and the Commonwealth had left their mark upon "educational and remedial" programs of the nation.[105] Indeed, among the numerous English educators influenced by Lane, the most controversial were the founders of the so-called freedom schools, J. H. Simpson, A. S. Neil, and W. David Wills. Each assumed that the child has only to be given his "freedom" to ensure that he will develop along healthy and normal lines. Their faith was based upon the perfectionist doctrine explicitly stated by Lane.

Human nature is innately good; the unconscious processes are in no way immoral. Faults are not corrected by, but brought about by suppression in childhood. If the child is allowed to express himself at different stages without restriction, he will himself eliminate the unethical, and, as altruism begins to unfold from the unconscious mind at adolescence, will develop the ethical being. For it is suppression of the primitive that makes the unethical persist in adult life. The freer a child is, the more it will be considerate and social, the more its chief interest will be progressive.[106]

Educational nihilism, some branded the doctrine. Progressive romanticism, others sneered. And, in truth, A. S. Neil's marvelously chaotic and anarchistic Summerhill School was but a natural projection of the child-centered educational philosophy first enunciated by Willard Hotchkiss, and later

[104] *Ibid.*, 24–25.
[105] The Earl of Sandwich to George, April 13, 1926.
[106] *Talks to Parents and Teachers*, 148.

developed by Gill, Welling, and Lane. The outlines of Dewey and Freud, of course, unmistakably loom in the background, but they are not as important as one might suppose. More relevant, I suggest, are the longer shadows of Bronson Alcott, Horace Mann, and the ante-bellum romantic perfectionists. Beginning with a reform impulse that was politically and socially conservative, driven by the need for social control, and led by such men as Lyman Beecher Stowe, the George Junior Republic began where the work of Charles Loring Brace had left off. In many ways child-centered education replaced the perfectionist's individualism. Each of the child-centered pedagogues assumed that the child was a "reservoir of possibilities" who only needed to be freed of the artificial restraints of an oppressive social order, and they shared with the romantic perfectionists a nostalgic proclivity for rural values. Rejecting politics for humanitarian and anti-institutional reforms, they struggled to establish ideal communities where poverty, suffering, crime, filth, and corruption would be banished. Both "Daddy" George and "Daddy" Lane would have agreed with John Humphrey Noyes that the common purpose of their endeavors was *"the enlargement of the home—the extension of family union beyond the little man-and-wife circle to large corporations."* [107] Reminiscent of the perfectionists at Oneida, Fruitlands, and Brook Farm, they founded anti-institutional institutions which throughout their history balanced precariously between anarchy and tyranny.[108] What had begun as a movement to adjust the child to "things as they are" was to culminate in a radical attack on the social order.

[107] John H. Noyes, *History of American Socialisms* (Philadelphia, 1870), 23.

[108] John L. Thomas' article, "Romantic Reform in America, 1815–1865," *American Quarterly*, XVII (Winter 1965), 656–681, suggested the outline for the above paragraph.

VI

A NEW PENOLOGY

———————— In 1910, the delegates to the International Prison Congress, by the simple miracle of the railroad, were able to study in orderly succession New York's three major contributions to American penology: the Auburn Prison, the Elmira Reformatory, and the George Junior Republic. The outing was an excursion through American penal history. In 1910, each of these institutions still reflected its original penal philosophy, enabling the delegates to make a firsthand comparison of prison function, organization, and discipline. At Auburn the lockstep and the striped uniform had disappeared, but the silent system of the Old Penology still prevailed.[1] Behind its Bastillelike walls Elmira appeared little different from Auburn, yet within the institution Zebulon Brockway, emphasizing individual treatment and vocational training, had eased the rigors of the Auburn system. The George Junior Republic, with its open spaces and self-government, completed the transition from the Old to the New Penology. To the foreign visitors, each of the institutions appeared to be archetypal of the penal philosophy it represented. The George Junior Republic, of

[1] Orlando F. Lewis, *The Development of American Prisons and Prison Customs, 1776–1845* (Albany [?], 1922), 88, cited in W. David Lewis, *From Newgate to Dannemora: The Rise of the Penitentiary in New York, 1796–1848* (Ithaca, N.Y., 1965), 276.

course, was regarded by nearly everyone as the most "Progressive" and interesting, if not the most desirable, of the three.[2]

At the same time, the Republic was an enigma to the foreign dignitaries and their American hosts. Auburn Prison, even with its new electric chair, was entirely familiar to them; and the Elmira Reformatory, though new to some, was easily comprehensible. But the visitors were unsure whether the youth Republic was a school or a correctional institution. Frederick Wines, for example, wrote that "self-government in penal institutions is merely an application of the educational principle that people learn by doing."[3] But Alexander Forbes, whose brother as governor-general of the Philippines introduced self-government into the Islands' penal system, requested Lyman Beecher Stowe not to emphasize the reformatory aspect of the Junior Republic to the detriment of the educational principle.[4] Furthermore, George, Osborne, and others kept insisting that the Junior Republic was not a penal institution. "The name 'institution,' in the ordinary meaning of the word, hardly applies," according to Osborne. "It is the belief of many who have looked most thoroughly into the workings of the Republic that its founder and superintendent, William R. George, is there developing *educational* methods of great importance in the manner of dealing with friendless and unfortunate children."[5] A decade later (and with typi-

[2] New York *Sun*, Sept. 20, 1910; J. Simon van der Aa, "An Excursion into Reformatory America," *Survey*, XXV (Nov. 5, 1910), 239; Paul U. Kellogg, "The International Prison Congress at Washington; A Layman Interprets It," *ibid.*, 211; William R. George to Albert Shaw, Oct. 18, 1910, and to Allen D. Peck, Sept. 22, 1910.

[3] Frederick Wines, *Punishment and Reformation: A Study of the Penitentiary* (rev. ed.; New York, 1919), 364.

[4] Forbes to Stowe, May 25, 1912.

[5] Thomas Mott Osborne, address before the National Conference

cally Progressive rhetoric), A. E. Winship, editor of the
Journal of Education, praised Riis, George, and Lindsey for
"rescuing rascals through the schools." [6] Frederick Almy,
Junior Republic trustee and secretary of the Charity Organization Society of Buffalo, turned the matter around when he
described the Republic as "a handsome school at which boys
and girls are fitted for college. The college idea is in the air
at this 'reformatory.' " [7]

The confusion between the school and the prison is obvious
and understandable. Responding to similar social needs, the
vocational school and the juvenile reformatory developed concurrently. Since both institutions sought to save and rehabilitate roughly the same class of children, it is not surprising that
they borrowed heavily from each other. Often the only difference between the student admitted to the industrial school
and the delinquent committed to the reformatory was that the
first had been sent by his guardian, while the second had been
sentenced by the juvenile court. In the annual reports of the
Conference of Charities and Corrections, and in institutions
such as the Berkshire Industrial Farm, the Children's Village
at Dobb's Ferry, and the George Junior Republic, even the
formal distinction between student and delinquent was
blurred.[8]

---

of Charities and Corrections, Washington, D.C., May 13, 1901, in
Proceedings, 1901, 23–25 (italics mine).

[6] A. E. Winship, "Rescuing Rascals through the Schools," *Journal
of Education,* LXXIX (Jan. 8, 1914), 31–32.

[7] Frederick Almy, "The George Junior Republic," in Hastings
Hart, ed., *Preventive Treatment of Neglected Children,* vol. IV of
Charles R. Henderson, ed., *Correction and Prevention* (New York,
1910), 42.

[8] For example, note the section on "Juvenile Reformatories and
Industrial Schools," National Conference of Charities and Corrections, *Proceedings,* 1901 (Washington, D.C.), 245–283; Charles D.

In addition, officials of the George Junior Republic actually encouraged the ambiguity. It was an open secret among juvenile court judges and social workers that the Junior Republic could not function properly if more than one-third of its citizens were sent to Freeville through suspended sentence or probation by the courts.[9] Bona fide juvenile self-government only worked when a majority of the citizens came from "dependable" classes. Children of Republic helpers made up an important segment of the stable youth community. Together with the students who enrolled on their own volition, they held most of the offices and positions of responsibility. Thus Republic officials, having no trouble whatsoever obtaining large numbers of delinquents, devoted their major recruiting efforts to enrolling "normal" students.[10] Yet despite their efforts to publicize the educational advantages of the Junior Republic, close observers increasingly identified the Republic as a correctional institution, a fact which the visit of the International Prison Congress only underscored.[11]

Thomas Mott Osborne was less reluctant than George to

Hilles, "What I Am Trying To Do [at the Children's Village]," *World's Work*, XXVII (April 1914), 642–649; Burnham Carter, *The Berkshire Industrial Farm* (Canaan, N.Y., n.d.) *passim*. In many instances, of course, the term "industrial school" was only a euphemism for reform school.

[9] George, *Junior Republic Principles and Bulletins* (Freeville, N.Y., 1941), 2.

[10] Rudolph Chamberlain, *There Is No Truce: A Life of Thomas Mott Osborne* (New York, 1935), 226–227; George, "The Delinquent Child and Education," MS, c. 1916–1918 (dated by Mrs. William R. George).

[11] George never relented on this issue, however, and in his last publication still insisted that some way must be found to dispel "the idea that the Junior Republic is a sort of reform school" (*Junior Republic Principles and Bulletins*, 2). He even refused to cooperate with Warner Brothers' Studio when they offered to film a movie on the Junior Republic, portraying it as a model reform school (George to Isador Witmark, Dec. 1, 1932).

admit the primacy of the penological function of the Junior Republic. If Osborne called the Republic a "laboratory experiment in democracy," he also regarded its self-government system as "the true foundation of prison reform." Fully convinced that self-government was the practical remedy for the evils of the prison system, Osborne paraphrased Gladstone when he wrote, "the prison must be an institution where every inmate must have the largest practicable amount of individual freedom, because 'it is liberty alone that fits men for liberty.' " [12]

Osborne's testimonial occasioned a second, more subtle, and potentially more divisive misunderstanding. When observers and friends looked at the model correctional school, exactly what did they see? There are two possibilities. First, they may have viewed the Junior Republic as a continuation of the revolt against the formalistic, classical Old Penology begun by the advocates of reformatory system in the 1870's. Repudiating the "dead-end" penology of the Auburn system, George and Osborne could easily be viewed as allies of Zebulon Brockway. With the prison walls, uniforms, and discipline stripped away, the George Junior Republic appeared to have liberalized and extended the work begun at Elmira. "Reformatory penology completed its cycle about 1910," Blake McKelvey noted. "For half a century it had run its course, an integral phase of American life. Developing within the old Auburn system the reformatory technique had slowly displaced the older traditions so that by the end of the era only the architectural shell of [the] system remained." [13] The George Junior Republic simply completed the task by shucking the vestigial husk of the

[12] Osborne, "The True Foundation of Prison Reform," paper delivered at the annual meeting of the National Prison Association, Albany, 1904; Osborne, *Society and Prisons* (New Haven, Conn., 1916), 153–154.

[13] Blake McKelvey, *American Prisons: A Study in American Social History Prior to 1915* (Chicago, 1936), 230.

Old Penology. How simple and logical it would be to place the Junior Republic along a reform continuum reaching from Auburn, through Elmira, to Freeville.[14] It is even possible that professional penologists who were sympathetic to the Junior Republic were defensive in their inclination to view the juvenile institution as the natural, almost inevitable, product of years of penological evolution, rather than as a radical and threatening assault upon the reformatory system itself.[15] Viewed as a fascinating and picturesque by-product of the growth of the reformatory system, the Junior Republic movement could be highly praised, but largely ignored.

Interpreted as a challenge to both the Auburn and reformatory systems, however, the Junior Republic commanded much more serious consideration. The second point of view removes the Junior Republic from the reformatory movement and asserts that George's creation was one of the forerunners of the New Penologist's anti-institutional attack on both the Auburn Prison and the Elmira Reformatory. If perceived in this fashion, Freeville represented the beginning of a new departure, and not the end of the line.

As early as 1880, the noted penologist E. C. Wines had warned that "a perverted nature can never be righted through a contravention of Nature's laws." Reflecting the educational theories of Pestalozzi and Froebel, Wines criticized the refor-

[14] Delavan Pierson, "The Little Republic at Freeville," *Missionary Review of the World,* XII (Nov. 1899), 801–809; Arthur J. Pillsbury, *Institutional Life* (Sacramento, Cal., 1906), 36–42; "Management of Prisons," Ithaca *Journal,* Jan. 7, 1915.

[15] Edwin P. Wentworth, "Origin and Development of the Juvenile Reformatory," National Conference of Charities and Corrections, *Proceedings,* 1901 (Washington, D.C.), 245–255; C. D. Hilles, "Expansion as Applied to Reformatories for Juvenile Delinquents," *ibid.,* 269–276; John L. Gillin, *Criminology and Penology* (New York, 1926), 581–617; Louis N. Robinson, *Penology in the United States* (Philadelphia, 1923), 120–152.

matory for not recognizing that "a man who has fallen away from virtue can never be restored to it against his will." [16] Later, Hastings Hart, chairman of the Russell Sage Foundation, declared that the juvenile reformatory was not designed as a permanent institution in which to raise children: "However good an institution may be, however kindly its spirit, however genial its atmosphere, homelike its cottages, however fatherly and motherly its officers, it is now generally agreed among those who are familiar with the needs of children of this class, that institutional life is at best artificial and unnatural." [17] Thomas Mott Osborne joined the disaffection with the reformatory. Granting to reformatory advocates the best of intentions, he wrote:

No system for the punishment of criminals which leaves wholly out of consideration that the beings who are to be punished are human will ever be successful; and this is precisely where the reformatory system has come to grief. You cannot treat men in terms of machinery or logs of wood; nor can you appeal to them with success if you force them against their will—not even if your aim is their highest intellectual or physical development. [18]

In his own simple way George summed up the Progressive indictment against the Old Penology and the reformatory system. "I care not how elaborate an institution may be," he reminded his followers, "or how beautiful its buildings, how perfect its sanitary arrangements, or how well officered, how well clothed its inmates may be, how well they perform their military drill, how beautiful their trade work may be done,

[16] E. C. Wines, *The State of Prisons and Child-Saving Institutions in the Civilized World* (Cambridge, Mass., 1880), 616.

[17] Hastings H. Hart, "The Juvenile Reformatory of the Twentieth Century," National Conference of Charities and Corrections, *Proceedings*, 1905 (Portland, Ore.), 101–118.

[18] Osborne, *Society and Prisons*, 115–116.

it amounts to nothing if its charges have not gained self-respect, self-reliance, responsibility and habits of industry." [19] Whether objecting to the reformatory system as applied to children or to adults, the New Penologists looked to the George Junior Republic as a model of the anti-institutional institution.

The question of whether the George Junior Republic marked the beginning or the conclusion of a reform movement now seems simply answered. As an alternative to the institutionalization of delinquents, the George Junior Republic was a bold step in the direction of the New Penology. The objective of the New Penology was not simply to create more humane and efficient penal institutions; rejecting severe and rigidly uniform discipline and totally abandoning mass regimentation, the Junior Republic represented one of the Progressives' first attempts to create a flexible, individualized, and scientific treatment center whose major function was not simply to punish or rehabilitate the delinquent, but to protect and nourish the child as well. The New Penology concerned itself as much with prevention as it did with correction. "Crime in the last analysis is not to be overcome after arrest, but before," wrote Edward T. Devine. The stronghold of crime is social misery. Thus all agencies for social betterment and reform—schools, churches, playgrounds, settlements, trade unions, charitable societies, and Junior Republics— were handmaidens of the New Penology. Only when reform agencies transformed the society itself, Devine believed, would it be possible to permanently reform the prison and the prisoner.[20]

[19] George, "The Care and Treatment of Delinquent Children," undated MS.

[20] Edward T. Devine, *The Spirit of Social Work* (New York, 1912), 125.

It could still be argued, however, that the founding of the
George Junior Republic did not represent a significant departure in penal history. Just as the New Penology is separated from the Old Penology by the transitional period of
the reformatory, so the George Junior Republic is separated
from the Elmira Reformatory by the Berkshire Industrial
Farm. Founded in 1886 by Burnham Carter, the Berkshire
Industrial Farm reproduced the juvenile reformatory on a
less institutionalized scale. Military in his discipline, Carter
nevertheless hoped that delinquents placed upon a large farm
would develop mind and body, becoming "industrious, honest, worthy citizens." [21] Before George had founded his first
Fresh Air camp, the Berkshire Industrial Farm was well on
its way to success.

How, then, does the George Junior Republic relate to the
history of penal reform that went before it? The answer is
double-edged and to understand it we will have to consider
briefly the histories of the Old and the New Penology.

i

In 1914, Thomas Mott Osborne recalled:

Many years back, in my early boyhood, I was taken through
Auburn Prison. It has always been the main object of interest in
our town, and I was a small-size unit in a party of sightseers. No
incident of childhood made a more vivid impression upon me.
The dark, scowling faces bent over their tasks; the hideous striped
clothing, which carried with it an unexplainable sense of shame;
the ugly close-cropped heads and shaven faces; the horrible
sinuous lines of outcast humanity crawling along in the dreadful
lockstep; the whole thing aroused such terror in my imagination
that I never recovered from the painful impression.[22]

[21] Carter, *The Berkshire Industrial Farm*, 12.
[22] Osborne, *Within Prison Walls* (New York, 1914), 1.

Years later, Osborne would be surprised to discover that the fortress-like institution known as the penitentiary had not been conceived by vengeful sadists, but by gentle, humane Quakers and rational, enlightened reformers. Indeed, it must be noted that in 1890 the "Old Penology" was not particularly old. Sometime after the American Revolution, a small group of Pennsylvania and New York humanitarians became distressed over the sad plight of convicted criminals who languished in the unspeakable squalor of colonial jails or who had suffered mutilation or beatings in punishment for their crimes. Disciples of the great English prison reformer John Howard, and led by such ardent reformers as Thomas Eddy, the founder of Newgate Prison, and Louis Dwight, the major advocate of the Auburn system, American penologists created the world's first penitentiary systems between 1790 and 1833.[23]

Harsh as their prison discipline now seems, the ante-bellum reformers did not consider imprisonment an end in itself. Five major considerations entered into the maintenance of their severe prison regime: punishment, retribution, deterrence, incapacitation, and reformation. To accomplish these ends, they founded the Pennsylvania and Auburn systems of prison discipline.[24]

Penal reform in ante-bellum America was dominated by the struggle between the two prison systems. The chief par-

[23] W. David Lewis, *From Newgate to Dannemora*, 1–110. Lewis' book is the best on the subject.

[24] A detailed comparison of the Pennsylvania and Auburn systems can also be found in Harry Elmer Barnes and Negley K. Teeters, *New Horizon in Criminology* (rev. ed.; Englewood Clifts, N.J., 1959), 337–346; and Edwin H. Sutherland and Donald R. Cressy, *Principles of Criminology* (7th ed.; Philadalphia and New York, 1966), 507–510.

ticipants in the controversy were the Boston Prison Discipline Society, led by the Reverend Louis Dwight who supported the Auburn system, and the Philadelphia Society for Alleviating the Miseries of Public Prisons, spokesmen for the Pennsylvania system. Both societies were religiously devoted to the reformation of criminals, and both were convinced of the absolute perfection of their own methods of prison discipline. Dwight leveled three serious charges against Pennsylvania's Eastern State Penitentiary. First, solitary confinement as practiced at Eastern State was far too expensive in construction and operation; the congregate system of Auburn was more economical for the taxpayer. Second, the Philadelphia prison did not make full use of its labor force, as the prisoners were confined to their cells. Auburn, on the other hand, with its "congregate but silent" system was able to exploit all the advantages of the new power machinery. Third, at Eastern State strict solitary confinement did not produce reform, but led to insanity and mental derangement. The Pennsylvanians easily parried the third charge, claiming there was as much evidence of insanity at Auburn as at Eastern State. The Philadelphia Society was not able to overcome Dwight's economic arguments, however, and by 1833 the Auburn system had been generally adopted throughout the country. Still, the New Yorkers were embarrassed by countercharges that the Auburn system was not only horribly cruel, but was in fact "a repudiation of the tenets of the new dispensation of imprisonment in the treatment of crime." [25] Such prisons were often administered by men more interested in protecting the public than in reforming the criminal, and many wardens placed greater emphasis on balancing the books and thwarting escapes than on preventing the moral contamination of

[25] Barnes and Teeters, *New Horizons in Criminology*, 344.

their prisoners. In time, most Auburn-style prisons became little more than congregate jails—the very institutions they were designed to replace.[26]

In the meantime, as the controversy between the two penal philosophies raged in the 1840's, Captain Alexander Maconochie (1787–1860) was developing a third system of penal discipline. Warden of the Norfolk Island Penal Colony off the coast of Australia, Maconochie determined to prepare his prisoners for release rather than to exact repentance from them. Believing that a convict should neither be returned to society until he was rehabilitated nor be kept in prison after he was reformed, Maconochie introduced the indeterminate sentence, the "mark system," and parole. The mark system was not unlike George's "Nothing without Labor" scheme. Each prisoner earned a certain number of "marks" which he used to secure his food, clothing, and ultimate release. Although Maconochie suffered repudiation and dismissal by his superiors, the endemic fate of reform wardens, his methods were imported to Ireland and England, and in 1863 they were introduced into the United States as the "Irish system" by Gaylord Hubbell, an enlightened warden of Sing Sing Prison.[27]

In 1870, the Reverend Enoch Cobb Wines invited prominent prison administrators and reformers to attend a National Prison Congress in Cincinnati. Zebulon Brockway, who was to become the first superintendent of the Elmira Reformatory in 1876, addressed the delegates: "The central aim of a true prison system is the protection of society against crime, not

[26] Zebulon Brockway, *Fifty Years of Prison Service* (New York, 1912), 49–50.

[27] John V. Barry, "Captain Alexander Maconochie," *Victorian Historical Magazine*, XXVII (June 1957). Barry, "Pioneers in Criminology, XII: Alexander Maconochie (1787–1860)" *Journal of Criminal Law and Criminology*, XLVII (July–August, 1956), 145–161.

the punishment of the criminal. Punishment, the instrument, protection, the object; and since it is clear that there can be no real protection against crime without preventing it, *prevention* must be placed fundamentally in the principles of a true prison system." [28] The convention subsequently adopted its famous Declaration of Principles which endorsed the Irish system, and called for the establishment of the indeterminate sentence, the mark system, parole, vocational education, productive labor, and religious instruction, all intended to reform the criminal and prevent recidivists.[29]

Disheartened by the Auburn system, New York State legislators authorized the construction of a secure prison in which the new techniques of the Irish or reformatory system could be tried. At Elmira, military organization replaced the lockstep, plain denim was substituted for stripes, and a library, newspaper, and entertainment supplanted the silent system. Athletics, a gymnasium and bath, hobbyshops, and intellectual education were introduced.[30]

At the turn of the century, the prospects for the new reformatory were bright. It had the support of a well-established professional society, and was being hailed in scholarly journals and popular magazines. More than a dozen institutions had adopted its methods for dealing with young criminals and first offenders, and states throughout the North and

[28] Zebulon Brockway, "The Ideal of a True Prison System," paper given before the National Prison Congress, Cincinnati, 1870, as printed in *Fifty Years of Prison Service*, 389.

[29] For a listing of the principles adopted by the National Prison Congress in 1870, see American Correctional Association, *Proceedings*, 1956, xiii–xix; or Corinne Bacon, *Prison Reform* (New York, 1917).

[30] Brockway, "The American Reformatory Prison System," in Charles R. Henderson, ed., *Prison Reform and Criminal Law*, Vol. I of Henderson, ed., *Correction and Prevention* (New York, 1910).

West passed indeterminate-sentence and parole laws. Courts had stilled all doubts concerning the constitutionality of the new penal laws, and as a result, the probation laws were extended to include all criminals. Eventually, the major provisions of the reformatory system began to be adopted by the state prisons themselves. Massachusetts, Colorado, Indiana, and Illinois were among the first states to liberalize their penal systems with reformatory techniques. Gradually the Auburn system disintegrated as the principles, and techniques of the reformatories reshaped the older prison system.[31]

For many attending the International Prison Congress of 1910 the victory of the reformatory system was bittersweet. Auburn still stood as a symbol of the old ways, but the eventual victory of the reformatory program had been assured. In attacking the older prison discipline, however, the reformatory system had assimilated many of its most unsavory aspects. The reformatory movement had almost no impact on prison architecture or administration. The fortresslike style continued to dominate prison and reformatory construction, thus physically limiting penal experiments. More seriously, reformatory superintendents and administrators were infected with what Barnes and Teeters called the "jailing psychosis" of the Old Penology. The reformatory system failed to fulfill its ultimate goals, they argued, because it was never given a chance to succeed.

The most important explanation for the failure of the reformatory is that it was blocked at the outset by the ever-present jailing psychosis with the frenzied preoccupation of counting and double-checking inmates. No rehabilitative program, however excellent in theory, can ever be a success, so long as safe and secure custody is regarded as the prime purpose of institutional activity, and administrators are judged to be efficient or incom-

[31] McKelvey, *American Prisons,* 206–230.

petent almost wholly by their success in preventing escapes. The public seems willing to accept a high price for such success: brutal and repressive programs, not to say complete failure to rehabilitate inmates.[32]

Given the structure and administration of American prisons, it was perhaps inevitable that the enlightened principles of 1870 proved disappointing. Little, after all, was changed within the shell of the old prisons. All the abnormalities of prison life continued; the contamination of prisoners, feuding among inmates, sexual perversion, sadism on the part of keepers, and others. Even Brockway ultimately reverted to corporal punishment. Indeed, it has been reported that fifty years after Elmira was founded convicts were pleading with judges to send them to Auburn rather than to Elmira, where the discipline was reputed to be excessively severe.[33]

The reformatory system failed for reasons that parallel the failure of the Auburn system. Once the system was universally adopted, the overexpanded reformatories were further taxed by growing populations that overburdened their facilities. The indeterminate sentence, the "mark system," and parole were intended to individualize the treatment of each prisoner. Instead the results were quite the reverse.[34]

ii

The George Junior Republic was first understood, even by Osborne, as an extension of the reformatory principle. Organized on a military basis like that of the Elmira Reformatory, the early Republic did not hesitate to condemn its criminals to the jail, dress them in stripes, work them ten hours a day on the rock pile, and confine them behind bars at

[32] Barnes and Teeters, *New Horizons in Criminology*, 428.
[33] Sutherland and Cressy, *Principles of Criminology*, 510.
[34] See, for example, McKelvey, *American Prisons*, 232.

night.[35] A point-by-point comparison of Brockway's thirteen principles of reformatory management with the actual operation of the Junior Republic reveals significant deviation at only two points: the architecture of the prison and the clothing of the inmates.[36] Even the application of additional principles such as self-government at the Junior Republic did not entirely liberate the Freeville institution from the reformatory tradition. Brockway claimed to have introduced "a system of almost complete self-government" when he was superintendent of the Detroit House of Correction in the 1860's.[37] Other penologists and reformers noted that Junior Republic principles could be more easily adapted for use in the juvenile reformatories than in the public schools.[38] Delighted at the segregation of youthful offenders from hardened criminals, Homer Folks thought the Junior Republic was a promising extension of the principle of inmate classification. "The experiment is of great value in demonstrating the extent to which such methods can be introduced in institutions," he wrote. "While not distinctly a reformatory institution, the children are mostly of a class who otherwise could be committed for correctional treatment." [39]

When Junior Republic officers and advocates modestly proclaimed that their method was merely a new application of old ideas, their contemporaries dismissed what appeared to be

[35] John R. Commons, "The Junior Republic, II," *American Journal of Sociology*, III (Jan. 1898), 437.

[36] Brockway, "The American Reformatory Prison System," in *Fifty Years of Prison Service*, 419–423.

[37] Brockway, *Fifty Years of Prison Service*, 96.

[38] Theodore F. Chapin, "Boy Government in a Reform School," National Conference of Charities and Corrections, *Proceedings*, 1901, 41–45.

[39] Homer Folks, in Herbert Baxter Adams, ed., *The Care of Destitute, Neglected and Delinquent Children*, Monographs on American Social Economics, XXI (New York, 1900), 107–108.

conventional humility.[40] What the National Association of Junior Republics should have stressed was not simply that the Junior Republic enjoyed historical precedents, but that Junior Republic principles, although independently discovered, were developed within the context of a long and continuous anti-institutional assault on the American penitentiary system. The conflicts between the Pennsylvania, Auburn, and reformatory systems have obscured the fact that there has existed throughout our history still another uniquely American alternative to the treatment and reformation of criminals and delinquents.

The anti-institutional approach obviously has been handicapped in its struggle against the dominant methods of prison discipline. Generally lacking the official support of prison discipline societies, anti-institutional techniques were most successfully employed in the care and training of nondelinquents —we have seen that the educational features of the George Junior Republic were easily confused with its penological functions—and anti-institutionalists rarely concentrated their efforts on the criminal classes, but instead achieved some of their most startling successes among the deaf and blind, the insane and idiots, the orphans and paupers.[41] Because they dealt with children rather than adults, and because they often appeared as educators rather than penologists, the ante-bellum forerunners of the New Penology have been largely over-

[40] William R. George and Lyman Beecher Stowe, "A New Old Idea," in *Citizens Made and Remade* (New York, 1912), 59–64; Osborne, "A Letter from Thomas Mott Osborne," *The Delinquent*, Feb. 1918, 22.

[41] Robert H. Claridge, "The Rise and Fall of the Reformatory: The Anatomy of a Reform Tradition, 1790–1930" (senior honors' thesis, Williams College, 1968). I owe a considerable debt of gratitude to Robert Claridge whose work has greatly influenced my own thinking.

looked, and historians of ante-bellum prison reform, have neglected two important anti-institutional leaders, E. M. P. Wells, superintendent of the Boston House of Reformation from 1826, and Joseph Curtis, founder of the New York House of Refuge in 1824.[42]

The importance of the anti-institutional critique of classical penology becomes more evident when it is remembered that, in 1827, one in six inmates at the Auburn Prison was under twenty-one. Only the most primitive classification of prisoners was attempted by the Old Penology; the separation of males from females, of children from adults, of vagrants and insane from felons, and of blacks from whites. Lesser offenders were housed in county jails and workhouses, or in state houses of correction. At best, ante-bellum prison segregation was crude, and often incomplete. In 1827, agents of the Boston Prison Discipline Society were horrified to find twelve-year-old children languishing in the Walnut Street Jail.[43] The first impulse of the anti-institutionalists of the ante-bellum era was to protect children from the harshness of the classical prison regime.[44]

The anti-institutional approach to the problem of reforming delinquents, in both the ante-bellum and Progressive eras,

[42] Robert S. Pickett's *House of Refuge: Origins of Juvenile Reform in New York State, 1815–1857* (Syracuse, N.Y., 1969) is the first complete study of the refuge movement. Pickett only generally relates the refuge movement with developments in education and adult penology, however.

[43] "Report of the Boston Prison Discipline Society" (Boston, 1827), 18, as quoted in Orlando F. Lewis, *Development of American Prisons and Prison Customs*, 293. In the states of Maine and New Hampshire, one in five prisoners was under twenty-one. The ratio was one in seven in Vermont and in Richmond, Virginia.

[44] Gustave de Beaumont and Alexis de Tocqueville, *On the Penitentiary System in the United States and Its Application in France*, trans. Francis Lieber (Philadelphia, 1833).

was rooted in a similar estimate of the nature of children; "child-saving" was possible because the child's personality was believed to be malleable. Strongly influenced by romantic perfectionism, ante-bellum advocates of more humane treatment for children accepted Bronson Alcott's dictum that "children were more susceptible to good than people imagined." [45] The philosophy of E. M. P. Wells summed up the perfectionist's attitude toward the young criminal:

Most people imagine, when they see or hear of bad boys, that they are a worse kind of boys, worse by nature than others. If my observations be of any value on this subject, it is not so, for though at first there be strong sproutings of evil principle and passion to be lopped off, we often find him as good a stock and as rich a soil as in other cases. . . . However bad a boy may be, he can always be reformed while he is under fifteen years old, and very often after that age; and he who has been reckoned and treated as if incapable of anything like honesty and honor, may be worth the most entire confidence. . . . We live happily together (in the House of Reformation) as a family of brethren, cheerful, happy, confiding, and, I trust, to a greater or less degree pious.[46]

As we have noted before, the Progressives also believed that children had natural instincts which could be directed toward good or evil. Juvenile instincts were "handles" the reformer could grasp in order to steer the child in the direction of social behavior. If ante-bellum reformers believed children possessed equal propensities for good and evil—the good to be nurtured and the evil suppressed—the Progressives defined children's instincts as amoral—variously turned to good or

[45] John L. Thomas, "Romantic Reform in America," *American Quarterly*, XVII (Winter 1965), 664.

[46] Quoted in Orlando F. Lewis, "Inmate Self-government a Century Ago," *The Delinquent*, VIII (Jan. 1918), 10.

evil behavior. Most importantly, both the Progressives and the ante-bellum perfectionists rejected the theory that any child was naturally or irreclaimably bad. In the Progressive Era, William R. George echoed E. M. P. Wells' sentiments almost exactly. Claiming that "every boy was like every other," George wrote: "Boys of all classes and conditions of society the world over have the same general characteristics. The benevolent person who assumes that all normal boys are good makes as great a mistake as the vindictive person who assumes that they are all bad. They are neither the one nor the other. The term 'angelic savages' aptly describes them." [47]

Among adult criminals, Tocqueville noted, corruption was inveterate and deeply rooted. But in a youth the finer sentiments still existed. Even the infamous Elam Lynds confessed to Tocqueville and Beaumont that youthful offenders might be completely reformed. The Frenchmen concluded that a system which corrected evil dispositions, inculcated correct habits of thrift, industry and self-respect, and taught elementary education and religious principles, would solve the problem of juvenile reformation. Only girls of bad morals, who were generally considered unreformable, would have to be excluded from the scheme. It remained for the George Junior Republic to include even the female "unredeemables." [48]

George's anti-institutionalism was complex, but not confusing or anarchistic. He accepted and promoted some institutions without question, such as capitalism and democracy. Yet his own experiment covertly undermined others, such as the church and family, and self-consciously rejected impor-

[47] *Citizens Made and Remade*, 139.

[48] *On the Penitentiary System in the United States*, 163–164, 150–151. For an excellent discussion of the care and treatment of the female criminal, see W. David Lewis, *From Newgate to Dannemora*, 157–177. For a discussion of girls at the Junior Republic, see below, 299–301.

tant sexual conventions. More important, George was firmly opposed to the "institutionalization" of children in either the school or the reformatory. The quintessence of the anti-institutional approach, however, was not the absence of a regular "school" or even a formal "institution." The George Junior Republic, for example, had definite boundaries, a board of trustees, a distinct administration, and a formalized citizen government. Rather, anti-institutionalism advocated the abandonment of inflexible and uniform regimes of prison discipline in favor of individualized programs of rehabilitation. Typical prison discipline regulated, or attempted to regulate, every detail of the prisoner's daily life by means of severe punishment for the slightest infraction of the rules. Not a minute of the convict's day escaped the scrutiny of his keeper. Often he lost his name, always he lost his autonomy. Anti-institutional features not only freed the prisoner from the tyrannical discipline of the Old Penology, but they assumed that the felons and delinquents would play an active role in their own reformation. Anti-institutional "institutions," then, typically incorporated some measure of "inmate participation."

The George Junior Republic methods were anticipated in the United States as early as 1824. In that year, the Society for the Prevention of Pauperism, which subsequently became the Society for the Reformation of Juvenile Delinquents, founded the House of Refuge in New York City.[49] Distressed at the conditions in Newgate Prison, fifteen prominent citizens met in the winter of 1815–1816 at the home of Joseph

[49] Probably the first attempt at partial self-government can be traced to Walnut Street Jail in the 1790's. Robert J. Turnbull described the "system" in his pamphlet, "A visit to the Philadelphia Prison; Being an accurate and particular account of the wise and humane administration adopted in every part of the building" (Philadelphia, 1796); noted in Negley K. Teeters, *The Cradle of the Penitentiary* (Philadelphia, 1955), 46, 95.

Curtis to discuss the causes of crime and pauperism. In the group were Thomas Eddy, the leading spirit in the founding of Newgate, and John Griscom, educator and philanthropist, whose tour of England in 1818–1819 had included conversations with the noted English penal reformer Elizabeth Fry and a visit to a juvenile reformatory.[50] Upon his return from England, Griscom was made chairman of a committee to establish an independent juvenile reformatory. Curtis was chosen to be the first superintendent of the House of Refuge, as the new institution was called.

Griscom's committee determined that the House of Refuge would accept both sexes, housing them in separate buildings, and two classes of inmates: children who had been convicted of a crime, and children who had committed no crime but who were so destitute or neglected as to be judged potential delinquents. Anticipating the Elmira Reformatory, the sentences were to be indeterminate, while the institutional discipline was to remain well regulated and inflexible.[51]

The administration of the first superintendent, Joseph Curtis, proved a surprise to the Society for the Reformation of Juvenile Delinquents. Taking full advantage of his institution's rural setting (the House of Refuge occupied four acres at the crossroads of the Bloomingdale Road and the Old Post Road, where Madison Square is now located), Curtis introduced a discipline based upon the family. Children who had been good throughout the entire week received cake and coffee on Sunday morning. Any boy who finished his work by noon on Saturday could go swimming and have liberty for the afternoon. Especially well-behaved children were allowed

[50] W. David Lewis, *From Newgate to Dannemora*, 160–161; Orlando F. Lewis, *Development of American Prisons and Prison Customs*, 294–296; Pickett, *House of Refuge*, 21–49.
[51] Orlando F. Lewis, *ibid.*, 298–299.

to visit their friends in the city, and runaways who returned voluntarily were forgiven. During recreation hours, Curtis played ball games and marbles with the children, made kites with them, and generally ran and romped with his charges. In the evenings, they read narratives aloud, or would gather for group singing and storytelling.

Discipline was not lax, however. Curtis insisted upon absolute silence at dinner and enforced discipline through the curtailment of recreational privileges, enforcement of solitary confinement, reduction of food to bread and water, and, in flagrant cases, infliction of corporal punishment (stripes).[52] But his discipline was not arbitrary. Introducing a modified form of self-government, Curtis sat as judge upon cases in which the boys tried each other by jury. Only at the recommendation of the boys themselves did he reluctantly administer corporal punishment.[53]

How far Curtis would have developed his system is unknown. After he had been superintendent slightly over a year, he was dismissed by the board of management. When Curtis refused to whip a runaway who returned voluntarily, the managers demanded that a definite system of rules and regulations be established and administered. Curtis objected that the House of Refuge could not be managed as a "factory." "Many things may be done that to a casual observer may seem inadmissible, but still, rightly managed, are productive of good." Orlando F. Lewis noted that family life and the rule of love replaced institutionalism as the major factor in Curtis' management.[54]

[52] Beaumont and Tocqueville, *On the Penitentiary System in the United States,* 145.

[53] Orlando F. Lewis, "Inmate Self-government a Century Ago," 12–13.

[54] Lewis, *Development of American Prisons and Prison Customs,* 301; "Inmate Self-government a Century Ago," 14. See also B. K.

A second juvenile institution, even more strikingly similar to the George Junior Republic, was founded in Boston in 1826. In contrast to the privately operated House of Refuge in New York, the House of Reformation was opened by the City of Boston on more than thirty acres of land in South Boston donated by the State of Massachusetts. Nominally under the direction of the Common Council, in fact the management of the institution was entirely given over to E. M. P. Wells, a young Episcopal priest who served as superintendent from 1828 to 1832.

According to Beaumont and Tocqueville, Wells established "a small society, upon the model of society at large." [55] Wells completely abolished corporal punishment and the practice of placing the children in solitary confinement at night, as they were in the Houses of Refuge in New York and Philadelphia in 1828. Anticipating Pestalozzi and Montessori, Wells adopted a Lancasterian method of mutual instruction, and introduced drastic curricular innovations which devoted five and a half hours of each day to labor and vocational training, four hours to academic instruction, and two and a quarter hours to recreation. Like Joseph Curtis before him and William R. George after him, Wells played with the children. The Frenchmen were not surprised at the success of the unusual school. Believing that the class of children committed to the House of Reformation were more resourceful than most, they wrote: "It is therefore not surprising that they should make rapid progress in their learning. Most of them have, moreover, a restless, adventurous mind, anxious for knowledge. This disposition, which first led them to ruin,

---

Pierce, *A Half Century with Juvenile Delinquents, or the New York House of Refuge and Its Times* (New York, 1869); Pickett, *House of Refuge,* 67–85.

[55] *On the Penitentiary System in the United States,* 142.

becomes now, in the school, a powerful cause of success." [56]
Wells, too, found the elusive secret of the anti-institutional
method: fit the institution to the needs, personality, and instincts of the child so that the institution might fit the child
for the demands of the larger society.

Beaumont and Tocqueville were astonished, however, by
Wells' methods of prison discipline. Allowing the children to
dress and conduct themselves at will, the young superintendent treated his boys and girls "as if they were men and
members of a free society." [57] The children were divided into
two grades, "bon" and "mal"—the members of the "bon"
grade participating by vote in the administration of the school.
No child was subjected to rules outside the moral law, the
law of the land, or the administrative regulations of the institution, and no child was required to inform on another.
The inmates were allowed to decide what punishments they
would face and voted to abandon the ferule, preferring an
honor system enforced by themselves. A book of conduct
was kept in which each child recorded his own merits and
demerits at the end of the day. The children, the Frenchmen
observed, were prone to judge themselves more harshly than
others would judge them. There was also a court, similar to
the one at the New York House of Refuge, conducted by
Wells as judge and "twelve little citizens" who composed the
jury. The jury and other offices selected by the children were
elected by the "bon" class, and "nothing is more grave," the
visitors reported, "than the manner in which these electors
and jurymen of tender years discharge their functions." [58]

Beaumont and Tocqueville were ambivalent toward the

[56] *Ibid.*, 143.   [57] *Ibid.*, 145.
[58] *Ibid.*, 147. It should be remembered that the presence of outsiders, rather than upsetting the institution's routines, usually ac-
centuates its formal behavioral patterns.

Boston House of Reformation. They conceded that in a democratic country the early exercise of liberty and self-government was undoubtedly beneficial. Young delinquents taught to obey their own rules later might become law-abiding adults. But they did not consider the House of Reformation "an infant republic in good earnest." They observed no system they could grasp, no set of rules or routine they could transcribe. They preferred, after all, a more uniform system based upon a less elevated and complex theory which was not dependent upon the personality of the superintendent. They found the New York and Philadelphia Houses of Refuge less noble, but more systematic, and undoubtedly better suited to the needs of France.[59]

The interest which the distinguished foreign visitors paid the House of Reformation stimulated the concern of the Boston Common Council. Paying the institution an official visit in 1832, the councilors were shocked at what they found. According to their investigation, the scholastic instruction was inadequate, the industries produced insufficient income, and there was generally lacking a settled plan of institutional discipline and order. In repudiating Wells, they declared that the purpose of the House of Reformation "was not *recreation* and *show* but 'convertible practical utility.' "[60] Shortly thereafter Wells resigned as superintendent.

The work of Joseph Curtis and E. M. P. Wells was of greater significance than was realized at the time. Although similar methods were being employed by Bronson Alcott and Samuel Gridley Howe, only Francis Lieber recognized the potential of using anti-institutional methods in the treatment

[59] *Ibid.*, 154; Alice Felt Tyler, *Freedom's Ferment* (Minneapolis, 1944), 287–290.

[60] Orlando F. Lewis, "Inmate Self-government a Century Ago," 12.

A New Penology   249

of delinquents.[61] Both Curtis and Wells were willing to subordinate system to personality as a method of education. Each stressed the development of character rather than fixed routine or curriculum. Although both men hoped to strengthen the individuality of the child and bring out his powers of self-expression, Wells was especially concerned that each child find himself through a maximum of play, a wide range of schooling, a variety of experience, and an absence of mandatory industrial training.[62] The ante-bellum era, however, demanded efficiency and uniformity in the prison routine. Boards of managers wanted something measurable, something regular and easy to understand. Beaumont and Tocqueville perceptively and prophetically defined the objection to Curtis and Wells. "It is not a *profession* which they perform," the Frenchmen wrote, "it is a duty they are happy to fulfill." [63]

iii

It is difficult to demonstrate continuity between the experiments of Curtis and Wells and the application of anti-institutional techniques at the George Junior Republic. Almost by its nature, anti-institutionalism is ahistorical. Evidence that links together Curtis, Wells, and George is largely circumstantial. W. David Lewis has argued that there was a bridge between the reform ferment of the ante-bellum era and the New Penology of the Progressive Era, but the relationship is ill-defined and vague. Orlando F. Lewis and Frederick Wines definitely linked William R. George and Thomas Mott Os-

[61] Translator's note in Beaumont and Tocqueville, *On the Penitentiary System in the United States*, 120–121.
[62] Orlando F. Lewis, "Inmate self-government a Century Ago," 13; Pickett, *House of Refuge*, 67–102.
[63] Beaumont and Tocqueville, *On the Penitentiary System in the United States*, 149 (italics mine).

borne to the earlier reformers (Wines described Osborne as "one of Mr. Wells' recent followers"). There is no doubt that George, Osborne, and the National Association of Junior Republics were aware of the unsuccessful experiments that preceded them, but there is no direct evidence that they studied closely the work of Curtis or Wells.[64] Perhaps the National Association of Junior Republics had difficulties enough of its own without associating itself with the unfortunate experiments of others. As we shall see, certain features of the Junior Republic seem to have been suggested by earlier models, but the "official" histories of the Republic hardly mention, and never stress, antecedents.

In the less sensitive area of education, the National Association officials were more willing to legitimize their own efforts by recognizing guiding precedents.[65] Tracing its historical roots back to Catherine Beecher's Hartford School and Bronson Alcott's Temple School, the National Association of Junior Republics placed itself in the anti-institutional, antiformalistic tradition of the romantic perfectionists to which Joseph Curtis and E. M. P. Wells most certainly belonged. Thus, when it is remembered that Beaumont and Tocqueville could not decide whether the House of Reformation was a prison or a school,[66] the relationship between the Junior Republic and House of Reformation, and the historical con-

[64] W. David Lewis, *From Newgate to Dannemora*, 285; Orlando F. Lewis, *Development of American Prisons and Prison Customs*, 309; Frederick Wines, *Punishment and Reformation*, 380. Osborne mentions the New York House of Refuge in his book *Society and Prisons*, 111–112.

[65] Richard Welling, "Pupil Self-government as a Training for Citizenship," National Education Association pamphlet (San Francisco, 1921); Jacob G. Smith, " 'Daddy' George," introduction to William R. George, *The Adult Minor* (New York, 1937), xvii.

[66] Beaumont and Tocqueville, *On the Penitentiary System in the United States*, 139.

tinuity of the anti-institutional penology becomes evident.

That Junior Republic officials failed to recognize their historical heritage is no mystery. In 1901, *World's Work* described the New York House of Refuge, by that time located on Randall's Island, as the very antithesis of the Junior Republic. Although some faint outlines of Curtis' work were still evident, the House of Refuge served as a perfect "institutional" foil against which to compare the Freeville Republic.[67] On the other hand, the Elmira Reformatory, the Junior Republic's *bête noire*, had not been entirely unaffected by anti-institutionalism, a fact which has led most historians and penologists to list Brockway among the New Penologists. Brockway rejected the classical penology which attempted to meet the severity of crime with equally severe punishment, and he earnestly sought greater flexibility and leniency in the administration of prison discipline. The indeterminate sentence, a necessary prerequisite to all anti-institutional schemes, had been successfully tested in the houses of refuge and was appropriated by Brockway as the central feature of the reformatory scheme. In company with the anti-institutionalists, Brockway had hoped to individualize convict treatment through the use of the indeterminate sentence. The failures of Elmira Reformatory have already been noted, but even the reformatory system at its best would have been scorned by the members of the National Association of Junior Republics. Professing to see little relationship between themselves and Brockway, George and Stowe noted that the indeterminate sentence, when applied within the institutional setting of the reformatory, tended to "institutionalize" Brockway's inmates. "Under an indeterminate sentence," they wrote, the convicts at Elmira "behave themselves in an ex-

[67] R. E. Phillips, "The Art of Saving Children," *World's Work*, II (Oct. 1901), 1296–1306.

emplary manner according to the negative standards of prison virtue." [68] At the George Junior Republic, on the other hand, it was asserted that even a long period of residency did not lower individuality, check initiative, or "institutionalize" the child.[69] Granting that prisoners were materially better off under the Elmira system than they had been under the Auburn system, Osborne saw no parallel between the use of the indeterminate sentence in Elmira and Freeville. Elmira sought immediate results through training. The difference, Osborne believed, was that the reformatory produced good prisoners, while the Junior Republic prepared good citizens.[70]

iv

Most Progressives were unconcerned about the theoretical origins of the Junior Republic's anti-institutional methods. Lillian Wald at the Nurse's Settlement was simply thankful that she had a place to send a runaway boy without having him committed to Elmira.[71] Settlement house workers and juvenile court judges were among the most active supporters of self-government for juvenile delinquents. Julian W. Mack, the prominent Chicago Juvenile Court judge who assisted in the founding of the Western Pennsylvania George Junior Republic, helped lead the fight against the reformatory system.[72] Instead of making decent citizens out of delinquents, Mack charged, the state

[68] George and Stowe, *Citizens Made and Remade*, 233.

[69] David F. Lincoln, "The George Junior Republic," *The Coming Age*, Jan. 1900, 42–43.

[70] Osborne, *Society and Prisons*, 212.

[71] Lillian Wald to George, Feb. 20, 1911.

[72] George, *The Junior Republic*, 242; George, Diary, May 30, 1910. On Julian Mack, the juvenile court, and midwestern Progressivism, see H. H. Lou, *Juvenile Courts in the United States* (Chapel Hill, N.C., 1927), 113; and M. R. Werner, *Julius Rosenwald* (New York, 1939), 90–91.

permitted them to become the outlaws and outcasts of society; it criminalized them by the very methods that it used in dealing with them. It did not aim to find out what the accused's history was, what his heredity, his environments, his associations; it did not ask how he had come to do the particular act which brought him before the court; it put but one question, "Has he committed the crime?" It did not inquire, "What is the best thing to do for this lad?" [73]

For Julian Mack, Lillian Wald, and others the answer was clear; send them to the George Junior Republic. Rose C. Barran, agent for George Montagu, noted the difference between the ordinary reformatory with its forbidding walls and the Junior Republic through which a stranger might pass without recognizing anything out of the ordinary. The children at the Junior Republic led happy, varied lives, full of interest, challenge, and responsibility. "Compare this," she wrote, "with the life of repression in a penitentiary, where day after day there is the same dull, monotonous existence, the strict rules, the many hours of silence, in which minds must lie dormant or full of the thoughts of their former evil lives, which as they have nothing else to talk about, they discuss with their companions, contaminating others more innocent than themselves." [74]

Once again, anti-institutional methods for treating juvenile delinquents were being called for, and this time from abroad as well as from home. From the National Conference of Charities and Corrections, the Penal Reform League in England, and Professor William Stern of Breslau University came en-

[73] Julian W. Mack, "The Juvenile Court," American Bar Association Reprint (n.p., 1909), 5, 14–15.

[74] Rose C. Barran, "The George Junior Republic," *Nineteenth Century*, LXVI (Sept. 1909), 503–508. Comparisons between the Junior Republic and the Reformatory are multiple. In addition to those in sources already mentioned, see Los Angeles *Herald*, Feb. 5, 1907; Plainfield (N.J.) *Currier News*, Oct. 16, 1908.

dorsement of the principle that "the best way to care for delinquent youth is to place them in an environment that is as normal as possible." [75] Indeed, an observer from the *Pall Mall Gazette* was enraptured on visiting the open village where discipline was hazy and ill-defined and young delinquents were not kept under any physical control. How amazed he was to find a man whom everybody called "Daddy" governing a reformatory settlement.[76]

How did the anti-institutional institution function? Mindful of the criticism encountered by Curtis and Wells, and still smarting from the investigation of the State Board of Charities in 1897, Frederick Almy warned that the answer was not found by analyzing the surface merits and faults of the Republic. That was precisely what was wrong with the institutional approach; it concerned itself too much with cleanliness, order, and discipline, which covered a multitude of latent sins. Almy understood that public opinion demanded surface correctness in public institutions, but he feared the public paid a high price for their "jailing psychosis." In a real Junior Republic, on the other hand, one would inevitably encounter indolence, disorder, confusion, dirt, and even violence. When the germ of pauperism or vice could not be killed, Almy noted with a medical metaphor, it was best to let the social disease "run its course in a mild form in order to prevent future attacks." It was absolutely necessary, he

[75] Elizabeth Putnam, "Dependent and Delinquent Children in this Country and Abroad," National Conference of Charities and Corrections, *Proceedings*, 1890 (Baltimore, Md.), 192. "Review of Citizens Made and Remade," *The Record*, published by the Penal Reform League (Jan. 1913), British Museum, London, England. William Stern, "Die Jugendrepublik," *Zeitshrift für angewandte psychologie und psychologische sammelsorschung* (Leipzig), III (1910), 334–345.

[76] *Pall Mall Gazette*, June 12, 1912.

argued, "to let a boy be idle and lazy for a time, and suffer all the consequences of hunger and cold; to let him be violent, and as a penalty be duly and severely punished by his peers; in fact, to give him a brief rehearsal of life under natural conditions which will be very profitable when life arrives in grim earnest." [77]

It was obvious to critics and friends alike that the success of anti-institutional methods at the Junior Republic was largely dependent upon the charismatic personality of William R. George. The Junior Republic, like the Boston House of Reformation and the New York House of Refuge, found cohesion through the dynamic leadership of its founder rather than through institutional regulations. Love is a force which the ordinary reformatory cannot sufficiently employ. Yet in the tradition of Wells and Curtis, "Daddy" George treated the children as if they were his own. He shocked prison authorities by hugging and kissing the inmates. The children, in turn, were free "to take hold of him at any time, catch as catch can, to stroke his chin, and ruffle his hair with the fond familiarity of the wife of his bosom." [78] Not content simply to referee or umpire, George joined the roughhousing and ball games. Rollicking fun and comradeship, which were always high on George's scale of values, played a central role in his reform program. From the children's point of view, the most serious consequences of being jailed were banishment from "Daddy's" presence and disqualification from the athletic teams. Penitent prisoners often listened longingly to the happy singing around the campfire, or to the boisterous cheering of an athletic rally. Perhaps unique

[77] Almy, address, in the Second New York Conference of Charities, *Proceedings*, 1901; Almy, "The George Junior Republic," in Hart, ed., *Preventive Treatment of Neglected Children*, 48.

[78] Pillsbury, *Institutional Life*, 36–42.

among correctional institutions, the George Junior Republic had its own yells, songs, and alumni association.[79]

Members of the National Association of Junior Republics recognized, however, that their principles had to rest on a foundation other than "Daddy" George. As long as anti-institutional principles depended solely on the personality of the superintendent, there was little chance that Junior Republic methods could find wide applicability. Although such prominent figures as Theodore Roosevelt and Andrew Dickson White suspected that the Junior Republic was a "one-man affair," none of the National Association workers, including George, accepted that verdict.[80] Republic theoreticians Osborne, Stowe, and George, cleverly argued that the success of their anti-institutional methods was rooted in the nature of convicts and delinquents themselves. Not ironically, the perfect Junior Republic superintendent was an "anti-superintendent." At best his function was negative; that is, keeping

[79] John Commons thought the "Republic Yell" significantly condensed the Republic's spirit of manliness and mutual responsibility.
"Ssz! Boom! Hear Ye This!!
Down with the boss; down with the tramp;
Down with the pauper; down with the scamp.
Up with the freeman; up with the wise;
Up with the thrifty; on to the prize.
Who are we? Why—We—are—the CITIZENS of the G.J.R.
We love our land and we would die
To keep Old Glory in the sky" (Commons, "The Junior Republic, II," 443).
Founder's Day, originally an annual alumni day held on July 10, is still celebrated (Jack M. Holl, "Founder's Day Address," Sept. 4, 1965). For the spirit of love and fellowship at the Junior Republic, see also Almy, "The George Junior Republic," 46; Wilbur F. Crafts, "A Day at the Boys' Republic," *Christian Endeavor World*, XII (Feb. 17, 1898), 415–416.

[80] Theodore Roosevelt, "The Junior Republic," *The Outlook*, C (Jan. 20, 1912), 119; Andrew Dickson White to Joseph H. Choate, Jan. 21, 1914, Andrew Dickson White Papers, Cornell University.

adult helpers, boards of trustees, and others from meddling unnecessarily in the affairs of the institution.[81]

In theory, the "delinquent-centered" correctional institution, like the child-centered school, was permissive only in the sense that the children's natural instincts and needs, and not an administrator's discipline and curriculum, determined the daily routine. George Junior Republic methods were universally applicable because the character and nature of juvenile delinquents was everywhere the same. In other words, Republic advocates asserted, self-government methods were learned through an understanding of the child.

The techniques and assumptions used to reform the delinquent were predictably similar to those used to Americanize the immigrant and educate the student. Basically, George, Stowe, and Osborne believed that human nature was everywhere, universally and uniformly, the same. "Boys are boys the world over," Osborne advised, rejecting the notion of inherent criminality in children. A child who has broken the law is not a criminal, George added, but rather an individual whose instincts of daring, leadership, initiative, and adventure have not been channeled into socially constructive paths.[82] How familiar and simple was the Junior Republic's solution to crime.

Take the boy off the streets; place him in an environment of fresh air; free space and healthy surroundings; try to instill in him the great moral lesson taught by the wonders and beauties of nature, and you are more apt to develop manly resource and moral courage in the street arab than the restricting influence and

[81] George, "The Junior Republic Superintendent," *Junior Republic Principles and Bulletins* (Freeville, N.Y., 1941), 17–19.
[82] Osborne, "The Way to Train a Boy," Buffalo *Express*, Feb. 10, 1902; George, "The George Junior Republic," *Fellowship*, Feb. 1909, 30–31; Osborne, Address before the National Conference of Charities and Corrections, Washington, D.C., May 13, 1901.

arbitrary discipline of the conventional reform schools of our states.[83]

If only given the chance, Osborne argued, all children would demonstrate their natural tendency to throw off the evil effects of a bad environment and heritage.[84]

One by one, Osborne refuted the current theories of criminality. Is there a physical criminal type? Phrenologists had thought there was, and the Italian physician Cesare Lombroso advanced a theory that criminal types often carried the physical traits of primitive ancestors. The criminal type, Lombroso postulated, could be recognized by discernible stigmata, certain facial, physical, and even moral birthmarks that he bore. Lombroso's studies had given hope to some who wanted to establish a new science—criminology. But Osborne, relying on the researches of Dr. Charles Goring, contemptuously dismissed Lombrosian theory, noting, with some levity, that Oxford graduates were physically more similar to English criminals than they were to Cambridge graduates.[85]

Is there a moral criminal type? Osborne admitted that this question was not open to scientific investigation, but from his own experience he concluded that there was no more reason for belief in a mental or moral criminal type than Goring had found for belief in a physical type. "When we talk about 'confirmed criminals' and a 'criminal type' and a 'crim-

[83] Osborne, "The Way to Train a Boy."

[84] Osborne to Mrs. L. F. Deland, April 11, 1900, Letterbook, Osborne Papers, Syracuse University. For a supporting argument from John R. Commons, see *Races and Immigrants in America* (New York, 1907), 170–171.

[85] Osborne, *Society and Prisons*, 23–26; Cesare Lombroso, *L'Uomo Delinquente* (Rome, 1884); Charles Goring, *The English Convict* (London, 1913).

inal class,'" he wrote, "we are trying to lay upon God the blame which belongs upon ourselves." Even mental defectives, Osborne maintained, did not possess inherently criminal traits. There was, however, a "prison type," which Osborne thought was often confused with a criminal. But the prison type—men who shuffled out of the prisons year after year, broken in health and spirit, white-faced with "prison pallor," with shifty, restless eyes and "the timidity of gods" —these creatures were the finished product of the prison system. Osborn rejected the whole notion that the propensity to commit crime was inherited, either physically or mentally. Heredity provided the amoral instincts which could be turned toward good or evil. In youth, the child's nature is almost infinitely pliable and susceptible to the influences of environment, he believed.[86]

Is crime a disease? The disease theory of crime, Osborne thought, was the most malevolent explanation of criminality, for it contained a certain superficial plausibility. Osborne admitted that the disease theory was valid to a certain extent, but only as a metaphor. The criminal's illness was neither physical nor mental; it was spiritual. The criminal was socially ill, he argued, "ill of selfishness—of a peculiar form of civic egotism, which causes him to be indifferent to the social rights of other men." In other words, Osborne distinguished between disease which is physical, dementia which is mental, and crime which is spiritual. A lawbreaker might be afflicted in two or three ways, he conceded, but that did not alter fundamental differences: "A man may commit a crime because he is insane; nevertheless the two things spring from different causes; and to call criminality a disease of which

[86] Osborne, *Society and Prisons*, 27, 28; "The Way to Train a Boy."

crime is a symptom is to juggle with words—to fall into just the kind of verbal fallacy we have been trying to avoid." [87]

Osborne was not unmindful of his own semantic juggling. What he really objected to was any theory of crime that denied the criminal's responsibility for his own acts. Once the convict was released from the personal responsibility for his crime, once society determined that the prisoner's defects were inherent, Osborne feared that all attempts to reform the man might be abandoned. Yet he recognized his theoretical dilemma. "How, then shall we reconcile the fact that we are to hold a man responsible for his act," he asked, "and yet not responsible for the motives which led him to commit it?" [88]

William R. George and Lyman Beecher Stowe attempted to solve Osborne's dilemma. In *Citizens Made and Remade* they proposed a theory of crime designed to undergird the penological methods they had already developed. All human behavior, they wrote, can be divided into four categories. Each category, in turn, was controlled by one of two motives, "principle" or "policy." Simply stated, humans (1) did right for sake of principle, (2) did right for the sake of policy, (3) did wrong for the sake of policy, and (4) did wrong for the sake of principle. But the categories were only logical constructs, the Republic theoreticians confessed, since few humans behaved on the basis of disinterested principle, and hardly anyone committed evil for evil's sake. Most human behavior, for good or evil, was based upon a calculation of individual self-interest, they believed. The criminal type, the person who did evil for the sake of principle, might exist, George and Stowe continued, but his numbers were so insignificant that penology directed at him was bound to fail. Extending Osborne's arguments, they denied the existence of a "criminal type," for all intents and purposes, and maintained

[87] Osborne, *Society and Prisons*, 32.   [88] *Ibid.*

that the world's lawbreakers had broken the law for selfish reasons—and had been caught.[89]

Once Junior Republic officials had rejected all forms of determinism, the possibilities for reformation became vast. If crime were the result of natural motives turned in antisocial directions, the perception, if not the task, of reformation was simple. As we have seen, the Junior Republic was organized so that the maintenance of "law and order" was in every citizen's self-interest. Yet even in the idyllic physical and psychological environment of the George Junior Republic there was a "class of children" who simply could not stay out of trouble and jail. Superficially, at least, they seemed to be incorrigibles, individuals who were in no way motivated by self-interest. This class, small in the Junior Republic but large in the reformatories, provided the greatest challenge to Junior Republic methods.

George, Osborne, and Stowe did not view delinquents and convicts with naïve sentimentality and optimism. They knew the vicious nature of crime, and recognized that many individuals who were incarcerated in the penitentiaries ought to be permanently placed in maximum-security mental hospitals. Their task was not to reform the "defective delinquent," but to save the vast majority of delinquents whose physical and mental faculties were perfectly sound. Nor was their analysis of the problem especially simplistic. "A man's actions are the resultant of many forces," Osborne stated. "His heredity, his environment, his training, all react upon that mysterious something—the man's own individuality." [90] At first, it had been enough merely to indict the prisons for crushing "individuality" and thus destroying the convicts' personality and hope for reform. But when the Junior Republic failed to re-

[89] George and Stowe, *Citizens Made and Remade*, 220–222.
[90] Osborne, *Society and Prisons*, 34.

form all delinquents by encouraging their "individuality," it became evident that there was need to distinguish the Republic's failures from those of the reformatory.

Republic officials made little or no distinction among "individuality," "personality," and "character." Each was measured by the strength of the individual "will." After years of study, George concluded that both heredity and environment played important roles in shaping strong character, but neither factor was as important as will. Stated most bluntly, George declared that "the volitions of such an individual are stronger than his inherited tendencies." [91] The strong-willed individual may rise above, fall below, or simply follow his inherited tendencies. Obviously the Junior Republic believed it had the greatest success with the strong-willed. They were the individuals who, after perceiving their self-interest, could pursue it within the Junior Republic scheme. Failures were found among those who, although perceiving their self-interest, lacked sufficient will power to pursue it. Among the weak-willed, heredity and environment often were determining factors in shaping character. "Will power is, in short, the controlling factor in the development of the individual—the common denominator between the two forces of heredity and environment." [92] The strong-willed could transcend his heredity and environment, the weak-willed could not.

The argument veered perilously close to the very determinism that Junior Republic theoreticians wanted to avoid. But they were not led to the conclusion that the weak-willed delinquent was unreformable. The strength of will was neither inherited nor innate. George made the crucial assumption that all physically and mentally normal persons possessed equal potentiality for developing strong wills. He carefully distinguished between genius and will. Genius belonged to a

[91] *Citizens Made and Remade,* 154.   [92] *Ibid.,* 161.

few who sometimes gained remarkable fame on the basis of their talents. But in the weak-willed, genius often consumed the whole personality, becoming a self-destroying passion. In addition, genius, unless developed, atrophied, often never to be regained. On the other hand, George believed that will could be developed by anyone. Thus will was a faculty or an "ever present potentiality" that was developed in the same manner by which one built up his physical powers—through exercise.[93]

The George Junior Republic, its adherents thought, was ideally designed for the exercise of will power. The economic and self-government features of the juvenile community forced its citizens to make willful decisions. The weak of will who could not develop "stick-to-itiveness" usually wound up in jail, but they were not allowed simply to languish there. After learning a short but pointed lesson regarding the wages of sloth, they were readmitted to the Republic community without stigma.[94] Jail terms, although usually short and efficacious, also reflected the tenacity of the Old Penology. Clearly a major function of the jail was to provide an occasion for introspection and repentance, to be re-enforced on the child's release by the loving encouragement of "Daddy" George.[95]

[93] *Ibid.*, 160–161; William J. Koerner, "The Junior Republic—Best Model of Prison Reform," *The World*, Aug. 7, 1910.

[94] Mary T. Eagger, "A Visit to the George Junior Republic," *Landmark*, VII (July 1925), 423–426.

[95] It should be noted that the most common crime was smoking. Punishments and jail terms for crimes such as theft, assault, vandalism, and truancy committed in the Junior Republic were estimated to be about one-tenth of what the child would receive for similar crimes at the hands of New York State.

The National Association of Junior Republics claimed an outstanding record of success. They counted only children who had stayed at the Junior Republics for at least three months, however.

William R. George's understanding of the function of will in criminal reform was not unusual. Wells and Curtis before him had based their experiments on the assumption that only children who were allowed to exercise their "free will" could be reformed.[96] Later, E. C. Wines reflected that "a system of prison discipline to be truly reformatory must gain the will of the convict. . . . No system can hope to succeed which does not secure this harmony of will, so that the prisoner shall choose for himself what his officer chooses for him." [97] But George and his colleagues were unique among prison reformers when they argued that no physically or mentally normal person could be classified as "incorrigible." Almost all penologists, even Elam Lynds, agreed that little children could be reformed. Fewer held out consistent hope for youths between ten and sixteen. Only the most optimistic believed that all adolescents might still be reformed. And none, except the officials of the George Junior Republic, held out universal hope for adults. Encouraged especially by Osborne on this point, no one was ever rejected as incorrigible by the Junior Republic.[98]

Republic officers legitimately claimed that they could not be held responsible for the recidivism of children who simply passed through their institutions. On the other hand, if a child survived the Junior Republic regime for three months, the probability that he would "succeed," i.e., stay out of further trouble, was high. In 1914 Freeville claimed 87 per cent success with reforming delinquents; the National Junior Republic claimed 94 per cent; the Western Pennsylvania Junior Republic claimed 88 per cent; the Carter Junior Republic claimed 87 per cent; and the Litchfield Junior Republic claimed 85 per cent (Lyman Beecher Stowe to William R. Hereford, July 21, 1914).

[96] Orlando F. Lewis, "Inmate Self-government a Century Ago," 10.
[97] E. C. Wines, *The State of Prisons and Child Saving Institutions*, 50.
[98] *Literary Digest*, March 30, 1901; *Harper's Weekly*, Jan. 12, 1901; New York *Evening Post*, Dec. 31, 1913; Abigail Powers, "The George Junior Republic," *The Puritan*, IX (Feb. 1901), 737–756.

The emphasis on will and the tenacious insistence that no individual was incorrigible reflected the depth of George's and Osborne's religious, romantic perfectionism, and the extent of their rejection of all scientific determinism. Taking a cue from E. A. Ross's *Sin and Society*, they suggested that there were no criminals, just "criminaloids." Ross's radical literature of liberation complemented their anti-institutional penology, for Ross, too, had stressed the importance of discipline, mastery, and control of the environment by the will. The concept of the "criminaloid" was ideally suited for Junior Republic theoreticians. According to Ross, the criminaloid was the "quasi-criminal" whose pursuit of self-interest was not guided by an evil impulse, but by moral insensibility.[99]

Yet not even the most selfish convict pursued evil all the time, George and Osborne argued, and even the saintly individual occasionally committed antisocial acts. The difference between the convict and the citizen was not an absolute difference between good and evil, but a relative difference in social and antisocial behavior. The history of the Junior Republic had demonstrated that anti-institutional penological methods became educational methods when applied to better classes of citizens. Encouraged by Ross's observation that Republic theory cut across a number of sociological generalizations,[100] George concluded that Junior Republic methods, which worked so successfully in the reformation of young delinquents, might be applied with equal success inside the walls of the penitentiary itself.

At first Osborne thought George's proposal was preposterous, but on subsequent reflection he became convinced that

[99] E. A. Ross, *Sin and Society* (New York, 1907), 43–71, esp. 50; George and Stowe, *Citizens Made and Remade*, 222; Ross, *Social Control* (New York, 1901); Christopher Lasch, *The New Radicalism in America* (New York, 1965), 171.
[100] Ross to George, Dec. 19, 1911; Ross to Stowe, March 24, 1913.

George's scheme had exciting possibilities. Osborne noted, for example, that upon release from institutional restraints, all boys, even Junior Republic graduates, tended "to go to pieces." But more encouraging, he observed that a large percentage of boys who had been in a reformatory became recidivists, while most of the Junior Republic alumni were able to "pull themselves together." The difference, of course, was that the Junior Republic had prepared its citizens to cope with the frustrations of the adult world, and the reformatory had not.[101]

In 1904 Osborne launched his anti-institutional attack on the citadels of the Old Penology. Addressing the National Prison Association at its annual meeting in Albany, Osborne outlined "the true foundation of prison reform." Predictably, he condemned the old prison system which made men industrious by driving them to work; which made them virtuous by removing all temptation; which made them law abiding by forcing them to submit to an autocratic regime; which gave them initiative by removing all choice; and which prepared them for re-entry into the society by subjecting them to a dystopian environment. Outside the prison walls, Osborne reminded his listeners, a prisoner once again had to choose between work and idleness, and between honesty and crime. The convict's presence in prison indicated that he had failed to make successful choices in the past. Even if the prisoner became sincerely repentant, Osborne asked, was there any reason to not believe that he would slip back into his old habits upon release? [102]

[101] Osborne to George, April 22, 1901, Letterbook, Osborne Papers, Syracuse University.

[102] Osborne, "The True Foundation of Prison Reform," address to the National Prison Association, Albany, 1904; *Society and Prisons*, 153–154.

The answer was self-evident. Unless prisoners were allowed to freely exercise their wills in meaningful choice while in prison, no permanent reformation would be hoped for. Although Osborn became convinced that self-government was the practical remedy for the shortcomings of the old prison system, in 1904 the details of the plan eluded him. Preoccupied by the management of the George Junior Republic, Osborne temporarily forgot his scheme for the reformation of New York State's penal system.[103]

v

Others saw the same possibility for prison reform that Osborne observed. In 1904, across the Pacific Ocean in the Philippine Islands, W. Cameron Forbes (past trustee of the George Junior Republic, later governor-general of the Philippines) became Secretary of Commerce and Police. Confronted with the need to relieve the horribly crowded conditions at Bilibid, the great prison in Manila, Forbes established an experimental penal colony on the island of Palawan. Situated on 22,000 acres, later expanded to over 100,000, the Ilwahig Penal Colony was populated with 1,200 long-term prisoners, most of whom had been convicted of such crimes as murder, rape, arson, and highway robbery. The idea of the colony had been derived from Forbes' experience with the George Junior Republic. Forbes accepted George's and Osborne's belief that even "hardened" criminals, once given responsibility and hope, could be reformed.[104]

[103] Osborne, *Society and Prisons*, 159; Rudolph Chamberlain, *There Is No Truce*, 236–237.

[104] W. Cameron Forbes, *The Philippine Islands* (New York, 1928), 228–231; Lyman Beecher Stowe, "A Prison That Makes Men Free," *World's Work*, XXVII (April 1914), 626–628. Charles B. Elliott, *The Philippines* (Indianapolis, Ind., 1917), 199, 390–392.

Accordingly, in 1906, with the encouragement of Samuel J. Barrows, President of the International Prison Commission, Forbes ordered that the Ilwahig Penal Colony adopt the self-government and self-support principles of the George Junior Republic. The colony was fortunate in the selection of Colonel John R. White of the Philippines Constabulary as superintendent. No one suspected that White could put the plan into literal operation. Arriving at his new post on Palawan, Colonel White found most of the prisoners too ill to offer resistance to the new regime. Purging the colony of the worst trouble-makers by sending them back to Bilibid, White succeeded in building a self-governing penal colony which quickly became a show-case that astonished even its most ardent supporters.[105]

White graphically demonstrated that if properly treated and gradually given increased responsibilities and liberty most of the convicts sent to Ilwahig could be transformed into good citizens. He vigorously opposed stationing paid guards in the colony or expressing distrust of the prisoners in any other way. All firearms were banned in the colony with the exception of White's shotgun which he used for bird hunting. Prisoners, on the other hand, were allowed to carry bolos, axes, and other implements used in their work. They were free to escape through the jungle or in boats readily available to them, but few did so, knowing that survival was unlikely and that recapture meant return to Bilibid. The only other protection given White and his five assistants was a telephone connection to the nearby army post at Puerto Princesa.

The colonists at Ilwahig were divided into grades. The

[105] Forbes, *Philippine Islands,* 229, 284; John R. White, *Bullets and Bolos* (New York, 1928), 314-337. White candidly admitted that the possibility of being sent back to Bilibid was the ultimate threat used to enforce the self-government scheme. George also used the jail to "exile" troublemakers. Few prisoners, once sent back to Bilibid, returned to Ilwahig, however.

scheme varied from that used by E. M. P. Wells and Alexander Maconochie, but the principle was essentially the same. The prisoner moved up and down the scale of grades, according to his conduct. The higher the prisoner's grade, the more privileges, liberty, and responsibility he assumed. As they progressed, colonists were given wider choices of occupation in agriculture, fishing, forestry, carpentry, industry, and clerical positions. They were allowed to save all income above a minimum paid to the colony and, as they advanced, were given access to the Ilwahig store where they could enrich their menu and purchase luxuries. At the most advanced grade, a prisoner was allowed to participate in the administration of the colony, serving as police officer, judge, prosecuting attorney, and so forth. Further, on demonstrating his industry and ability, the prisoner was permitted to have his wife and children live with him. When qualified, he was given a plot of land, a bull, farm implements, and seeds. Then fellow colonists voluntarily helped their comrade clear his land, plant his crops, and build his house. Working as an independent farmer (or at whatever trade was available) he paid the government shares which were gradually reduced. Upon release from the penal colony, he was fully independent but usually chose to stay in the colony and retain the farm on which he had labored.[106]

An unexpected dividend of America's colonial venture at

[106] Forbes, *The Philippine Islands*, 233; Stowe, "A Prison That Makes Men Free," 627; William L. Altdorfer, "Unique Penal Colony: Novel and Successful Experiment in the Philippines," Los Angeles *Times*, July 16, 1911; James F. Smith, "Report of the Secretary of Public Instruction," *Report of the Philippine Commission, Bureau of Insular Affairs—War Department*, part three, 1906 (Washington, D.C., 1907), 319–336; Robert Ladow, "United States' Prisons and Prisoners," in Charles R. Henderson, ed., *Penal and Reformatory Institutions*, Vol. II of Henderson, ed., *Correction and Prevention* (New York, 1910), 179–180.

the end of the nineteenth century was the excellent testing ground that Cuba and the Philippines provided for adventurous Progressives. Earlier, after finding resistance in New York City, Wilson Gill had demonstrated the practicability of student self-government when adopted in Cuban schools. Now from the Philippines came evidence that the theory of self-government could be successfully applied to adult criminals. The test given the self-government principle at the Ilwahig Penal Colony had been a severe one, all observers agreed, and even General Aguinaldo reportedly was willing to commend Forbes' efforts at prison reform.[107] By 1913, no prisoner released from the Ilwahig Penal Colony with the recommendation of the superintendent had been returned to a Philippine prison, an astounding record which could not be overlooked even if the authenticity of the self-governing regime were questioned. The second superintendent, Charles B. Lamb, spent months in the United States studying penal methods and institutions, which included an extended visit to the George Junior Republic. When Lamb returned to Ilwahig and successfully assumed John R. White's position, the new superintendent graphically demonstrated that the penal colony was not a "one-man affair," and that the principles and methods of anti-institutional penology, like any other principles and methods, could be taught and mastered. Colonel Lamb's testimony was firm evidence that the rehabilitation of adult criminals through anti-institutional methods had been transferred from the realm of penological theory into a workable scheme of prison discipline. "To my mind," Lamb wrote, "Ilwahig furnished a practical method of reform based on opportunity and justice, which conveys to the prisoner an understanding of the inviolable law of compensation, and which

[107] Forbes, *The Philippine Islands*, 231; Altdorfer, "Unique Penal Colony"; Alexander Forbes to George, Feb. 15, 1914.

has proven itself practical, and is a method which has a real value for reformation purposes." [108]

The Philippine experiment set off a wave of interest among Progressive penologists in the United States. George began to receive regular inspections and inquiries from prison administrations and reformers in addition to the numerous visits from educators. Unlike E. M. P. Wells and Joseph Curtis, who received little or no support from such organizations as the Boston Prison Discipline Society, George enjoyed the official sanction of the National Association of Junior Republics, and the self-government plan had been endorsed by juvenile-court associations and settlement-house workers in such major urban centers as New York, Chicago, Los Angeles, Denver, Seattle, Pittsburgh, Boston, Baltimore, and Philadelphia. The New York Society for the Prevention of Cruelty to Children, the New York School of Philanthropy, and the American Institute of Criminal Law and Criminology invited George to address their annual meetings on the topic of institutional reformation of juvenile delinquents. [109] In Massachusetts, Lewis M. Palmer, a Trustee of the State Training Schools, proposed the adoption of Junior Republic methods. [110] Perhaps

[108] Quoted in Altdorfer, "Unique Penal Colony." See also Victor G. Heiser, *An American Doctor's Odyssey* (New York, 1936), 53. Heiser noted that released prisoners from Ilwahig found it easier to obtain employment than those who had not served time there. The success of the Colony is testified to by the fact that 52 years after its establishment, Ilwahig, grown to 3,500 population, still functioned as a model prison colony (Bruno Shaw, "Prison Without Bars," *Collier's* [May 11, 1956], 56–57).

[109] H. Clay Preston, secretary, NYSPCC, to George, July 5, 1911; Henry W. Thurston, Child Welfare Division, N.Y. School of Philanthropy, to George, April 12, 1913; Edwin Mulready, secretary-treasurer, American Institute of Criminal Law and Criminology, to George, Oct. 18, 1912.

[110] Palmer to Stowe, Sept. 19, 1913, and to George, Oct. 3, 1913.

even more encouraging was the report from Oregon that Governor Oswald West, a noted prison reformer, favored the establishment of self-government in the state reform school.[111] Actual experiments in self-government for prisoners, based upon the George Junior Republic, were tried in such diverse areas as Illinois, California, Manitoba, and New Zealand.[112] And after the outbreak of World War I, a curious and intriguing report from London indicated that the British government, at the suggestion of prominent British penal reformers, had established a self-governing camp for German prisoners of war with hopes of countervailing Prussian *Kultur*.[113] The New York *Times*, in 1915, was certainly not alone in calling for a "sane, unsentimental, and logical prison reform" by the extension of the republic idea into the entire American penal system.[114]

[111] West to George, April 16, 1912; Mrs. M. E. Shafford to Stowe, Nov. 26, 1913; "Prison Reform," editorial in *The Outlook*, CVI (March 21, 1914), 613–614. A reluctant state legislature objected that the governor's proposal was too expensive, however.

[112] M. M. Mallary, superintendent of the Illinois State Reformatory, attempted to establish a Junior Republic inside the reformatory walls shortly after his visit to Freeville in 1906 but was forced to abandon the work and resign his position after the experiment set off extensive political opposition (George, Diary, May 15, 1906; Mallary to George, Dec. 16 and Dec. 29, 1909). Calvin Derrick, "Institution Management," *The Junior Republic* (journal published by the citizens of the California Junior Republic), IV (March, 1915), 3–10. In Manitoba the experiment was carried out at the Boy's Industrial Farm at Portage la Prairie (Manitoba *Free Press*, Aug. 26, 1916). The New Zealanders observed both the Ilwahig Penal Colony and the George Junior Republic (Robert Stout, "Interim Report of the Department of Justice, Prisons Branch: Prisons Board," Session II, General Assembly, Wellington, New Zealand, May 20, 1912).

[113] Richard Welling to the editor to the New York *Times*, Dec. 7, 1915.

[114] Review of *Citizens Made and Remade*, New York *Times*, Nov. 3, 1912.

vi

As the broader potentialities for prison reform became evident, Thomas Mott Osborne became more and more restive with the limitations of the George Junior Republic. His relationships with George and the Junior Republic Board of Trustees were none too satisfactory, and Osborne, who was as impatient with the day-to-day management of the Junior Republic as he had been with the operation of D. M. Osborne and Company, gradually began to expand his horizons. The former mayor of Auburn and member of the State Public Service Commission under Governor Hughes allowed himself to be boomed for governor in 1910.[115] After accepting an appointment by Governor Dix to be Commissioner of Forest, Fish, and Game, perhaps it was inevitable that, sooner or later, Osborne would carry through his perennial threat to resign from the Republic Board of Trustees.

Still, the break came somewhat accidentally. During an illness in 1912, Osborne read Donald Lowrie's sensational *My Life in Prison*, which stimulated his latent thoughts on prison reform, and according to Rudolph Chamberlain, "jolted him out of his irresolution."[116] He had found his mission, but he was still not sure what he would do. After the election of Governor Sulzer in 1913, Osborne, an anti-Tammany reform Democrat, recognized a unique opportunity to translate his own reform ideas into reality.

Osborne petitioned Sulzer to accept the proposal of Dr. George Kirchwey, dean of the Columbia University Law

[115] Charles F. Rattigan, "Honorable Thomas Mott Osborne" (published by the Democratic General Committee of Cayuga County, 1910).

[116] Lowrie, *My Life in Prison* (New York, 1912); Osborne, *Within Prison Walls*, 1–10; Chamberlain, *There Is No Truce*, 238.

School, for the creation of a State Commission on Prison Reform. To Osborne's great surprise, despite the fact that Sulzer was under great pressure from Tammany to reject the idea, he not only established the Commission, but made Osborne its chairman. In addition, Sulzer appointed Kirchwey as vice-chairman and Professor E. Stagg Whitin, also of Columbia, secretary.[117] When Charles F. Rattigan, Democratic "boss" of Cayuga County and Osborne's old campaign manager, was appointed warden of Auburn Prison at Osborne's behest, the way appeared open to gain positive reforms in the very heart of the New York prison system.

Some of Osborne's old friends questioned the propriety of the Rattigan appointment. Oswald Garrison Villard of *The Nation* was especially distressed at Osborne's political insensitivity. For years Osborne, along with other Progressives, had protested against the political corruption and spoils in the prison system. Rattigan's appointment made the Progressives appear hypocritical, Villard believed. But Osborne, who regarded Progressive politics as an instrumental means to his social ends, was clearly more interested in the realities of penal reform than in the niceties of political strategy. Whether he was unconcerned or unaware that he was giving his enemies a potent weapon, Osborne was content with the knowledge that with his friend as warden of Auburn great things could be accomplished.[118]

Shortly after he resigned from the George Junior Republic, the new chairman of the Prison Reform Commission launched a series of investigations, visiting prisons, reformatories, and jails, interviewing administrators and inmates, and noting obvious deficiencies. With the cooperation of Warden Rattigan,

[117] New York *Evening Sun,* Sept. 29, 1913; Osborne, *Within Prison Walls,* 5.

[118] Chamberlain, *There Is No Truce,* 239.

Osborne concentrated his studies on the Auburn Prison, where he was able to attack immediate problems.[119] Thomas Mott Osborne possessed the investigator's suspicion of surface appearances and the reformer's drive to "get inside" every system. Given his determination to discover at first hand the horrors of the Auburn system and his propensity for secret masquerades, Osborne decided to enter Auburn Prison incognito and become a regular prisoner. When Osborne put the scheme before the warden, Rattigan, who feared for his own position as well as for Osborne's safety, persuaded his friend not to show bad faith with the prisoners by spying on them. Rattigan knew his man well, and the logic worked perfectly. Although Osborne was never averse to deceiving his friends, he did not want to risk being discovered by the convicts and thereby lose their confidence. After announcing to the assembled prisoners his intentions of investigating penitentiary life and conditions by becoming a prisoner, Osborne turned himself over to the prison authorities, was fingerprinted, photographed, dressed in a prison uniform, registered as Tom Brown, prisoner 33,333x, and placed in a cell. Thus began one of the most celebrated and dramatic episodes in all of American penal history.[120]

Osborne was not completely naïve about his experiment. He was fully aware that the prison routine and prisoners would not be quite normal during his stay, and that it was impossible for him to experience and understand the Auburn system in a week. He also knew that as chairman of the Commission on Prison Reform he would not have to suffer the subtle indignities and torments that the common prisoner was

[119] *Ibid.*, 239–240; Frank Tannenbaum, *Osborne of Sing Sing* (Chapel Hill, N.C., 1933), 63; Osborne, *Society and Prisons*, 139–152.
[120] Osborne kept a fascinating daily journal which was later published as *Within Prison Walls*.

subjected to daily. Yet with minor exceptions (Tom Brown
was allowed to have his daily paper, pen and ink, toilet articles) Osborne lived the daily routine of the convict to the
extent of spending a night in the "hole" for insubordination to
an officer. It was Osborne's greatest charade. Just as the boys
back at the Junior Republic did not fully accept a comrade
until he had "done his time" in the jail, so Osborne viewed
his imprisonment almost as a rite of passage. His obvious bias
against guards and administrators probably muted his appreciation of their problems. But despite the fact that this unscientific, suspicious, sentimental and romantic reformer was
likely to discover for himself all of the prison horrors described by Donald Lowrie, Osborne's indictment of the Old
Penology remains convincing. Reflecting on his sixteen years
as president of the Junior Republic Board of Trustees and his
week inside Auburn Prison, Osborne simply declared that
"our prison system, from the orphan asylum through to the
prison, had been a gigantic failure." [121]

Characteristically, Osborne claimed that his major contribution to penal reform, the Mutual Welfare League, was
dramatically suggested to him by a "fellow convict," Jack
Murphy. The basis for the Mutual Welfare League, however,
had already been long established in his work with the George
Junior Republic. Three of Osborne's principles, worked out
slowly in the first decade of the century, stood behind the
League:

First. —The law must decree not punishment, but temporary
exile from society until the offender has proven by his conduct
that he is fit to return.

Second. —Society must brand no man as a criminal, but aim
solely to reform the mental conditions under which a criminal
act has been committed.

[121] Osborne, "Prison Reform," in Corinne Bacon, ed., *Prison Reform* (White Plains, N.Y., 1917), 152.

Third. —The prison must be an institution where every inmate must have the largest practicable amount of individual freedom, because "it is liberty alone that fits men for liberty." [122]

Orlando F. Lewis, secretary of the Prison Association of New York, reportedly declared that Memorial Day of 1914 was the most significant date in Progressive penology.[123] On that day, after several months' gestation, the Mutual Welfare League was born. Founded at Auburn Prison, and later introduced in Sing Sing where Osborne became warden in December of 1914, the League represented Osborne's attempt to introduce self-government principles into adult prisons. It way simplistically organized; every inmate in the prison was eligible for League membership after meeting qualifications set by the League itself. Candidates for League office, unscreened by prison officials, were elected by the prisoners. Thus in no way was the Mutual Welfare League a "warden's club." League members were granted special privileges in return for self-discipline and loyalty to the prison administration. Misconduct of one member could result in suspension of privileges for all members. A Board of Review, inspired by the Junior Republic court and composed entirely of League officers, ruled on all violations by MWL members, except in cases involving assault, refusal to work, strike, and attempted escape. The only punishment that League officers could impose was suspension of membership, which meant that the offending prisoner lost his League privileges.

Given the prison environment of 1914, the suspension of privileges was not an insignificant punishment. League mem-

[122] "Thomas Mott Osborne Heads Prison Labor Committee," *Survey*, XXX (June 7, 1913), 320; "Introducing Warden Osborne," *ibid.*, XXXIII (Nov. 28, 1914), 205–206; Osborne, "New Methods at Sing Sing Prison," *Review of Reviews*, LII (Oct. 1915), 449–450.
[123] F. M. White, "Prisons of Freedom," *World's Work*, XXX (May 1915), 114–120.

bers were not bound by the awful rule of silence, but were allowed to talk and laugh during recreational hours. "Blue Sunday" was also abolished for League members. Under the old system, Sundays and holidays were especially torturous for prisoners who were locked in their cramped and foul cells for the entire day, except for a brief moment in the morning when they were allowed to empty their night buckets and eat a small breakfast. Under the new regime, the Sunday afternoon assembly, with its lectures, concerts, or debates, became one of the most valued breaks in the otherwise changeless prison routine. Other League privileges allowed prisoners to purchase their own postage stamps instead of being dependent on contributions from friends and relatives, allowed prisoners to keep daily papers in their cells until they had finished reading them, and allowed men to receive non-regulation shoes and sweaters as gifts from the outside. Some cripples and epileptics were transferred from bunks in their cells to beds in the prison dormitory.[124]

Perhaps the League's most daring innovation was the introduction of outdoor athletics in the prison yard. Sunday afternoon concerts within the confines of the prison chapel had been tolerable to the defenders of the old silent system, but the prospect of a thousand convicts set loose in the prison yard sent chills of anxiety through veteran guards and administrators. Memorial Day, 1914, was warm and sunny. At the order from the warden, the cells were unlocked, and 1,400 men, each wearing on his chest the green and white button of the Mutual Welfare League, marched in perfect order into the prison yard, guarded only by sergeants-at-arms of the MWL. No such perfect discipline had ever been seen before in Auburn Prison, Osborne thought to himself. His description of the scene merits notation, for it accurately reflected the

[124] *Ibid.*

Progressive's sense of historical moment: "Each group stood at attention until the last man was in the yard; then at the trumpet call ranks were broken, friends rushed across the yard to greet each other, and brothers who for long years had never been able to speak, clasped hands and walked away together, their feelings too sacred for the common gaze." [125] With a blast from a trumpet, the Old Penology was at last overthrown.

The system of inmate self-government introduced at Auburn and Sing Sing was not simply another "honor system," Osborne believed, but was fundamentally different in kind. Under the honor system, such as used at Elmira, the warden was cast as a benevolent autocrat instead of a brutal autocrat. Prisoners preferred the honor system to the old regime, of course, but it only succeeded in making model prisoners out of the inmates. Inmate self-government, on the other hand, trusted not only the individual but the entire prison community. Under the old system, the prisoner answered to the warden; under the self-government principle he was held accountable by the whole body of his fellow inmates. The self-government scheme succeeded in eliminating some of the worst features of the old regime: repression, suspicion, spying, and informing. [126]

Statistically, the success of the Mutual Welfare League was impressive. During the three years preceding the Osborne administration at Sing Sing, the prison hospital treated an average of 373 wounds per 1,450 inmates. After Osborne became warden, the prison population rose to over 1,600, but the

[125] *Society and Prisons,* 178.

[126] Osborne, "New Methods at Sing Sing Prison," 451; Osborne, "Prison Efficiency," *Efficiency Society Journal,* Nov. 1915; "The New Prison System," in Bacon, *Prison Reform,* 144; F. M. White, "Great Meadow and Sing Sing," *The Outlook,* CV (Dec. 20, 1913), 846–854.

number of wounds treated dropped to 155. Previously many of the wounds had been inflicted by keepers in retaliation for prisoner assault. Under Osborne, there was only one instance of an assault on a keeper, and in this case the officer refused to make a complaint because he believed the prisoner was deranged. For each of the three years prior to Osborne, an average of thirty-five convicts were committed to the Dannemora State Hospital. In the two years Osborne was warden only nineteen were transferred to Dannemora. Industrial productivity increased 21 per cent under Osborne. There were not significantly fewer escapes during Osborne's administration, but perhaps for the first time in Sing Sing's history, some escapees returned voluntarily to the prison when they learned that their actions had brought discredit on the warden and the League. Perhaps the most significant statistic was reported by Judge William H. Wadhams of the Court of General Sessions of New York City, who noted on January 17, 1916, that he had not had a single recidivist from Sing Sing since the creation of the League.[127]

Osborne's success can be explained several ways. Almost any change in the stultifying routine of the Old Penology would have met with dramatic success. The novelty of the League's activities and the memory of the silent system worked decidedly in Osborne's favor. But once the silent system had been abolished, and other humanitarian reforms had been taken for granted, it was impossible to impose the old system on prisoners who would not cooperate with the League. Young first offenders, especially, gave Osborne trou-

[127] F. M. White, "The True Sing Sing," *The Outlook*, CXII (Jan. 5, 1916), 42–47; H. B. Bolasky, "The Call of the League," *Survey*, XXXIV (Feb. 5, 1916), 557–558; "The New Prison System," in Bacon, *Prison Reform*, 144–145; Frederick Wines, *Punishment and Reformation*, 405–406.

ble. At Sing Sing he did not have a "Republic jail" with which he could periodically remind convicts of the horrors of the Old Penology. Some of the new prisoners regarded the new comforts and privileges not as benefits which they had earned through self-discipline and sacrifice, but "as the natural order of things, their inalienable right for which they need feel small gratitude." [128]

During his tenure as warden, Osborne's personality was certainly the most important single asset the League possessed. Even the warden's most severe critics did not doubt that he had the bona fide loyalty of most of the prisoners. Like Curtis, Wells, Maconochie, Gill, White, and George, Osborne understood the dynamics of personal loyalty. As Tom Brown, he had earned the respect, admiration, and sympathy of most of the prison population. No doubt he was assisted by the fact that advocates of the Old Penology heaped abuse and ridicule on his adventure. Osborne's personality was so powerful, in fact, that once again the old question was asked of his anti-institutional methods: Could the Mutual Welfare League succeed under the direction of any other warden? [129]

Osborne, of course, believed his system was rooted on the firm foundation of universal human nature. Although he often misunderstood his colleagues and was frequently guilty of running rough-shod over their sensibilities, as George could abundantly testify, he had, nevertheless, an unusual empathy and understanding of the psychology of the delinquent and convict. Osborne wasted no sympathy on the criminal; the lawbreaker belonged in prison, or at least in exile. Yet, he realized that most individuals in prison were failures. One cannot reform them by making them think right or act right,

[128] Chamberlain, *There Is No Truce*, 281.
[129] Bolasky, "The Call of the League," 557–558; Chamberlain, *There Is No Truce*, 281.

he declared. The Mutual Welfare League rescued men because it trusted them to accomplish what they were capable of doing. The tasks were often simple, but they generally succeeded in re-enforcing self-esteem. Osborne encouraged ethnic and racial minorities to organize subgroups within the League, special interest committees were also formed, and most critically, an employment bureau was established. For a prisoner suspended from the League, loss of privileges was only a secondary matter as long as the MWL remained under convict control. More serious to the inmate was his loss of face and a sense of ostracism which accompanied the revocation of his right to wear the MWL's green and white badge.[130]

The latent radicalism of the self-government scheme was underscored when Max Eastman, noting that, after the emancipation of women and labor, prison reform would become the next focus of American radicalism, hailed Osborne's work at Sing Sing: "There is still poverty of interest, poverty of instruction, poverty of remediation at Sing Sing. It is a thin life for sick men, a dull life for rebels. But all that a fearless will and an exceedingly wise human heart can do, under the law and with the appropriation, Mr. Osborne has done or is doing in that notorious and forlorn place." [131]

Osborne was the first to admit that the League did not solve all penal problems. Wherever there were power and authority, there were politics; and wherever there were politics, there was corruption. In all probability no penal system could be perfect, he insisted. In spite of all the failures, maladjustments and shortcomings of the League, Osborne argued, one could not deny that it worked.

[130] Osborne, *Society and Prisons*, 185–186; "Prison Efficiency"; "New Methods at Sing Sing Prison," 449–456.
[131] *The Masses*, VI (June 1915), 5–6.

It may take many years to convince reluctant prison officials and stupid politicians that we have at last found the true principles of prison government; but the past, at any rate, is secure. In Auburn prison for more than two years, in Sing Sing prison for more than a year, the new system has been in operation and *the thing works*. The truth of that fact no reluctant official and stupid politician can argue out of existence. It is a rock which affords a solid foundation for the future of prison reform.[132]

Unfortunately, the future of the New Penology was not as secure as Osborne believed. His struggle against the Old Penology, begun in 1897 at the George Junior Republic, was all but over by the time the manuscript for *Society and Prisons* reached the publishers in 1916. Twice indicted in 1916 and twice acquitted (once on appeal), Osborne was temporarily suspended as warden of Sing Sing. The charges brought against him by his enemies were those traditionally made against reform wardens: mismanagement tinged with favoritism and homosexuality. Although exonerated of the charges, Osborne never again enjoyed the full confidence of American reformers. Reinstated as warden in July 1916, he unaccountably resigned two weeks later. His book, which was intended to be an introduction to the New Penology, became instead a *l'envoi*.

It was unfortunate that George, Osborne, and Lane could not speak with one voice concerning their anti-institutional methods. The idea of the anti-institutional institution was difficult enough to grasp without the constant disagreement among its proponents. At times, George, Osborne, and Lane seemed simply to want freedom from the regular supervision of boards, trustees, and state agencies. Each was fiercely independent, and it was often charged that their institutions

[132] Osborne, *Society and Prisons*, 222–223.

were anti-institutional only in the sense that they were one-man affairs which could not survive the departure of the charismatic leader. In another sense, their anti-institutionalism was interpreted as a revolt against the "jailing psychosis" of the Old Penology. Prison walls and prison routine were substituted for a normal environment, either of the family or the village. But "honor farms" and "country schools" represented only the most literal understanding of anti-institutionalism. Neither George, Osborne, nor Lane thought it ironic that they worked within an institutional structure. For them, anti-institutionalism, whether practiced by the Junior Republic, the Mutual Welfare League, or the Little Commonwealth, meant the rejection of the rigid, inflexible discipline of formalistic education and penology. Yet, if most Progressive educators and penologists would grant the desirability of individualized programs, the anti-institutionalists went even further by insisting that students and prisoners themselves should play a major role in determining their fate. Through inmate self-government the anti-institutionalists hoped to guarantee meaningful "citizen" participation in education and rehabilitation.

Critics of self-government had always been sensitive to the possibilities of disorder and abuse. By 1916 they added another charge: self-government permitted only crude and ineffectual inmate classification and treatment. Not only was the anti-institutional scheme too vague and dangerous, too romantic and unprofessional—it was also too unscientific.[133]

[133] Barnes and Teeters, *New Horizons in Criminology*, 501.

VII

"NOTHING WITHOUT LABOR"

———————— "In 1914 progressivism was triumphant; six years later it was apparently dead as a doornail." Such is the conclusion of William E. Leuchtenburg. What killed progressivism? The obvious answer, Leuchtenburg suggested, was the war. "In 1913 progressive intellectuals were giving the United States its first intelligent analysis of modern society and blueprinting an ebullient, buoyantly hopeful program of reform. By 1919 they were a disenchanted lot; discouraged by the war and peace that followed, they had become, as Walter Weyl wrote, 'tired radicals.' " [1]

Leuchtenburg's thesis is appealing to the student of the George Junior Republic. As he stood in 1911 with Theodore Roosevelt on a hillock overlooking Freeville, William R. George was clearly in the forefront of Progressive reform. Yet by 1920 the Junior Republic was so crippled that it never regained its former stature. George dreamed of universal reforms in the summer of 1913, and by 1922 he was disillusioned and bitter. It would be a mistake, however, to conclude that the Junior Republic was simply an unfortunate war casualty. There is no doubt that the war left its marks, but George and other Republic leaders gamely compared the wartime to the "pioneering" years of the early Republic. Far from having

[1] *The Perils of Prosperity* (Chicago, 1958), 120–124.

285

tired and lost their faith in progress, democracy, and humanity, George's friends were confident that the postwar years would witness a vital resurgence of the Republic doctrine. There is little evidence of flagging resolve among key Republic partisans in the 1920's. The war did not leave them emotionally or spiritually exhausted.

Actually, the decline of the George Junior Republic was well under way before America became involved in the European conflict. The war contributed to George's difficulties, but it did not create them in any important way. In the words of Henry May, World War I can only be credited for "speeding, widening and altering in kind a movement already underway." [2] To understand what happened to the Republic movement in the 1920's, one must keep in mind that it became hopelessly factionalized in 1913, increasingly isolated from the social welfare movement after 1914, and absolutely irrelevant to the cult of social science in the postwar decade. When George joined the New York Child Labor Committee in 1902, he joined his friends V. Everit Macy, Lyman Abbott, Jacob Riis, Bishop H. C. Potter, and Frederick Almy in a coalition for social justice.[3] Learning of his opposition to the child labor amendment in 1924, a bewildered Lillian Wald could only ask, "what does 'Daddy' George mean by his action?" [4] The question is worth answering, for it presents us with another perspective on the fate of Progressivism in the 1920's.[5]

[2] "Rebellion of the Intellectuals, 1912–1917," *American Quarterly*, VIII (Summer 1956), 125.

[3] Jeremy Felt, *Hostages of Fortune: Child Labor Reform in New York State* (Syracuse, N.Y., 1965), 46.

[4] Lillian Wald to Richard Welling, Dec. 27, 1924.

[5] Once a neglected subject, Progressivism in the 1920's now boasts an extensive bibliography. See Clarke Chambers' bibliography in *Seedtime of Reform: American Social Service and Social Action,*

i

When William R. George agreed to move from Freeville to Ithaca in 1912, he also promised not to launch a rival Junior Republic. He was still national director of the National Association of Junior Republics, however, and in that capacity George planned to continue his self-government work. He was especially encouraged to expand his vision by Lyman Beecher Stowe, the national secretary whose main interest was not in Freeville. Stowe believed that Junior Republic methods could be introduced into any reformatory or educational institution for children or adults. "Only where the community is of sound mind and body can the full principle of the Republic, 'Nothing Without Labor,' take hold," Stowe noted. "But even where the conditions of soundness do not exist," he continued, "modified application of the Junior Republic principles are useful." [6]

At first, George opposed plans to introduce modified self-government into schools, prisons, institutions, and clubs. Too many moribund institutions, he contended, had already tried to save themselves by "cashing in" on Junior Republic popularity. Polluted self-government was only a sham which hurt the entire movement, he maintained. The NAJR must repudiate all so-called junior republic, junior state, or junior settlement schemes that did not conform strictly to Junior Republic principles, George thought, or risk being associated with

1918–1933 (Minneapolis, 1963). Three additional books, which have influenced the present study, are: Jeremy Felt, *Hostages of Fortune;* Roy Lubove, *The Professional Altruist: The Emergence of Social Work as a Career, 1880–1930* (Cambridge, Mass., 1965); Otis L. Graham, Jr., *An Encore for Reform: The Old Progressives and the New Deal* (New York, 1967).

[6] "Memorandum of the Application of the Junior Republic Idea to Other Institutions," MS, 1914.

men and methods it could not condone.[7] He admitted to being thrilled when a Boys' Club or other organization adapted the Junior Republic plan, but he feared that his work would become so popular that its greatest possibilities would be lost sight of. "The thing I fear principally," he confided to the NAJR, "is that people may become too much contented with the self-government name and make self-government *fact* a secondary consideration."[8]

But after his move from Freeville, George could not turn a deaf ear to the pleas for help and advice which poured into his office. It was best, he knew, to render as much assistance as possible, for the general public would not make a careful distinction between the good work at Freeville and the bad work done elsewhere. Furthermore, in need of a job himself, George became convinced that promoting partial self-government was better than not promoting self-government at all. This notion was especially impressed upon him by Stowe and Richard Welling. Both men, although members of the NAJR, were active in New York City reform. As members of the National Self-Government Committee, they advanced the cause of self-government in New York City public schools. Welling especially desired the founder's blessing, admitting, however, that with it or without it he would continue his work. At a meeting with Stowe and Welling in New York City, George finally conceded that partial self-government could serve as an effective pedagogical and training tool in situations where the complete Junior Republic regime was impractical. He was finally persuaded that Junior Republic methods were not only beneficial to children with antisocial

---

[7] George to Samuel L. Stiver, Nov. 12, 1909; George, "Report to the NAJR," Oct. 16, 1911; Minutes of the NAJR, April 20, 1912; George to Frederick Almy, Aug. 29, 1910.

[8] George, "Report to the NAJR," May 31, 1912.

tendencies, but were appropriate for the training of all boys and girls, the world over.[9]

This outward shift, quietly taken, represented a major departure in Junior Republic theory. Gone was the simple plan "to fit the child for society" by removing him to the bucolic environment of Freeville. For years, Frank Sessions noted, American reformers had sought to reform the criminal, restore the insane, quicken the wits of the feeble-minded, remove temptation from the drunken and the licentious, and place the feet of the dependent on the rock of independence. These efforts were costly, Sessions believed, and in the main ineffectual. The new Junior Republic plan was to begin at the beginning: to grasp hold of the child and, with him in hand, reform the larger society.[10]

George's plans for universal reform developed slowly and remained somewhat vague throughout his career. As early as 1909, he accepted in principle the idea of establishing "George Junior Republic Boys' Homes" for the care of working children between the ages of twelve and sixteen.[11] Already Juvenile Court Judge Mathewson of New Haven had successfully established a self-governing boys' home using modified Republic methods when George proposed a similar project of his own. Working as a probation officer in conjunction with the Juvenile Court of New York City, he planned to establish a "City Junior Republic." Boys referred to George by the court would form the nucleus of his new colony. Each would obtain outside employment, pay room and board to the

[9] George, "Report to the NAJR," Nov. 18, 1912; George to E. Molenaar, Aug. 23, 1909.
[10] Frank J. Sessions, "The George Junior Republic," paper read before the Contemporary Club of Davenport, Iowa, Nov. 23, 1911.
[11] George to Robert D. Klees, Baltimore, Dec. 22, 1909; Fred G. Bale, Mayor of Westerville, Ohio, to George, Nov. 9, 1909; George to Bale, Nov. 17, 1909.

City Republic, and be subject to the community's rules and regulations. The City Republic would duplicate the Junior Republic as much as possible, eventually occupying a city block or more, and containing its own stores, banks, jails, schools, and girls' cottages. Once under way, the City Republic would accept all children as citizens, even country youths who came to New York to seek the advantages of urban life, and young adults who were interested in doing social settlement work among children. George saw no reason why such City Republics, like privately endowed colleges and universities, could not be established in every major city in the nation. As an ultimate goal, he would have had all youth automatically become citizens of a junior form of government, just as at twenty-one years of age all individuals become voting citizens of the Great Republic.[12]

George realized, however, that it was not economically or politically feasible to establish incorporated Junior Republics or City Republics in every community in the nation. Therefore he developed still another scheme which he called the "Junior Municipality." Precursor of the American Legion's "Boys' State," and the Y.M.C.A.'s "Youth Legislature" programs, the Junior Municipality established a permanent youth government which cooperated with the adult government of the community. Ideally including all youths between the ages of sixteen and twenty-one, the Junior Municipality elected its own mayor, police chief, judges, and other necessary youth officers.[13] In Ithaca and Cortland, New York, where Junior Municipalities were first established under official city sponsor-

[12] George, "The City Junior Republic," Ithaca *Journal,* Aug. 26, 1914; "A Republic in a City," MS, Jan. 30, 1912; *The Adult Minor* (New York, 1937), 51; "City Republic Youth, a National Factor," *Junior Civics,* I (May 1928), 14.

[13] George, "The Junior Municipality," MS, June 26, 1913, and MS with the same title dated 1921.

ship, the youth government performed many of the functions which later were to become regular duties of high school student governments. In addition, the Ithaca youth officers caught a forger and a prowler and significantly cut down on truancy.[14]

Initially George's new scheme appeared to be an unlikely amalgam of his old Law and Order Gang and the Junior Republic. But the revival of the law and order idea shifted the emphasis of the junior government from a passive learning of the rights and duties of citizenship to an active exercise of governmental power. The officers of the junior government were not simply to study and play the roles of their adult counterparts, as in most educational programs. Rather, in addition to having control over most of their own affairs, they were to keep watch over the corresponding adult official. "Officials inclined to be lax are likely to take more real cognizance of their duties when they know that sharp young eyes are following their moves with critical appraisal," George commented with some humor. He assumed that once the junior officer mastered the duties and possibilities of his office, the youth would turn his attention to the community and seek out needed reforms and improvements.[15]

During an era in which community leaders were less than attuned to the demands of student activists and youthful radicals, few adults took George's scheme very seriously, and none of them took it literally. George himself probably did not appreciate the consequences of his plans if fully developed. Yet, as always, if he accepted something short of absolute self-government in the Junior Municipality, it was not

[14] Lyman Beecher Stowe, "Junior Citizens in Action," *The Outlook*, CVIII (Nov. 18, 1914), 654–656.

[15] *The Adult Minor*, 64; "The Junior Municipality," MS, June 26, 1913.

because he had compromised his ideals. In words strikingly similar to Randolph Bourne's, George reminded his generation that America's youth would not stand idly in the wings waiting for their entrance into history. "Student responsibility" was the Progressive equivalent of "student power." Both Bourne and George called for increasing responsibility among youth. "Is it not sound doctrine that one becomes responsible only by being made responsible for something?" Bourne inquired in a question that could have been asked by George or Osborne.[16] By means of an elaborate system of guides and instruction, American institutions brought the nation's youth to the threshold of life, George observed, and then demanded they wait until "maturity" before experiencing the realities of living. *"But can they stand still?"* George demanded. "The answer to that is written in the daily grist of the newspapers, in police records, in thousands of homes made desolate by unaccountable, often violent outbursts of thwarted young folks." America's most urgent problem, he believed, was to devise immediate, natural and inexpensive means of including "adult minors" in the life of the community.[17] George's solution became the slogan of a later generation: participatory democracy. "Let us consider the proposed solution to the situation, this participation mentioned above," he wrote just before his death. "Why not grant participation in local government to such an extent that adult minors feel themselves real, working members of the community. . . . Adult Minor citizenship can be started anywhere, in large or

[16] Randolph Bourne, *Youth and Life* (Cambridge, Mass., 1913), 41. Bourne's affinities with George are evident throughout this book, esp. 1–52.

[17] *The Adult Minor*, 61–62. George used the term "adult minor" to refer to all youths over the age of sixteen who were physically adults but legally minors.

small communities. Its appeal is directly to young people between the ages of sixteen and twenty. Its scope and possibilities are unlimited." [18]

One can only speculate just how far George would have
pushed his Junior Municipality–Junior City scheme, or what
impact, if any, fully developed self-governing juvenile communities would have had on American urban life and culture.
In addition to the prewar experiments in Cortland and Ithaca,
there were unsuccessful attempts to revive the movement
with postwar projects in New York City and Glen Ridge,
New Jersey. *The Outlook, Survey*, and *World's Work* hailed
the new Junior Municipalities as encouraging harbingers of
renewed Progressive effort. "*The Outlook* knows and trusts
the men behind this movement," noted a 1921 editorial which
called for more than a hundred Junior Municipalities by the
end of the year.[19] Junior Cities established in connection with
urban universities would help bridge the gap between professors, students, and the urban poor, George and the National
Self-Government Committee believed. With the aid of the
Columbia University Settlement and the Social Service Council of Columbia University, the NSGC planned a Junior City
in the vicinity of Morningside Heights, but lack of funds and
student apathy forced them to abandon the project. For his
own part in the matter, George had hoped that the Junior
Republic could serve as a training center for Junior City personnel, and that the Junior City, in turn, could act as a "half-

[18] George, *The Adult Minor*, 62. See also " 'Daddy' George's
Latest Plan," editorial, Ithaca *Journal*, Aug. 27, 1914; Williamsport
(Pa.) *Gazette Bulletin*, Feb. 19, 1916.
[19] "For Our Inevitable Citizens," *The Outlook* CXXIX (Oct. 5,
1921), 160–161; Hermann Hagedorn, "Citizens through Understanding," *Survey*, XLVI (Sept. 16, 1921), 676–678; "Junior Governments," *World's Work*, XLIII (Nov. 1921), 11–12.

way house," assisting Junior Republic graduates on their return to the city.[20]

Although none of the postwar plans was successful, they
reflected how far George had come in his willingness to support varied forms of self-government. Speaking before the
Johnstown, Pennsylvania, Chamber of Commerce, George
proposed that prisons and reformatories be abolished and Republic Cities be erected in their stead. The difference between
the convict and the citizen was not the absolute difference
between good and evil, George asserted, but a relative difference in social and antisocial behavior. The history of the
George Junior Republic and its imitators had proven that
penological methods became educational methods when applied to the better classes of citizen.[21] In 1913, when George
had argued that the bad boy could only be reformed through
association with the good, he was already on the brink of
universalism. By 1921, he had tumbled in declaring: "It will
be a long step in the right direction when there is a universal
belief that self-government should be given an opportunity
for self-expression in every individual and community." [22]
The theoretical distinction between the Junior Republic and
the Great Republic had been lost.

[20] National Council for Democratic Training, Bulletin No. 4, Sept.
1920, and Bulletin No. 9, Dec. 1920; Florence Yoder Wilson, "Pav-
ing the Way for Good Politics in Newark," *Woman's Age*, I
(May 1, 1922), 8–9; Newark *Evening News*, March 21, 1921; George
to G. Spencer Miller, Aug. 13, Nov. 3, and Nov. 20, 1920; George
to George Christiancy, Jan. 11, 1921; George to E. D. Bruner,
April 25, 1927, Western Pennsylvania George Junior Republic Papers, Cornell University.

[21] Johnstown *Leader*, Jan. 18, 1917.

[22] "Good, Bad, and 'Daddy George,'" *Survey*, XXX (Aug. 2,
1913), 565–566; "Social Sanitariums and Social Doctors," *The Outlook*, CXXVII (Jan. 5, 1921), 21.

ii

George's theoretical fantasies were always tempered by the reality of conditions at Freeville. He did not move naturally or comfortably toward his radical conclusions, and he embraced "universalism" only out of a sense of desperate necessity. Before 1913, George's major problem was to protect the purity of Republic doctrine as institution after institution adopted his methods. After 1913, however, the problem was the opposite. Interest in the Junior Republic continued, to be sure, but increasingly George found himself in the unfamiliar role of promoting Republic principles among skeptical social workers. Fifteen years had elapsed since he first had brought young toughs to Freeville, and techniques in child-saving which had seemed so progressive in 1895 were no longer regarded adequate or appropriate in 1913. In addition, during the two and a half decades of the Progressive Era, the public image of the George Junior Republic was gradually transformed. Viewed originally as a rural settlement and refuge for immigrant children, and then as a vocational and preparatory school for the poor, by 1913 the Junior Republic was most frequently described as a private reform school. George stoutly resisted the change, but the professionalization of social work in the cities and the rapid expansion of public high school education continued to deprive his Republic of nondelinquent citizens. As immigrant and disadvantaged youth found more adequate educational and recreational facilities in the cities, the number of citizens who were enrolled voluntarily declined. Their places were largely taken by children assigned to the Junior Republic by the juvenile courts or committed to the institution by their parents. The comparatively simple task of outfitting the poor immigrant for his place in society was steadily superseded by the need to reform youth of deficient and delinquent character. At a time when George was arguing for the universal application of the Republic principle, it became evident that the Republic itself could no longer offer something for everyone. Tensions long hidden beneath the rhetoric of the Republic principle began to work their way to the surface.

Success had brought division within the Republic ranks, as it had in many other reform programs. The reformers so friendly in the 1890's became hostile rivals two decades later. When Thomas Mott Osborne resigned from the Junior Republic Board of Trustees in March 1913, he left the institution virtually leaderless. Calvin Derrick, the former superintendent, had already moved to California; William R. George was preparing to move to Ithaca; and Lyman Beecher Stowe remained in his NAJR offices in New York City. At this juncture, certain "friends of the Republic," who apparently had sided with Osborne and Derrick, hired a private detective to investigate the morals charges made against George, and also tipped off the State Board of Charities regarding the conditions at Freeville. The Board was obliged to act upon the report, because of numerous state and county dependents registered at the Junior Republic, and thus in the midst of the leadership vacuum burst the 1913 investigation of the State Board of Charities.[23]

The Junior Republic had not been without its critics. Once before, in 1896, the State Board of Charities had disclosed that the George Junior Republic did not meet minimum state requirements.[24] At that time a committee of seven, chosen by the Junior Republic Trustees to study the charges, recom-

[23] George, Diary, April–Dec. 1913; Minutes of the George Junior Republic Executive Committee, Feb. 15 through Nov. 18, 1913; Ithaca *Daily News*, Dec. 19, 1913.

[24] *Thirteenth Annual Report of the New York State Board of Charities*, I (Albany, 1896).

mended that additional facilities be provided for bathing, schooling, and manual training, including instruction in farming, carpentry, and smithing.[25]

Although the Junior Republic apparently satisfied the State Board of Charities, the 1896 investigation was not the last of the Republic's troubles. A few years later, the New York *Herald* printed reports of two runaway boys who complained of cruel treatment of prisoners, filthy conditions, lewdness among boys and girls, undernourishment, overwork, neglect of education, brutality, and the prisonlike appearance of the Junior Republic. The charges of these obviously bitter boys were investigated by the Syracuse Bureau of Labor and Charities and the Society for the Prevention of Cruelty to Children, both of which completely exonerated the managers at Freeville.[26]

George, Osborne, and others were acutely sensitive to the fact that certain features of the Junior Republic would always be a source of potential trouble, and that the Republic would never be completely safe from investigation and scandal. George intuitively recognized that his scheme of "Nothing without Labor" might raise qualms among certain social workers. Therefore, he insisted that all citizens be over sixteen years old. Young boys and girls were not wanted in the Junior Republic because they could not be expected to support themselves. George knew how hard it was to refuse the applications of the "little fellows" because it seemed so cruel to send them somewhere else. "But they always ball up things when they get here," he wrote Leonard Levine, "and knock the economic system topsy-turvey because some sort of conces-

[25] New York *Daily Tribune*, Feb. 5, 1898.
[26] New York *Herald*, Sept. 4, 1901; "A Report of the Bureau of Labor and Charities and the Society for the Prevention of Cruelty to Children" (Syracuse, N.Y., Dec. 1901).

sion has to be made for them in the way of labor." [27] Osborne was always careful to defend the State Board of Charities as a public guarantee "against abuses whose existence will always be a danger." On the other hand, he knew the Republic would have to be constantly vigilant. "There are faults in the very system," Osborne admitted to Agnew, "but we believe our faults to be less serious in character than those of the ordinary reform school." [28] The faults to which Osborne alluded were clearly summarized in the 1913 report of the State Board of Charities.

Their critique was comprehensive and reflected most of the old issues. Ironically, they felt that too much stress was put on "classical education," while too little was done with vocational training. The investigating committee noted the Republic's shaky financial condition and the institution's irregular administration. Serious violations of the Public Health Law were discovered. Venereal disease, chronic illness, and general uncleanliness demanded the employment of a full-time doctor, the investigators maintained. Furthermore, since too many of the Republic's absentee trustees were ignorant of the conditions at Freeville, the committee suggested that the Republic Board of Trustees be reduced to those active members who lived in the vicinity of Freeville.[29]

But the focus of the report was on the issues which had been the most controversial throughout the Republic's history: coeducation and self-government at Freeville.

[27] George to Levine, Jan. 26, 1910.

[28] Osborne to Hon. Benjamin Wilcox, Feb. 27, 1900; to Hon. E. G. Treat, Feb. 14, 1901; to Robert W. Hebberd, Sec. of the State Board of Charities, Oct. 25, 1901; to A. G. Agnew, Nov. 26, 1901; Osborne Papers, Syracuse University.

[29] "Report of the Special Committee on the George Junior Republic Submitted to, and Unanimously Adopted by, the State Board of Charities at Its Meeting of Dec. 17, 1913," *Forty-seventh Annual Report of the State Board of Charities of the State of New York* (Albany, 1913), 497–510.

George's attitudes toward the family and sex, along with his friendship with Ben Lindsey and Jane Addams, gave him a curious affinity with the "new radicals," even though he was conservative in regard to social, cultural, and ethical issues. It is noteworthy that throughout their public careers George, Thomas Mott Osborne, and Homer Lane were all haunted by accusations of sexual misbehavior that were never proven. Their anti-institutional doctrines presented no threats to traditional political or economic institutions, but they did pose a challenge to traditional sexual regulations within penal and educational institutions.

When the State Board of Charities first objected to the presence of girls at the Junior Republic in 1896, John R. Commons, Mrs. Gerrit Smith Miller, and others defended the girls with straightforward arguments. Anyone who thought that slum children learned anything new about sex at the Junior Republic was terribly naïve, Republic defenders asserted. In fact, John R. Commons noted, not only was Freeville a much more wholesome environment for children, but young girls were much safer from sexual assault at Freeville than they were on the streets of New York. The Junior Republic stripped away the forbidden mysteries of sex. "The frailties and meanness of all are too well known," Commons argued. "Taken altogether, the community seems to contain within itself a sufficient number of individuals of upright life, and enough consciousness of responsibility for others to make the relations between boys and girls more sensible and straightforward than could possibly be the case under the ordinary management of adults." [30] Susan Dixwell Miller justified in-

[30] "The Junior Republic, II," *American Journal of Sociology*, III (Jan. 1898), 444–445. It will be remembered that Homer Lane reached the same conclusion regarding girls at the Little Commonwealth (see above, 218). Roy Lubove discusses the sexual education of slum children in *Progressives and the Slums: Tenement House Reform in New York City, 1890–1917* (Pittsburgh, 1962), 70.

cluding girls in the Junior Republic from a much more traditional point of view, but in the end she was just as daring as Commons. In 1898 Mrs. Miller proposed increasing the number of girls at Freeville because "the few girls who are there now do not afford sufficient variety in character to help develop the best that is in each, or to stimulate the boys to better and higher ideas of woman's place in life." She concluded by observing that no one could reasonably expect disadvantaged and delinquent youth to develop normal and healthy sexual habits and relationships segregated from the opposite sex during the period of greatest sexual development.[31]

Commons' and Mrs. Miller's justifications became the official position of the George Junior Republic Association.[32] At Freeville, the "learn by doing" principle was as applicable to sex education as it was to civic and industrial training. This is not to suggest that the Republic encouraged or condoned promiscuous sexual behavior. George once wrote that there was nothing like hard work and plain clothes to control sexual appetites.[33] Still, he recognized that love and sex were natural in any coeducational situation. George believed that segregation of the sexes was far more dangerous than coeducation, and there is no doubt that he preferred to have his boys playing with the girls than to have them playing with one another.[34]

Critics of the Junior Republic were less concerned about

[31] "Girl Citizens," MS, c. 1898.

[32] George, "Girls as Citizens," in *The Junior Republic* (New York, 1910), 138–154; George and Stowe, "Girl Citizens," in *Citizens Made and Remade* (New York, 1912), 118–138; George, "Bulletin XVII—Girls," *Junior Republic Principles and Bulletins* (Freeville, N.Y., 1941), 67–70.

[33] George, "The Love-Bug," MS, Oct. 22, 1932.

[34] George, "Bulletin XVII—Girls," 67–68; "Girls in the Republic," MS, 1919; George to Henry W. Thurston, Jan. 30, 1912.

good girls becoming corrupted than they were about "fallen" girls polluting the citizenry. As George observed, "most of the women I meet in connection with this work have a heart for the boys, but to 'halifax' with the girls." [35] But George and Osborne insisted that even "foolish" girls could be saved, and prior to the troubles of 1913 they even talked about establishing courses in sex hygiene.[36] Under intense pressure they grudgingly gave ground on this issue, however, and in June 1912 agreed to establish the Strawbridge-Brophy Junior Republic at Morristown, New Jersey, for girls of questionable moral integrity.[37] The scheme collapsed during the investigations of 1913.

After coeducation, the most controversial features of the Junior Republic were the court and jail. Following the troubles in 1896, John R. Commons noted:

The treatment of criminals in the Republic sometimes meets with that maudlin sympathy from outsiders characteristic of prison sentiment in other quarters. It seems cruel for boys to condemn their fellows to stripes (bed-ticking), to bars and bread and water, to ten hours' hard work every day, and to terms as long as a month. But we must remember that these boys are hard cases. Over half . . . have been convicted of crime, some have served in prison, and two or three are now under suspended sentence.[38]

In 1896–1897, Washington Gladden, Jacob Riis, William I. Hull, professor of history and political science at Swarthmore

[35] George to Miss Sarah Mounce, Jan. 10, 1917.
[36] Mrs. William R. George to A. E. Winship, Feb. 21, 1912.
[37] Philadelphia *North American*, June 21, 1912; George to Emily Howland, June 25, 1911; Mrs. William R. George to Miss A. L. Opper, July 2, 1911; George to Mrs. Shoemaker, Oct. 5, 1911; Margarett Roberts to George, May 28, 1912.
[38] "The Junior Republic, II," 433–488.

College, and Frank Munsey's *Argosy* joined Commons in defending the Junior Republic jail.[39] Each of these early defenders noted that Republic jail terms normally ranged from two to six days. The longest term served in the Republic jail was one month for sodomy, a crime which in New York State might have resulted in a twenty-year sentence. Bars, striped garb, and the work gang were severe punishments, the men agreed, but they were nothing compared to what awaited the child in the state reformatory. George hoped that by giving his citizens an object lesson in the realities of prison life he could save young delinquents from the reformatory. All of George's friends agreed that it was better for the citizens to spend a month or two in the Republic jail than a year or two at Elmira. And without the jail, George believed, self-government would be impossible.

The jail was a constant source of trouble and a ready focus for discontent, however. Charges of cruel and rough treatment at the hands of Republic guards brought investigations by the State Board of Charities and the Syracuse Society for the Prevention of Cruelty to Children in 1901.[40] In addition, parents who thought they were sending their children to obtain a vocational education at the Republic were sometimes shocked to learn that they spent much of their time digging ditches alongside ex-convicts. One father was outraged to discover that he was paying $250 a year for the privilege of having his son work on the prison gang for nothing.[41] Other

[39] Gladden, "The Junior Republic at Freeville," *The Outlook*, LIV (Oct. 31, 1896), 778–782; Riis, "Introduction," MS; Hull, "The George Junior Republic," *Annals of the American Academy of Political and Social Science*, X (Aug. 10, 1897), 73–83; "The End of the Century: An Epitome of Things of Current Interest—The George Junior Republic," *The Argosy*, XXI (Jan. 1896), 301–305.

[40] Syracuse *Post Standard*, Oct. 27, 1901.

[41] Rochester *Herald*, April 13, 1909; Rochester *Evening Post*, April 14, 1909.

critics, such as Homer Lane and the State Board of Charities, believed that it was a mistake to re-enact scenes of the young delinquent's former life by subjecting him to arrest, trial, and sentence. The Republic should provide a radically new environment, they maintained, which taught the delinquent a new principle—"not so much to avoid certain wrong actions as to take the right path because it is the natural one on which to travel." [42] Finally, within the Republic family itself there were those who thought that the Republic jail was an ironic anachronism. How could the Republic hope to replace the old reformatories, they asked, when its own jail was hopelessly old-fashioned? [43]

For years Junior Republic officials had been able to contain incipient scandal. "There is absolutely certain to be . . . trouble" concerning the jail and coeducation, Osborne predicted to Agnew.[44] But a friendly inspector from the State Board of Charities, and the diplomatic skills of Thomas Mott Osborne had headed off all serious conflicts.[45] The internal fighting among Republic trustees in 1913 opened a Pandora's box, however, and the accumulated charges of brutality and sexual permissiveness, the evidence of sexual intercourse among citizens, and an incident of venereal disease in a newly arrived girl led the State Board of Charities to demand the abandon-

[42] Katherine F. Ellis, "A Boys' Republic," *The Outlook*, XCVIII (June 24, 1911), 427.

[43] Jacob G. Smith to G. Spencer Richardson, Oct. 22, 1912.

[44] Osborne to A. G. Agnew, Nov. 26, 1901. Twenty years later, Stowe expressed a similar conviction in his "Radio Talk on the George Junior Republic," WGBS, Dec. 8, 1922.

[45] William R. George, "Statement about the State Board of Charities and Its Secretary Robert W. Hebbard," MS, 1914. For example, in 1907 Superintendent Parker resigned after being charged with improper conduct toward a girl citizen. The State Board of Charities investigated the matter, was satisfied with the Trustees' action and kept the issue quiet. William R. George, Diary, June 20–Nov. 11, 1907.

ment of the Republic penal system, the dismissal of all girls, and the resignation of William R. George.[46]

Shortly thereafter, the trustees launched an investigation of their own. After hiring Emory R. Buckner of the firm of Elihu Root to serve as counsel for the Association, the trustees invited Joseph H. Choate, Lillian Wald, and Justice Samuel Seabury to independently investigate the morals charges brought against George and the Republic. The State Board of Charities had been unclear concerning George's personal morality. The three trustee-appointed judges absolved George of criminal conduct but censured him for "willful misconduct" which was in the "highest degree improper." [47]

What did the two reports add up to? Henry W. Thurston, writing for *Survey*, concluded that "the decision is . . . so indecisive that Mr. George's enemies, with apparent justification, declare it a condemnation and his friends, with equal warrant, hail it as an exoneration." [48] Where did the truth lie? Thurston believed that the report of the judges shifted the issue from one of crime and moral character to a question of conventionality, good judgment, and good pedagogy. In other words, the judges did not establish that " 'Daddy George' is other than he has always seemed; namely a big, warm-hearted, unconventional dynamo of a man whose consuming passion is to try to teach boys and girls to play a square game from free choice and not from external compulsion." [49] *The Outlook* and the Ithaca *Daily Journal* concurred that George's only

[46] "Report of the Special Committee on the George Junior Republic," 508–509.

[47] Quoted from the report of Choate, Wald, and Seabury, Feb. 17, 1914, as noted in Henry W. Thurston, "George," *Survey*, XXXI (March 14, 1914), 755–756.

[48] Thurston, "George," 756.

[49] Thurston, "The Junior Republic Idea," *Survey*, XXXII (May 16, 1914), 203.

indiscretion was his naïve belief that he could really be a father to adolescent girls. "Mr. George's attitude toward the citizens has been parental in its intimacy," *The Outlook* observed, "and it is this that has subjected him to severe criticism which, after several years of agitation by his opponents, brought about the grave charges made to the State Board of Charities and to the investigating committee of his own trustees." [50]

Both critics and defenders of the Junior Republic agreed that the basic question under dispute transcended the specific issues of moral laxity. The Ithaca *Daily News* attempted to dismiss the report of the State Board of Charities by suggesting that the Board still clung to the "old fashioned reformatory idea." *The Outlook* agreed that the Board had demonstrated an "utter lack of comprehension of the underlying principles of Mr. George's remarkable institution." In an impassioned and picturesque speech to the National Association of Junior Republics, Benjamin Lindsey charged that the attack upon the founder of the Junior Republic was analogous to the attack upon himself, the founder of the Juvenile Court. A. E. Winship supported Lindsey's defense, observing, "[George's] methods are so radically different than those of others, that the much greater success of his methods impeaches all official and institutional methods. The nationalizing of his work and the universalizing of it would put every board of state charities out of a job." [51]

[50] "Mr. George and the Freeville Republic," *The Outlook*, CVI (March 21, 1914), 622–624. See also, "Mr. George," *ibid.*, CVI (March 28, 1914), 656–657; Ithaca *Journal*, Sept. 15, 1914.

[51] Ithaca *Daily News*, Dec. 22, 1913; "Mr. George and the Freeville Republic," *The Outlook*, CVI, 622; Benjamin Lindsey before the National Association of Junior Republics, Jan. 3, 1914; A. E. Winship, "William R. George," *Journal of Education*, LXXIX (Jan. 8, 1914), 42.

The defenders of the George Junior Republic failed to realize that they were flogging a dead horse. Fundamentally, they were still fighting the battle against the institutionalism of the Old Penology. In 1913, however, the main threat to the Junior Republic came not from the reformatory, but from the professionalization of social work. Edward T. Devine, Frederick Wines, John Lewis Gillin, Calvin Derrick, Bernard Glueck, Maurice Parmelee, and William I. Thomas accepted the Junior Republic's indictment of the Old Penology and the reformatory system, but by 1915 their guide to penal reform was to become William Healy's *The Individual Delinquent* instead of *Citizens Made and Remade.*[52]

Healy's *Individual Delinquent* was a major turning point in American institutional history.[53] Healy, an associate professor in the field of nervous and mental disorders at the Chicago Polyclinic from 1903 to 1916, studied the mental, physical, environmental, and educational histories of numerous delinquents and mental defectives. He concluded that there was no simple solution to the problem of delinquency, and no single program sufficient to cope with the varieties of antisocial behavior. Healy stressed instead "the importance of multi-causal, differential diagnosis as the foundation of scientific casework.

[52] Edward T. Devine, *The Spirit of Social Work* (New York, 1912), 108–109; Frederick Wines, *Punishment and Reformation* (New York, 1919), 384 ff.; John Lewis Gillin, *Criminology and Penology* (New York, 1926), 616–617; Calvin Derrick, "Self-government," *Survey*, XXXVIII (Sept. 1, 1917), 473–479; Maurice Parmelee, *Criminology* (New York, 1918), 439–440; William I. Thomas and Dorothy Swaine Thomas, *The Child in America* (New York, 1928), 122 ff.

[53] Boston, 1915. At least two scholars have noted the importance of Healy's book: Roy Lubove, *The Professional Altruist*, 64–66; Robert Claridge, "The Rise and Fall of the Reformatory: The Anatomy of a Reform Tradition, 1790–1930" (senior honors thesis, Williams College, 1968), 168–175.

Social workers had to discard preconceived theories about behavior and investigate each case empirically and objectively, considering the relevant mental, physical and social facts." [54] Healy questioned the usefulness of traditional punitive methods used in homes, schools, and reformatories, a questioning which he would have extended to the George Junior Republic. Although Healy was also anti-institutional, his program was almost the antithesis of Junior Republic methods. The scientific rhetoric and methods of the new criminology, with its emphasis on testing and individual therapy, made the Junior Republic appear hopelessly obsolete. Increasingly the Junior Republic motto, "Nothing without Labor," was regarded as romantic, unscientific, and even repressive. As Progressivism entered its third decade, efficiency, objectivity, and professionalism in social work replaced the evangelical intimacy and volunteerism characteristic of the 1890's. In 1895, the George Junior Republic had ridden the front wave of Progressivism, but by 1913 it was swept aside by the onrush of professionalism and bureaucracy, and was left caught in a stagnant eddy of social reform. [55]

George was not oblivious to the threat Healy's philosophy presented to the Junior Republic. Following the 1913 report of the State Board of Charities, George confessed that it was impossible for the model of the anti-institutional New Penology to cling to the old jail system. Accordingly, he introduced into the Junior Republic a new scheme called the "Social Sanitarium" to be run by an officer known as the "Social Doctor." The details of the scheme are complex, but its purpose was simple and direct: George hoped to replace the discredited jail with a more "scientific" method of Republic discipline while at the same time protecting citizen self-gov-

[54] Lubove, *The Professional Altruist,* 66.
[55] Claridge, "The Rise and Fall of the Reformatory," 173–175.

ernment. The idea turned out to be a hodge-podge of new rhetoric and old methods:

The idea is based upon a system of successive enclosures, all self-governing and self-supporting communities. The commitment to the Social Sanitarium would not constitute the loss of citizenship in the community. The treatment for social illness would be substituted for punishment for crime, and yet maudlin methods should not prevail and upon occasion even heroic surgery might be in order.[56]

The establishment of the Social Sanitarium following the time of troubles might have reflected the deterioration of the interpersonal relationship between "Daddy" George and his children. This more "professional" scheme may have been George's reaction to his dismal failure to establish a close familial relationship with the citizens. More likely, the Social Sanitarium represented George's attempt to emulate recent social scientific ideas and thus regain part of his lost reputation by re-entering the mainstream of social work. George was driven to adopt the disease analogy and rhetoric which he and Osborne had earlier rejected. After Healy, the revival of the idea of "social illness" became popular among the new school of Progressive reformers because it gave them a basis for scientific treatment of delinquency.[57] George proposed the Social Sanitarium in the vain hope of reconciling his old friends.[58]

[56] George, "Practical Working of the Social Sanitarium," MS, 1916.
[57] Robert Bremner, *From the Depths: The Discovery of Poverty in the United States* (New York, 1956), 130. A book which purportedly influenced George was W. P. Capes' *The Social Doctor* (New York, 1913). A detailed description of the Social Sanitarium scheme can be found in George, *The Adult Minor* (New York, 1937).
[58] Ithaca *Daily News*, May 7, 1915; Pittsburgh *Sun*, Jan. 20, 1917. The George Junior Republic Papers contain several of George's

George promoted the Social Sanitarium concurrently with his new schemes on the Junior Municipality and the City Republic. In their last major feature on the Junior Republic, *The Outlook* and *Survey* dutifully hailed George's pseudo-scientific program.[59] Most of his former friends ignored the Social Sanitarium, however, and the venture into "experimental sociology" did not even fool George's most devoted followers. From Charles Dawson, an ex-citizen and member of the California Legislature, came an amused observation: "I note that you have a fancy name for the old jail. Shades of Chief of Police Spike McKean, do you mean to let us old timers understand that the 'hoosegow' is just a plain, everyday 'social sanitarium?' It used to be the 'can,' the 'jug,' and the 'pen' when Elmer Newman was judge."[60]

iii

The time of troubles left the Republic without a superintendent or citizens, and an $18,000 debt. After the removal of state wards from the Republic, the State Board of Charities ordered withdrawal of all state funds. At the same time, private support of the institution all but collapsed. By September of 1914, the Board of Trustees, seeing no alternatives for the empty Junior Republic, decided to close the doors. On October 1, 1914, the National Association of Junior Republics closed its New York office and the entire executive committee, with the exception of Leonard Levine and Stowe, re-

---

manuscripts on the Social Sanitarium, among them "The Social Sanitarium and the Social Doctor," "The Social Laboratory," and "Practical Working of the Social Sanitarium."

[59] George, "Prison Walls without a Prison," *Survey*, XXXIX (Nov. 3, 1917), 120–123; "Social Sanitariums and Social Doctors," *The Outlook*, CXXVII (Jan. 5, 1921), 18–21; "The Jail inside Yourself," *Survey*, XLIX (Oct. 15, 1922), 82–84.

[60] Charles Dawson to George, Jan. 28, 1923.

signed.[61] Stowe was pessimistic whether the Republic could survive. He wrote to George in mid-September: "My opinion is that the trustees would rather close the place up than turn it over to you and your new Board unless they have absolute assurance of the payment of the debts and a reasonable prospect that the Republic will be able to make both ends meet under the new management." Somehow George gave the old Board of Trustees the necessary assurances, and on September 24 he once again assumed leadership of the Junior Republic.[62]

It was obvious that some radical changes were in order in Freeville if George's program for rehabilitation of youth were to continue. The introduction of the Social Sanitarium was only a minor issue compared to the need for raising money and recruiting citizens. George decided to accept no more children from the State of New York, thus freeing himself from the scrutiny of the State Board of Charities. In addition, he enrolled no unsupported citizens unless scholarships were provided for them. He hoped to be able to attract a new core of "Republic pioneers," similar to the group he had gathered in 1895, and by November he reported he had enrolled more than twenty new citizens.[63] In addition to his recruiting drive, George launched two major innovations. First, he concluded that all citizens of the Junior Republic need not live within the boundaries of the institution. A variation of the Junior Municipality–Junior City scheme, George proposed that citizens be able to maintain their citizenship in the Republic while working for some outside employer. Second, he explored possibilities of establishing new industries within the

[61] Minutes of the George Junior Republic Association, Sept. 12, 1914; Minutes of the semi-annual meeting of the NAJR, Nov. 18, 1914.

[62] Stowe to George, Sept. 17, 1914; Ithaca *Daily News*, Sept. 23, 1914.

[63] Mrs. William R. George to Christian Jeremiason, Nov. 11, 1914.

Republic and obtaining outside employment for the older citizens.[64]

Throughout 1915 and into the spring of 1916, the new plan slowly took shape in George's mind. He wrote to Paul A. Davis of Union Theological Seminary: "It is my purpose to have established industries in the Republic. It is my hope that one or more reliable manufacturers will place a branch of their business in the Junior Republic." [65] George worked throughout the winter of 1915–1916 toward this end. In January, he opened negotiations with Hart I. Seeley of the Spencer Glove Company, Waverly, New York. George envisioned a small Spencer plant in Freeville as a beginning toward making the Freeville Republic self-supporting. But an acute shortage of leather brought on by the war stopped this plan.[66]

Finally, in April, a week after he wrote to Davis, George secured the promise of Charles A. Miller of Cortland to locate a branch of his corset factory in Freeville if George could provide thirty girls, ages 16–21, and the old print shop in which to work. In the meantime, Miller hired seven Junior Republic boys to work in Cortland. George immediately sent out a flood of letters attempting to recruit workers for the new factory.[67]

[64] George, "Annual Report to the George Junior Republic Association," 1916.

[65] George to Paul A. Davis, April 18, 1916.

[66] George to Hart I. Seeley, Jan. 19, 1916; Spencer Glove Company to George, Nov. 13, 1916.

[67] Mrs. William R. George to her daughter, May 11, 1916; George to Marion Erwin, April 27, 1916; to Elizabeth Shoemaker, April 28, 1916; to James Bell, April 29, 1916; to J. A. Mundell, April 3 and after. The girls were to get $6.00 per week starting salary for three weeks and thereafter placed on piece work. The boys were paid $8–10 a week. Out of this the Republic took $4.00 for room and board. The boys paid the cost of transportation to and from Cort-

While George had, as yet, no reason to suspect his own "Progressivism" or to anticipate his future alienation from certain social welfare groups, he nevertheless cautioned his old friend R. Montgomery Schell: "Don't tell anybody because they might misunderstand, but every boy and girl that comes here and pays for their board with the money which they earn accomplishes just the same for the Republic as a subscription for $200. . . . Formerly every citizen admitted meant more hustling for subscriptions to pay his keep. I like the new method much better." [68]

It was eventually decided to discontinue all attempts to raise money by subscription and place the whole emphasis on self-support. To this end the Republic began to accept only able-bodied boys over sixteen (or boys 14–16 if they had a work permit).[69] Within a year of his first success in getting outside employment for his citizens in Cortland, George arranged for boys to begin work at the Corona Typewriter Works in Groton, New York. Soon about one-third of the total population of the Junior Republic was commuting to Groton for work, a few reporting to the Groton Road Roller Company. There is further evidence that other Junior Republic citizens were "farmed out" to work and live in towns and cities within a forty-five-mile radius of Freeville. Whether

---

land. While debts were reportedly cut to $1,000, it is not known whether industrial work was the chief factor in this. The weekly cost per capita on 78 citizens from Oct. 1, 1915, to Oct. 1, 1916, was $3.00 (George Junior Republic Report on Cost of Maintenance, Oct. 1, 1916).

[68] George to Schell, May 15, 1916.

[69] George to A. S. West, Aug. 9, 1916, and to Charles O. Smith, July 24, 1916. The Junior Republic also accepted citizens who paid their own expenses; their annual fee, which entitled them to attend school rather than to work in the factory, was $330 for grammar school students and $350 for those in high school (George to R. G. Stoddard, Sept. 11, 1916).

the George Junior Republic received a reimbursement for their services has not been determined.[70]

While George found it easy to secure wartime work for his citizens outside of the Republic, he was unsuccessful in persuading manufacturers to locate in Freeville. Although the Corona Company sent some assembling work to the Junior Republic, which temporarily occupied about a dozen girls, George's promise, to "give the use of grounds or buildings . . . for manufacturing purposes on the most reasonable terms and such labor as the nature of our work brings," did not attract substantial offers.[71]

Through a contact in the Big Brother Organization of Syracuse, George arranged for war-industry employment for thirty-three more of his girls who were housed in what was called the "Syracuse Section of the George Junior Republic." [72] The war reduced the number of Republic boys to zero, leaving the struggling Republic in Freeville with but twenty-five girls who tended vegetable gardens and a small herd of dairy cattle.

[70] Mrs. William R. George to George Lamarche, April 21, 1917; George to Henry Schneider, April 27, 1917; Mrs. William R. George to Alvord A. Baker, May 18, 1917; George to Emily Howland, Aug. 2, 1917. The boys working at the Corona Works reportedly earned from $7–15 per week, $5.20 of which was turned over to the Junior Republic for room, board, and transportation. During this period the Junior Republic did not pay clothing, educational, or medical expenses. George admitted that it would be impossible to work and attend school (George to Charles O. Smith, July 31, 1916).

[71] George, MS, Dec. 1917. In December of 1916, a toy manufacturer declined such an invitation (R. E. Simon to George, Dec. 12, 1916), as did the Ithaca Gun Co. (Louis D. Smith to George, Oct. 13, 1917).

[72] These girls wore khaki uniforms and led a military life. Their reported salary was $12–30 a week; Syracuse *Herald*, April 17, 1918; Syracuse *Post*, June 9, 1918.

In the fall of 1918, George once again attempted to lure an industry to the Republic. On September 1, he signed a contract with Atlantic Woolen Mills of Dryden, which proposed to cut up old wool suits in order to extract used wool for sailors' uniforms. Unfortunately the enterprise went bankrupt before the year was out.[73]

The George Junior Republic did not escape the heavy blow the war dealt to many other welfare and reform agencies. The desperation which seems to have seized George can be measured, in part, by his ludicrous attempts to get a trouser factory established at Freeville and to secure Mrs. Andrew D. White as a "godmother" for a series of industries to teach girls the practical arts of dairying, chicken raising, gardening, and laundering.[74] This time of troubles weighed so heavily on George that, long after the rest of the country had returned to "normalcy," he lamented:

I feel sometimes as if we were almost deserted by the world, so far as financial help is concerned. Instead of rendering us aid in a life and death struggle, it seems as if the aforesaid world is standing on the sidelines vociferously applauding our struggle for existence and shouting, Bravo, Bravo and between the whiles arguing amongst themselves, how much longer we will be able to hold out.[75]

This bitter feeling of isolation and alienation became related to postwar xenophobia. Only gradually did George begin to realize how little he had in common with the left wing of the

[73] George, "Annual Report to the George Junior Republic Association," 1918. According to the terms of the contract, the bakery was rented to the war industry for $1.00 per year, and the girls were to be paid at a minimum rate of 2¢ per pound of processed wool.

[74] George to Mrs. A. D. White, Jan. 15, 1919; David Hershman to George, Sept. 30, 1919.

[75] George to Richard Welling, Jan. 2, 1922.

social welfare movement, but although the Red Scare seems to have solicited a belated response in George, it fully captivated him. Bewildered over the cause of the waning interest in the Junior Republic, George concluded that the enemies of "Americanism" must have singled out the Junior Republic as a special threat to communism. "I believe," George wrote in November 1922, "that if some person carefully and wisely outlined the far reaching and hellish work of this group who is trying to destroy our nation and placed beside it the idea of the Junior Republic as an antidote, people who believe in Americanism would gladly support our efforts financially to throttle Bolshevistic education." [76] It is not surprising that George began to wonder whether un-American tendencies had been displayed by those who apparently had abandoned the Freeville Republic.

Such a connection began to form in George's mind after he sent out a circular declaring that a strict adherence to the Junior Republic motto would "strangle communist sprouts of any chance to flourish in the heart of American Youth." [77] A patron of the Republic regretfully responded that she had been greatly misled by the slogan "Nothing without Labor" into supposing that the Republic was a progressive center for training youths in the principle of a cooperative commonwealth. As an old friend of the Republic she could only express her regret that George put himself and his citizens on record in such a reactionary light.[78]

While George was not dispirited by the withdrawal of financial aid by persons he labeled "parlor pink," it cannot be doubted that his increasing isolation from the mainstream of the social welfare movement drove him steadily into the camp

[76] George to Edmund Sinclair, Nov. 8, 1922.
[77] George, "Letter Number Two," MS, Jan. 1923.
[78] Mrs. A. B. Campbell-Shields to George, Feb. 27, 1923.

of the extreme right wing. In an attempt to find new allies, George wrote to Etta V. Leighton, civic secretary of the National Security League, that he hoped he might be able "to work in conjunction with those splendid men and women of the National Security League in the task of 'doing up' Bolshevism, Communism, Socialism and a few other 'isms' which are striving to throttle the one 'ism,' more important than life itself—Americanism!" [79]

The extent to which George's position was changing is graphically illustrated by his response to a questionnaire on settlement houses sent out by Etta Leighton. In it George stated that while he had always supported the aims and ideals of settlement houses, he suspected that they had "tendencies to lean to socialistic ideas destructive to our nation and life." [80] Thus, on June 2, 1924, when the United States Senate approved a resolution for a proposed twentieth amendment to the Constitution, which would authorize Congress "to limit, regulate, and prohibit the labor of persons under the age of eighteen," William R. George was well along the route which would allow him to fight against its ratification with embittered fury.[81]

George's first reaction to the threat of the proposed amendment was rather mild. As late as May of 1924, George still held his membership on the New York Child Labor Committee. In response to the Committee's circular soliciting support for the amendment, George wrote, "There is no one who believes more in a law of some sort regulating child labor up to the age of sixteen years than the writer of this letter, but

[79] George to Etta V. Leighton, Jan. 27, 1923.
[80] George to E. V. Leighton, Mar. 2, 1923.
[81] Richard B. Sherman, "The Rejection of the Child Labor Amendment," *Mid-America*, XLV (Jan. 1963), 3–17, presents a comprehensive analysis of the defeat of the amendment.

great was my distress when I discovered that the proposed amendment to the Constitution included the years sixteen to eighteen." In a note to the New York *Times*, he wrote: "The world has yet to awaken to the great truth that around the age of sixteen a child evolves both physically and mentally into a man, not as mature as one of twenty-five years, but nevertheless 90% more a man than a child." No person over sixteen years of age needed special protection from the United States government.[82]

But George realized that the point at issue was more than the right of sixteen-to-eighteen-year-olds to work. He also knew that the proposed amendment would not hamper the work of a vocational school. Rather, George believed that the child labor amendment was a "slap in the face to everything which the Junior Republic exemplifies in the line of civic and economic responsibility." He surmised that what was at stake was the vindication of the principles of the Junior Republic: "Is it not asking too much of any person—man, woman, or child who is physically and mentally fit, if from early youths they acquire daily experience in spiritual, social, recreative, economic, and civic activities?—the Junior Republic is a concrete exemplification of these attributes and its extension would be of inestimable value." The greatest fear that George harbored from his Fresh Air days was that idleness among teenagers would inexorably breed boredom and crime. "When a youngster can't work, his only economic outlet is a gift or stealing. When the first is impossible the second is inevitable."[83]

[82] George to Jennie V. Minor, May 9, 1924; George to the editor of the New York *Times*, June 16, 1924. A similar sentiment is expressed in a letter to Henry W. Thurston, June 9, 1924.
[83] George to Charles Dawson, Aug. 8, 1924; MS, 1924–1925; and undated MS.

Interpreters of the defeat of the child labor amendment have noted that it was the first and most serious defeat suffered by social reform during the first half of the twentieth century. There had been setbacks before, but the defeat of the amendment represented a more fundamental blow to Progressivism. According to the proponents of the amendment, the struggle to abolish child labor was one of the few clear-cut and unambiguous confrontations between liberal reformers and arch-reactionaries—and the reactionaries won. Few opponents of the child labor amendment defended child labor, and all gave lip service to the ideals of the reformers, but having proclaimed that state laws were sufficient to control the problem

they were free to denounce the amendment as the work of vicious plotters intent on destroying local self-government, nationalizing the children, and subverting the authority of the family, home, church and school. They represented the sponsors of the measure as fanatics determined to stop young boys from the wholesome exertion of milking the family cow, to prevent young girls from the maidenly task of washing dishes, and to spare all children under eighteen from the nightly chore of school homework.[84]

At first George was confused by the issue. He had long supported child labor laws, and had reservations about the amendment only because it included adolescents above the age of sixteen. George certainly did not defend the "right" of little children to work in the mines and textile factories. But he was concerned that the so-called child-centered society, which refused to enfranchise its adult minors, was taking one

[84] Bremner, *From the Depths*, 227. Jeremy Felt's *Hostages of Fortune* is an excellent history written from the records of the New York Child Labor Committee. See also Frank Bruno, Jr., and Louis Towley, *Trends in Social Work, 1874–1956* (New York, 1957), 160–167; Clarke A. Chambers, *Seedtime of Reform*, 29–58.

more step in the direction of isolating youth from meaningful participation and responsibility in the society. Eventually, George adopted all the rhetoric of the right-wing extremists, at first because it was a means of identifying himself with the opposition to the amendment, but in the end because he believed it. By 1925 he was able to write that "Americanism, our country, and its Constitution" could only be maintained by a stout defense against the dangerous elements which supported the child labor amendment:

I am more convinced than ever that the assaults on business interests of our country, by socialists, near socialists, parlor socialists, labor unions, certain social workers and their friends, are not only unfair, but are dangerous to our country, and something must be quietly,—slowly—but not too slowly—organized to bring the effort of these destructive forces to confusion.[85]

During the summer of 1924, George's activities against the amendment were largely confined to talking with visitors who passed through Freeville. It was not until the first of September that he wrote to the secretary of the Syracuse Chamber of Commerce about forming a committee to combat the amendment. On the same day, in a meeting with Carleton A. Chase, president of the First Trust and Deposit Company of Syracuse, George was introduced to the efforts of the National Association of Manufacturers to defeat the proposal. Immediately he sent a request to James A. Emery, general counsel of the NAM, for one hundred copies of a pamphlet that attacked the amendment. Later, George sent for a package of antiamendment leaflets printed by the American Constitutional League. On the same day that he appeared before a committee of the Republican State Convention to speak

[85] George to Samuel J. A. Page, Jan. 9, 1925; George, MS, Feb. 24, 1925.

against the amendment, George accepted an invitation to canvass Massachusetts.[86] For two weeks, October 5–20, George traveled through the state, speaking primarily before high school audiences and distributing tracts printed by the Franklin Print Shop of the George Junior Republic.[87] The amendment was defeated in Massachusetts by a three-to-one majority in a referendum on November 4, 1924.

George believed that by using the same tactics the amendment could be defeated in New York State, and he began extensive speaking tours. In Buffalo he publicly debated Julia Lathrop, vice-president of the League of Women Voters. In a spirited and exciting meeting, J. Doyle, a labor leader, charged from the floor that George was in league with the "interests." George vehemently denied the charge, and later piously asserted, "the story that the manufacturers flooded the state [Massachusetts] with money for propaganda and lecturers in opposition to the amendment is not true. I don't recall the name of a single manufacturer or the committee combatting the amendment." [88]

Also, in Buffalo, George debated his former colleague Owen Lovejoy, now secretary of the National Child Labor Committee. The Frontier Defense League, with which George was in correspondence, described Lovejoy as an intimate friend of Eugene Debs. This organization even went so far as to

[86] George, MS, Feb. 7, 1925; George to James A. Emery, Sept. 10, 1924; to Henry S. Carr, Sept. 12, 1924; to A. J. Philpot, Sept. 23, 1924; to James W. Wadsworth, Sept. 8, 1923.

[87] The literature George distributed was partly financed by the NAM (Richard Welling to the office of the president of National Association of Manufacturers, Oct. 4, 1924). George did not limit himself strictly to high school audiences, speaking occasionally before civic and service groups (Boston *Globe*, Oct. 8, 1924). Sherman considers the stunning defeat of the amendment in Massachusetts as the death blow to the movement in 1924.

[88] Buffalo *Evening News*, Oct. 24, 1924; George to Clara Sabo, Oct. 5, 1933.

charge that the amendment "follows the orders issued from Moscow to the Young Communists in the United States to work for the abolition of labor by minors under 18." [89]

As a result of these activities, George's association with right-wing organizations became rather close. He was appointed vice-chairman of the New York State Committee for the Protection of Our Homes and Children, a group described as most responsible for the dissemination of antiamendment propaganda which concentrated on the threat to the family and the menace of communism. He also joined an organization, headed by Louis A. Coolidge, treasurer of the United Shoe Company of Boston, which called itself the Sentinels of the Republic. The Sentinels, who opposed social and labor reform generally, asked George to be their recruiting officer for the Finger Lakes region.[90]

As George moved solidly into the conservative camp, his break with the left wing of the social welfare movement became complete. Though he attended a Conference of Charities and Correction in Buffalo, he described himself "as popular as a skunk at a Sunday School picnic."

My friends—perhaps I should have said "former friends"—in social work are beginning to regard me as an outcast, a "traitor to childhood." I am beginning to reap the whirlwind. Several of our best contributors love us no more!

One of these days we must organize the Social Workers of our country who are not swayed by sentiment but believe most heartily in the Junior Republic motto: "Nothing without Labor." [91]

[89] George to Cora D. Green, Jan. 9, 1925; Frontier Defense League, Bulletin No. 116, Jan. 19, 1925.

[90] Felt, *Hostages of Fortune*, 202–205; Katharine T. Balch to George, Mar. 24, 1925. The motto of the Sentinels of the Republic was, "Every Citizen a Sentinel, Every Home a Sentry Box!"

[91] George to Lewis Coolidge, Feb. 5, 1925. Several other citations are possible here, among them *The Advocate of the George Junior*

Yet George's new position did have its compensations. "I am coming into contact with a lot of very interesting people whom I know will help us later on the money business" he wrote as early as November 10, 1924.[92] Just after his lecture trip to Massachusetts in October, George met a Mr. Roberts who revived the old dream of establishing a factory at Freeville, suggesting that he might open a silk manufacturing plant. This time, however, the Board of Trustees would have nothing to do with such a scheme. Instead they suggested that the Republic might best be served by improving and expanding the existing work of the carpentry shop, the bakery, and the Franklin Print Shop.[93] Such a drive had long been contemplated. During the fight against the child labor amendment, George had suggested to Mark A. Daly, president of the Associated Industries of Buffalo, that a group of manufacturers might be persuaded to aid the Junior Republic. Daly at that time counseled patience and suggested that the drive be postponed until after the amendment was safely put away.[94]

By spring of 1925 the drive for ratification seemed a certain failure.[95] George now turned his full energies back to his Junior Republic. At first the plans for raising funds were vague, it being certain only that the manufacturers' associations, with which George had so recently and closely worked, would play a major role. George explained:

Republic, Mar. 1925; Dr. Harold E. B. Speight to George, Mar. 9, 1925. While George claimed not to be unduly troubled, he was undoubtedly saddened to hear that his dear old friend Judge Lindsey was leading the fight for the child labor amendment in Colorado.

[92] George to Richard Welling, Nov. 10, 1924.

[93] George to Welling, April 12, 1925; Welling to George, April 15, 1925.

[94] George to Mark A. Daly, Mar. 16, 1925.

[95] Sherman, "The Rejection of the Child Labor Amendment," 14.

The suggestion is that the manufacturers association either officially or unofficially request that the George Junior Republic Association permit the manufacturers to contribute to the Republic Association money to be used for the building trades or any other special project they desire.

The persons making these suggestions reason that it would place the burden of raising funds upon the manufacturers. Through an action of this sort it would probably be easier to collect money than it would if the manufacturers simply gave the Junior Republic Association an invitation to solicit funds from the manufacturers organizations.[96]

Eventually it was proposed that a $1,500,000 endowment fund campaign for the Republic be sponsored by "manufacturers *everywhere*" so that "we will be able to place the Republic on a firm financial foundation." [97] John E. Edgerton, president of the National Association of Manufacturers, was asked to be chairman of the National Campaign Committee. He refused. Later, John R. Finley, editor of the New York *Times*, accepted the chairmanship after Livingston Farrand, president of Cornell University, pledged his support. Franklin D. Roosevelt lent his name as one who would serve on the National Committee. John J. Pershing even agreed to write "To an Unknown Giver," a pamphlet appealing for endowment funds.[98] But the first flush of optimism eventually gave way to discouragement. Of the proposed $1,500,000, only $75,106 was raised. George admitted that the causes of the

[96] George to Jack Calder, April 23, 1925.

[97] John D. Strain to Mark A. Daly, Aug. 28, 1925. Strain, president of the Industrial Association of Utica, became a loyal friend of the Republic and a member of the Board of Trustees.

[98] John E. Edgerton to George, Dec. 14, 1925; John R. Finley to George, Feb. 1, 1925; Ralph Hedges to George, Feb. 2, 1925. A partial list of the National Committee is found in George to Mark Daly, Nov. 28, 1925.

failure seemed threefold: the isolation of Freeville from large cities; the belief that the Republic was self-supporting; and the fear that the George Junior Republic was, after all, a one-man affair.[99]

Rebuffed by the industrialists, separated from his former colleagues, George assessed the progress of the past decade with unconscious irony:

A strange yet unnatural evolution developed in this work. It was catalogued as one of many distinct activities in the multitude of other active movements for social betterment. . . . [But] the incident [of child labor] showed conclusively how far the Junior Republic and its policies were removed from most of its contemporaries. We were assailed with selling out to the textile industries and "interests" in general. It was an amusing statement for the Junior Republic was receiving nothing from any of the interests as such and little or nothing from any of their respective leaders.[100]

Only two alternatives appeared open. On the one hand, with no greater success then before, George revived the ancient plan to have an industry established in Freeville. On the other, he plunged deeper into right-wing activities. In *The Monitor*, a publication of the Associated Industries of New York State, George criticized the five-day, forty-hour work week, and vindictively charged the American Federation of Labor with being the American Federation of Anti-Labor. In a letter to Mark Daly, he even expressed opposition to state laws prohibiting child labor below the age of sixteen.[101] The only way to save the current situation, George

[99] Syracuse Chamber of Commerce, Committee on Solicitations, Bulletin No. 70, June 2, 1926; George to Charles Dawson, April 14, 1927.

[100] George, "To Whom It May Concern," MS, 1931.

[101] George to Board of Trustees of the George Junior Republic, Oct. 18, 1926; "Organization for the Future," MS, Dec. 10, 1926;

believed, would be to form on the right wing of the social welfare movement a viable organization, to counterbalance a left wing that was "top-heavy with communists, socialists and promoters of the closed shop." [102]

Thus George joined forces with those promoting "welfare capitalism." There followed conferences with Cameron Black of the Welfare Department and the Stock Exchange, and Erich Nicol, director of Western Union Messengers. On behalf of George, John D. Strain wrote to William J. Cronin, secretary of the New York and New Jersey Branch of the National Metal Trades Association, requesting $5,000 to enable George to promote right-wing activities from a New York City office. In November, George reported to Mark Daly that he had found few respondents when he attempted to drum up right-wing support at a meeting of the New York State Social Workers. Later in the month, he received financial aid from Strain to attend regional child labor conferences in Albany, Binghamton, and Rochester. How far and in what direction his work in "welfare capitalism" would have carried George can only be surmised. In March of 1929 he suffered a severe gall bladder attack; the next year, in March and November, he suffered two heart attacks.[103]

Although his strenuous activities were reduced, George could not resist hatching new schemes. Failing to attach himself firmly to "welfare capitalism," George proposed to found an organization in New York City called The League for

---

"The Five-Day Week," *The Monitor*, XIII (Oct. 1926); letter to Mark Daly, Oct. 18, 1926.

[102] George to Thomas Kelly, May 16, 1928; MS of speech George delivered before the Hartford Manufacturer's Association, June 14, 1928; George to Catherine M. Cummery, May 17, 1928.

[103] George to C. M. Cummery, May 17, 1928; John D. Strain to William J. Cronin, Aug. 8, 1928; George to Mark Daly, Nov. 15, 1928, and to John D. Strain, Nov. 30, 1928.

the Promotion of Civic and Economic Responsibility. The League's main purpose was to act as a backfire to "political liberalism." "La Follette–Pinchotism," and all radicalisms, including communism and socialism.[104] While the basic outline was acceptable to George's new right-wing friends, an assistant manager of the Industrial Bureau of the Merchants' Association of New York complained that the whole concept of the League and its program were too vague to allow concrete commitment.[105]

The Depression eventually forced George to abandon his New York office, but in doing so, he relinquished none of his visions. Shortly after his return to Freeville he was shocked to discover that many "perfectly good ministers and college professors of intimate acquaintance were beginning . . . to go over to Socialism, Communism, and peace-at-any-price pacifism or some other obnoxious absurdity to which I had supposed they were totally immune." [106] "All I want," George told Clayton R. Lusk, "is a few outstanding individuals who are opposed to Communistic, Socialistic and 'pink intellectual' propaganda to serve on a preliminary committee for the National Organization of the Phalanx." The Phalanx plan was an extension of his earlier League proposal. "People of wealth with whom I have some acquaintanceship," George continued, "are interested in our crusade. However, I believe it would be better not to approach them for contributions until we have an organization composed of reliable sponsors." George had learned some hard lessons. The Phalanx idea was initially received with some curiosity. After an article describing

[104] George, "Relative to Organization of a Phalanx," MS, 1931–1932; George to E. A. Smythe, Jan. 9, 1932; to Mrs. Edwin Gruhl, Feb. 22, 1932; to Mrs. Finley J. Shepard, Feb. 23, 1932.

[105] G. F. Bent to George, Nov. 11, 1931.

[106] George, MS, Aug. 26, 1934.

George's new activities appeared in the New York *Evening Post*, the Freeville Republic received numerous inquiries for more information. But, as in the past, interest soon waned, and lack of funds forced George to abandon the project.[107]

At this juncture, George's career entered its last and most tragicomic phase. George himself bluntly set the scene for the final act by declaring, "The Junior Republic is rapidly approaching a crisis which will mean its extinction if steps are not taken." [108]

The last panacea which George organized was called the League of Adult Minors. The Lams, as he affectionately christened them, were organized to fight the three forces threatening American democracy: "Communism, Socialism as propounded by such extremists as Karl Marx and Norman Thomas, and pacifism." The origins of the League of Adult Minors were diffuse. In part it descended from the old Law and Order Gang and the Junior Municipalities established in Ithaca and Cortland in 1913. Other roots can be traced to the defunct Phalanx and League for the Promotion of Civic and Economic responsibility. Mostly, the Adult Minors were a consequence of George's beliefs concerning adolescents. He had always argued that persons between the ages of sixteen and twenty-one were not children. "At the age of sixteen

[107] George to Clayton R. Lusk, Feb. 16, 1932; New York *Evening Post*, May 17, 1932; George, MS, Aug. 26, 1934. Some of those who expressed interest were: A. H. Seed, Jr., vice-president of the Young Men's Board of Trade, May 18, 1932; Charles P. Morse, chairman of the Americanism Committee of the American Legion, May 29, 1932; C. W. Hunt, research director of the Boy Scouts, June 11, 1932; Jesse Gordon of Kuhn, Loeb and Co., president of the Older Boys Council of New York City, June 11, 1932; Charles Tuttle, 1930 Republican candidate for governor; Edward Gray, director of the Wall Street Y.M.C.A.; Clayton Lusk; and Otis E. Smith of the National Electric Light Association, June 19, 1932.

[108] George, MS, June 27, 1933.

young people are actually adults, although legally minors. We shall therefore use the term *adult minor* from now on to designate those between the ages of sixteen and twenty-one." [109] The organization was never very large, with but two or three youths in the Syracuse area who prominently campaigned against social reform, and a small nucleus of college students in New York City who were holdovers from the Phalanx days. Predictably, the main difficulties were financial. George could never understand why some of his well-meaning friends would not "transfer some of the contributions they have been giving to causes masquerading under the plausible, appealing, and sometimes religious names, but are slyly and sometimes openly using the money to extend a propaganda that is destructive to our national life." [110]

When Governor Herbert Lehman, on August 14, 1933, in a message before a special session of the legislature, called for ratification of the child labor amendment, he inadvertently provided a shot in the arm for the sagging League of Adult Minors. Anticipating the governor's action, George had contacted old friends in the Sentinels of the Republic and a newly organized group called the Paul Reveres, announcing that his Lams were prepared to combat the child labor amendment. Just two days after the governor's message, George arrived in Albany to lobby against ratification, with John Kinane, president of the League of Adult Minors, in tow.[111]

George's activities now came to the attention of Jerome D. Barnum, publisher of the Syracuse *Post Standard*. George had written a letter to the editor of the *Post Standard* stating

[109] George to Captain H. E. Richards, April 27, 1933; *The Adult Minor*, 59, 69; letter to the editor of the New York *Times*, June 16, 1924.

[110] George to Walter Drew, April 24, 1934.

[111] George to Alexander Lincoln, July 13, 1933; to E. M. Hadley, July 13, 1933; to Mrs. John Balch, Aug. 23, 1933.

that the chief cause of crime and delinquency in the United States was failure of youth to get jobs. Passage of a child labor amendment, George contended, would only foster and promote crime. To the depression argument, "give father the job," George replied by arguing that it was actually safer to let the father go jobless while his son worked, as the father having familial responsibilities was less likely to turn to violence and crime.[112]

Barnum, who was strongly opposed to the amendment, provided ample space for two of the most active Lams to print their attacks on the amendment. The *Post Standard* also gave considerable coverage of the activities of the League of Adult Minors. One of the fears of the newspaper publishers was that a child labor law might be passed which would jeopardize their use of boys to sell and deliver papers. One device used to challenge the amendment was to organize the paperboys in claiming their rights to work. George, who realized that the newspapers might be charged with "vested interest," suggested that the Newsboys' Organization not oppose the amendment directly, but rather use the League of Adult Minors as a cover organization. At first George's idea was well received, but, as in the past, he suffered bitter disappointment. H. W. Stodghill, chairman of the Newspaper Boy's Welfare Committee of the International Circulation Managers Association, wrote to George on January 24, 1934, congratulating him on his plan, but observing that it was similar to one already being advanced by the ICMA. One week later, George again could state with a touch of irony, "I will be glad to make a sworn statement here tonight to the falsity of the charges of the proponents that the manufacturers —or the magnates of any other industrial groups financed or

[112] George to the editor of the Syracuse *Post Standard*, Oct. 24, 1933; George, MS, c. 1932.

used any other unscrupulous method to accomplish defeat of the measure." In March, *The Monitor* was only too willing to publish this denial.[113]

Again George was brought under the influence of right wing groups. Mary G. Kilbreth, president of the Women's Patriot Publishing Company in 1924, had been the first to charge at the Congressional hearings on March 1, 1924, that national child labor laws were part of a communist plot to acquire state control of children. Now returning to the fight, she requested from George a resolution from his League of Adult Minors that might be quoted in print.[114]

Nicholas Murray Butler, president of Columbia University, who lent considerable respectability to the antiamendment forces in 1924, had subtly suggested that the amendment might be subversive. Ten years later, Butler referred George to Mary G. Kilbreth and requested him to accept a position on the Permanent State Committee to fight the Child Labor Amendment, of which Butler was the chairman.[115]

In this period George joined a temporary organization called the National Committee for the Protection of Child, Family, School, and Church. He became a member of the American Liberty League, kept in close and frequent touch with the American Bar Association Special Committee to

[113] George to Karl H. Thesing, Dec. 17, 1923; E. S. Dobson, circulation manager, Brooklyn *Times Union*, to George, Jan 3, 1934; George to Dobson, Jan. 5, 1934; H. W. Stodghill to George, Jan. 24, 1934; George, "Paper on Proposed Child Labor Amendment" given during a debate with Ralph E. Himstead, professor of constitution law, Syracuse University, Jan. 31, 1934; *The Monitor*, XXI (Mar. 1934).

[114] Mary G. Kilbreth to George, Nov. 29, 1933.

[115] Nicholas Murray Butler to George, Jan. 4, 1934; George to Butler, April 9, 1934. This committee of sixty-eight prominent New York citizens (including Al Smith) was credited as being extremely influential in defeating the measure in committee.

Oppose Ratification of the Federal Child Labor Amendment, and continued his work with the Sentinels of the Republic and the National Association of Manufacturers. Indeed, it was one of the representatives of the National Association of Manufacturers who paid John Kinane's expenses on his lecturing trips against the amendment and communism in the CCC camps.[116]

The climax to this second drive for ratification of the child labor amendment in New York State came at two committee hearings held in Albany in 1935 and 1936. The Senate Judiciary Committee scheduled the first hearing on the amendment for January 23, 1935. Jerome D. Barnum requested that George and a couple of the Adult Minors be present. Appearing with former Chief Justices Frank H. Hiscock and Cuthbert W. Pound, both trustees of Cornell University, George was scheduled as the highlight of the opposition presentation. However, George's speech was cut short, much to his embarrassment, by the long-winded and impassioned plea for the amendment made by Fiorello H. La Guardia. Nevertheless, George managed to charge that persons who sought to secure legislation limiting child labor under all circumstances should be classified as public enemies. He called upon Republicans and Democrats alike to unite against those who would "pussy foot and play with socialists and communists avowedly supporting the amendment."[117]

Clearly the highlight of the proceedings for George was neither his own appearance nor the defeat of the measure, but

[116] Sterling E. Edmunds to George, Jan. 16, 1934; A. P. Fenderson to George, Feb. 21, 1935; George to William Guthrie, Mar. 18, 1934, and after. H. G. Torbert to George, Mar. 22, 1934; George to Noel Sargent, April 24, June 8, 1934, and after.

[117] Jerome D. Barnum to George, Jan. 16 and Jan. 26, 1935; Syracuse *Journal*, Jan. 24, 1935; Ithaca *Journal*, Jan. 23, 1935; Syracuse *Herald*, Jan. 23, 1935; Syracuse *Post-Standard*, Jan. 24, 1935.

rather the testimony of his three Adult Minors. George claimed that they were the first minors ever to testify before a legislative committee. Characteristically, he now believed that all across the country adult minors could be organized to perform the same service. To Sterling Edmunds, director of the National Committee for the Protection of Child, Family, School, and Church, George proposed to send delegations of youths to all state capitals. In another letter to William Guthrie, he complained that the conservatives were sleeping while radicals enlisted youths into their ranks by the thousands. Finally to Noel Sargent of the National Association of Manufacturers, George practically begged for "a few hundred dollars [so] that we could have youthful organizations of Adult Minors in every state of the Union to combat, not only the Child Labor Amendment, but the insidious forces which are destroying our form of government and private ownership. Can't some special committee, composed of industrialists, be formed to study conditions I have mentioned and make recommendations?" [118] Once again, George attempted to embark on a fund-raising campaign. This time he proposed the establishment of Adult Minor Citizenship Centers where young people might be trained in civic and economic responsibility. A budget of $4,290 was proposed but only $2,500 was solicited.[119]

Almost cruelly, the Depression anchored George in Freeville and limited his activities to writing his third book and training his daughters and sons-in-law as successors. His notebook recorded his agony:

[118] George to Sterling Edmunds, Jan. 26, 1935; to William Guthrie, Jan. 29, 1935; to Noel Sargent, Feb. 2, 1935.

[119] Malcolm J. Freeborn, "Report to the Executive Committee of the George Junior Republic," Feb. 4, 1935.

getting old. no money no automobile can't get arround Tied hand and foot in so far as seeing people is concerned. And it would help the world a lot if I could see people. Republic going to the dogs financialy. Loss of prestage Few Citizens Yet it has all the possibilities and even greater than it ever had in the past . . . I am overwhelmed with dissapointment I am heart sick.[120]

To Noel Sargent, George bitterly complained that his little colony could barely keep its head above water. How tragic it was, George lamented, that the only institution devoted to the principles of juvenile economic and civic self-determination should be left to languish. In an apparent fit of depression, George sought to resign from the Executive Committee of the Junior Republic, hoping that if he disassociated himself from it, the Junior Republic might again prosper. Still later he stated that he was convinced that all men with an original idea are doomed to persecution and frustration. In almost incoherent rhetoric, George proclaimed:

What our country needs today is "guts." "Guts" made us a nation . . . our ancestors were not angels. They were hard-boiled and killed Indians and burned witches. . . . In our spine-less "wishy washy" contemplations today we see some human bipeds that we have sound reason for thinking savages and witches and deserve crucifiction . . . but we haven't got the "guts" to do it.

In this day of alphabet soup and wild-eyed communism and shilly shally socialism and metaphorical exclamations of "naughty! naughty!" to nations that are spending their time industriously developing "guts" . . . let us revert to the spirit of our fore-fathers and get busy and regenerate ourselves before it is too late. . . . Brain, brawn and the will to use them, with "malice toward none and charity for all," will annihilate the maudlin

[120] George, Notebook, Oct. 7, 1935.

sentimentalism that has lulled us into imbecility and will vesture us into the nation that our fathers conceived.[121]

An editorial in the New York *Evening Post* caused the Senate Judiciary Committee to give a second and final hearing to the lifeless child labor amendment. At the request of Jerome D. Barnum and Sterling Edmunds, George girded himself for his last public appearance on March 31, 1936. Within three weeks he too would be dead. George's lackluster statement was given a perfunctory five minutes. Practically repeating the statement he had made a year before and on a thousand other occasions, George capitalized and italicized a conclusion which could be emphasized in no other way: "The amendment means the hamstringing of young Americans. If successful it will induce idleness and idleness is the germ of the three deadly cancers of society— *DEPENDENCY, DELINQUENCY AND DEGENERACY.*" [122]

iv

He died at the height of the New Deal, and Harry Elmer Barnes mourned his passing:

The death of William Reuben George marks the passing of one of the major figures in the history of American humanitarianism, reformative methods and education. Out of his experiments at the George Junior Republic have grown a number of major advances both in the reformation of delinquents and in the character building of youth. It is not beyond the bounds of possibility

[121] George to the Board of Trustees of the George Junior Republic, July 10, 1935; to Noel Sargent, Aug. 3, 1935; George, MSS, Jan. 30, 1936, and July 31, 1935.

[122] Jerome D. Barnum to George, Mar. 23, 1936; George, "Paper Read before Committee at Albany," Mar. 31, 1936; Ithaca *Journal*, April 25, 1936.

that his innovations will ultimately revolutionize the treatment of delinquents.[123]

Barnes was being kind. The George Junior Republic had long since made its last major contribution to penal and educational reform. Not only had George failed to keep up with the scientific advancement in his field, but he had never satisfactorily resolved the internal contradictions of his own scheme. He claimed universal applicability for the Junior Republic principle, only to exclude from its benefits those seemingly most in need of them. He assured Progressives that the Junior Republic was not a one-man affair, but never once gave his unqualified support to any work other than his own. He professed that the Junior Republic was a "village just like any other village," and yet was engaged in a constant struggle to maintain the community's normality. He repudiated professionalism in social work, and yet was himself a professional who relied heavily on the support and assistance of other professionals. Finally, he could not decide whether he wanted the Junior Republic to be a microcosmic reflection of the greater society wherein youth could learn how best to cope with the problems and frustrations of life, or whether Freeville was to establish a model community whose experiments in democratic living could be an example for American schools, penal institutions, and society at large. It made little sense, George realized, to reproduce an exact copy of the greater society on the Junior Republic campus. Junior political bosses, robber barons, and labor organizers were outlawed at the Junior Republic, to say nothing of atheists, socialists, and anarchists. George wanted to model his institution after American society "as it actually was," but he could find no suitable

[123] Harry Elmer Barnes, "William Reuben George, Pioneer in Reformation," New York *World Telegram*, May 4, 1936.

"actuality" except in the recesses of the dim, mythical past. As we have noted, George's frantic search for "reality" ironically transformed the Republic principle into a utopian doctrine.

Most reformers were willing to overlook the inconsistencies of this lovable, eccentric man. Though he often fulminated against Republic heretics, George was so inarticulate and vague that he alienated few of his friends. Besides, they cared most about the practical results of his work. If George wanted to stew unnecessarily over Republic principles, they were willing to indulge him as long as he did not interfere with their own work. Though George was horrified by the cannibalization of his ideas, most social workers bent on their own projects felt justified in picking and choosing from the Junior Republic what seemed most appropriate and useful. It is impossible to know the full extent of George's influence, and it is as easy to claim too much as it is to suggest too little. One young lawyer who came of age during the age of Roosevelt actually claimed that George was one of the spiritual forefathers of the New Deal.

When I think of George, I link his name with those of Jacob Riis, Theodore Roosevelt, William Jennings Bryan, Lincoln Steffens, and many another that I read about in my boyhood days. These men stood up in a hardboiled generation as champions of human rights as against property rights. From the seats of the mighty they were greeted with derision and abuse. They were called reformers. But they started a great movement, which has constantly gained in energy and scope so that today it is one of the greatest forces in our civilization.[124]

Latter-day liberals have not shared the enthusiasm of the young lawyer. They have dutifully granted George his con-

[124] Augustus L. Richards to Jacob G. Smith, Dec. 1, 1936.

tributions to student self-government and to Progressive penology. But liberals generally find no tragedy in George's final years. Antagonistic to his reactionary politics, indifferent to his conservative reform, and unsympathetic to his radical potentiality, few liberal intellectuals, then or now, can empathize with a man who failed to understand himself or his times. When they think about him at all, they find his anti-institutionalism chaotic, repressive, and threatening. But the tragic loss belongs to the liberal society itself, for it has forgotten George's conservative warning that peace and stability cannot be maintained in a patronizing society that refuses to give its mature youths meaningful tasks and responsibilities.

The old station that once proudly bore the sign FREE-VILLE lies abandoned along the Lehigh Valley line. An occasional car still unloads lumber into her baggage room, and migrant flocks of sparrows sometimes settle in the lobby for a night's roost before pressing south along the otherwise deserted tracks. Once the subject of a specially prepared tourist's brochure honoring the George Junior Republic, the Freeville station is no longer even a whistle stop. Passenger service was discontinued years ago, and with it passed not one era, but two.

BIBLIOGRAPHICAL NOTE

———————— The sources upon which this study rests are self-evident in the notes. The George Junior Republic Papers held by the Collection of Regional History and University Archives at Cornell University provided the basic manuscript materials. This collection is excellently described by Douglas A. Bakken in "William R. George and the George Junior Republic Papers, 1807–1967," published by Cornell University in conjunction with the Diamond Anniversary of the Junior Republic, June 1970. Also held by Cornell University are the papers of the Western Pennsylvania George Junior Republic, and oral history interviews conducted by Jack M. Holl and Frances M. Keefe. The Thomas Mott Osborne Papers are at Syracuse University.

George wrote three books (*The Junior Republic*, 1910; *Citizens Made and Remade*, 1912; and *The Adult Minor*, 1937) and more than forty published and unpublished articles, brochures, and speeches. Since they are not identical, the bibliographies of both Frances M. Keefe, "The Development of William Reuben (Daddy) George's Educational Ideas and Practices from 1866 to 1914" (Ed.D. dissertation, Cornell University, 1967), and Jack M. Holl, "The George Junior Republic and the Varieties of Progressive Reform" (Ph.D.

dissertation, Cornell University, 1969), should be consulted for primary and secondary materials relating to the Junior Republic movement. M. E. Norris, "The History of the California Junior Republic" (M.A. thesis, University of Southern California, 1930), provides an excellent account of the founding of that institution.

The annual reports of the Conference of Charities and Corrections contain a wealth of materials relating to juvenile reform and education, as do such journals as *Survey*, *World's Work*, *New Republic*, and *The Outlook*. Persons interested in pursuing the implications of George's work within the wider context of social reform should consult the excellent bibliographies in Robert H. Bremner, *From the Depths: The Discovery of Poverty in America* (New York, 1956); Allen F. Davis, *Spearheads for Reform: The Social Settlements and the Progressive Movement, 1890–1914* (New York, 1967); Lawrence A. Cremin, *The Transformation of the School: Progressivism in American Education, 1876–1957* (New York, 1961); W. David Lewis, *From Newgate to Dannemora: The Rise of the Penitentiary in New York, 1796–1848* (Ithaca, N.Y., 1965); and Otis L. Graham, Jr., *An Encore for Reform: The Old Progressives and the New Deal* (New York, 1967).

INDEX

National Education Association,
198
National Junior Republic (An-
napolis Junction, Md.), 10, 139,
264n
National Prison Association, 266
National Prison Congress (1870),
234
National Security League, 316
National Self-Government Commit-
tee (NSGC), 197, 199-201, 288,
293
Negro admitted to GJR, 187, 188
Neil, A. S., 221
New immigrants, 41, 75
New Jersey Junior Republic (Flem-
ington Junction), 158
New Penology, 223, 228, 230-231,
239, 249, 251, 283, 307
New York Child Labor Commit-
tee, 286, 316
New York House of Refuge, 109,
240, 243-248, 251, 255
New York School of Philanthro-
py, 271
Newbold, John, 139
Newgate Prison, 232, 244
Nicol, Erich, 325
Norfolk Island Penal Colony (Aus-
tralia), 234
North China Junior Republic As-
sociation, 208
"Nothing without Labor," 96, 101-
103, 110, 141, 176-177, 186, 192,
218, 234, 287, 297, 307, 313
Noyes, John Humphrey, 222

Olcott, E. E., 19n, 20
Old Penology, 223, 227-229, 231-
232, 240, 243, 263, 266, 276, 279-
281, 283-284, 306
Orton, William C., 118, 126
Osborne, Agnes Devens, 25, 26
Osborne, David Munson, 23, 25
Osborne, Eliza Wright, 23
Osborne, Thomas Mott, 4, 8, 19n,
21, 42, 43n, 49, 57, 109, 125,
126-127, 129-131, 141, 160, 163,
204
ancestry, 22
assessment of George, 132, 144

attracted to GJR, 27-28
Chief Justice of GJR court, 133-
134
compared to Montagu, 214
compared to Wells, 250
conflict with George, 133-134,
135-138, 140-141, 145, 165-172
on criminality, 258-261, 265
defends GJR court and jail, 303
defends "Nothing without Labor," 297-298
as educational reformer, 182, 194
on the GJR abroad, 205-206
and GJR trustees, 27, 131, 170,
274, 296
on human nature and will, 257-
258, 264-265, 267
on imperialism, 205
masquerades, 26-27, 53, 135
memories of Auburn Prison, 231
and Old Penology, 229, 266, 276
personality, 24-25
political career, 26
as prison reformer, 223ff., 273-284
seeks financial stability for GJR,
140-148, 151
sponsor of GJR citizens, 180-
181
as "Tom Brown," 275-276
warden of Sing Sing, 277-282
Otis, Harrison Gray, 156
Overstreet, H. A., 204

Palmer, Lewis M., 271
Parker, Francis W., 181, 192
Parker, John A., 146-149, 303n
Parkhurst, Charles H., 19n, 70, 125
"Parkhurst Cops," 71
Parmelee, Maurice, 306
Parole, 235, 237
Paul Reveres, 328
Peabody, Endicott, 194-195, 200
Penal Reform Society, 214, 253
Pennsylvania system, 233, 239
Perfectionism, 40
Perkins, Frances, 36
Pershing, John J., 323
Pestalozzi, Johann, 191-192, 195, 228,
246
Phalanx, 326-328